Education and the commodity problem: Ethnographic investigations of creativity and performativity in Swedish schools

the Tufnell Press,
London,
United Kingdom

www.tufnellpress.co.uk

email contact@tufnellpress.co.uk

British Library Cataloguing-in-Publication Data
A catalogue record for this book is
available from the British Library

ISBN   1872767729
ISBN-13   978-1-872767-72-7

First published 2007

Printed in England and U.S.A. by Lightning Source

Education and the commodity problem: Ethnographic investigations of creativity and performativity in Swedish schools

Dennis Beach and Marianne Dovemark

Contents

Introduction

There are a number of myths about education. One of these is that education is a stable entity that needs to be engineered for change; another is that it is a common social good with a positive value for each individual in society and a third is that it is a general good for society itself. These things are socially constructed myths. Education has never been a stable and uniform enterprise in any nation or region. It has always been an outcome of a resolution of different economic, social, productive, ideological and other cultural forces, constantly in flux (Peters et al, 2000). Moreover, education has no given positive value in and of itself, for individuals or the societies they are a part of, and nor has the value of education ever been evenly spread across societies for all social individuals. Lenin for instance described the value of education in respect of the distinct social classes that make up capitalist society. In his rendition an education for the masses was valuable in terms of its use in a struggle to counter the hypocrisy and lies of the bourgeoisie. The value of education for the bourgeoisie was oppositely indexed, in terms of its use as an instrument of class rule imbued with the bourgeois caste spirit. Here an ability to supply obedient lackeys and able workers to the capitalist economies of goods and signs in the interest of profit was central. Moreover, even within bourgeois concepts of education, there was never one kind of education that operated in the common interests of all (Beach, 2005a, b). Instead, there has always been one education for the poor masses of the population, one for the rich inheritors of wealth and yet a third for the middle classes, such as the book-keeping bureaucrats of the capitalist order (lawyers, accountants etc), who were to orchestra affairs in the dominant class interests.

Sometimes this 'trinity' of class reproductive education has taken very open and obvious organisational proportions, such as within the tripartite system of State education operating in England and Wales for much of the middle portion of the previous century, and the parallel school system operating in Sweden during most of the first half of the 20th century. These different school 'types' catered to the needs of the capitalist State with respect to its distinct social classes in school systems that were supplemented by an emphatic private sector of elite public schools and other private and quasi-private institutions, particularly in England.

However, at times the organisational form of education and its correspondences with the capitalist State are less obvious and more subtle than with respect to the tripartite system in England and the parallel school system in Sweden. Such is the case in current education provision through independent and State schools at secondary and upper-secondary levels in both Sweden and the UK (Broady and Börjesson, 2005; Ball, 2003; Beach, 1999a, 2001, 2003a, b, 2006c; Korp, 2006). The present book looks at these education practices and processes on the ground inside Swedish schools in the early 21st century.

These present day school forms are local outcomes of long national and global processes of development, which was accomplished in two stages in most European nations (Beach, 2005a). First through the development of church and voluntary organisations and second by the 'absorption' of the activities of these organisations into an expanding public domain as public services, by way of which the teaching labour originally carried out mainly by women within a system of kinship relationships and small family groups in the home, but also by men in association with productive labour, have successively been moved into the general economy: mainly as female work but in some sections also as male. This socialisation of labour and the creation of a new lower-middle class is described as occurring in the previous century in most European countries, earlier for some and later for others. Current developments are more in line with a massive habituation of education and the influx of neo-liberal principles of control (Beach, 2005a).

Organisational principles of democratic schooling in Sweden

The three general principles of parity, equal access and equality of qualifications that should have been governing school policy since the 1950s in Sweden are questioned by the suggestions of class division introduced above. These principles and their current negations in practice are ethnographically described in the present book. The following table summarises the principles and our main findings in respect of them:

Table 1: Principles of education in Swedish education policy and there negations

Principles	Concrete negations of principles in practice
All citizens should have access to an equivalent education regardless of gender, social class, and geographic background	There is a myth about 'one school for all', but little equivalence in the education availed of by different classes
All public education should be free of charge to individuals	Education consumption is always privately subsidised and supplemented. 'Subsidies' are unequal between classes

Principles	Concrete negations of principles in practice
All curricula, examinations and grading should be valid nation-wide	As access is socially skewed there is little class equality in school qualifications

The three principles described above have been discoursed very differently in policy over previous decades and have led to different local and national State measures and reforms. Lisbeth Lundahl (2002a, b) has examined these issues (Beach and Dovemark, 2005a). She characterised Swedish education policy up to the end of the 1970s as centralised and regulated in collective interests, noting reforms that included mechanisms such as detailed national curricula, earmarked State subsidies and tight central control over the constitution of organisational resources, curricula, staff time and learning practices. More recent State strategies are depicted in opposite terms by Lundahl. Things are becoming less collectivistic with more individualised instruction and increased moves toward deregulation and decentralisation (Gustafsson, 2003; Wass, 2004; Sundberg, 2003; Dovemark, 2004a; Dovemark and Beach, 2005a; Henning-Loeb, 2006; Båth, 2006). There has been a transition from governing by rules to governance by objectives (Lindblad et al, 2005).

Lundahl names three distinctive organisational periods from the second half of the previous century onwards. These are *1945-1975, Construction of the (strong) modern welfare State; 1991-1998, Recession and Reform; and 1999-2002, Educational Problems Remain.* The latter period, from 1991 onwards, is the one we are most concerned with. This period represented a period of neo-liberal economic restructuring in welfare State education, with experimental roots from the mid-late 1980s (Beach, 2005b; Beach and Carlson, 2005; Carlson, 2005). Within it Sweden's schools were transformed from being amongst the most highly regulated education systems in the world to being amongst the least regulated. Restructuring took place in two phases, or by two means (Beach, 2004a; Wass, 2004; Lindblad et al, 2005; Dovemark, 2004a; Henning-Loeb, 2006; Båth, 2006). These were firstly discursively, through new ways of discoursing schooling, and secondly in social and material terms. The present book uses ethnographic research to consider what this has involved on the ground for teachers and learners in school.

The discursive and social practices of restructuring

From having been recognised at home and abroad as one of the World's most successful post-WW2 national economies and most egalitarian societies (Ball and Larsson, 1989; Beach, 2005b), in the beginning of the 1990s, a new public discourse emerged about Sweden as a nation in economic recession with high unemployment rates and increasing poverty. This discourse described financial and political needs of change and put pressure on the public sector to transform in accordance with what was conceived of as a new set of global political realities (Henning-Loeb, 2006; Båth, 2006). The public sector as a provider and regulator of services was questioned (Wass, 2004), even on the ground amongst practising teachers (Henning-Loeb, 2006), and the highly egalitarian system of strongly State funded and regulated education was no longer officially expressed as a politically and economically feasible project (Lindblad et al, 2005). The highly socialised and low-commercialised public service sector came increasingly under media threat and was also successively challenged. A new discourse emerged about the value of public choice in a new 'third way' welfarist society. A new concept of Stakeholder Welfare emerged.

The deconstruction of strong welfare State education politics and the mobilisation of resources supporting a new 'stakeholder form of welfarism' (Loxeley and Thomas, 2001) marked a clear break with past ideologies and democratic interests in Sweden (Båth, 2006) and the Nordic countries more generally (Gordon et al, 2003), because despite the continuing class-markings of and in education during the mid 20th century (Beach, 2003a, 2005b), the socialisation of education as a public service in a collective (folk-home) interest had still formed a main kernel of development there (Beach, 2003a). This applies also according to Lundahl (op cit.) and is apparent in several other European countries (Beach, 2005a), where the establishment of a welfare State and the inclusion of education in the public welfare system has created massive infrastructures of education supply through State efforts to (at least on paper) improve educational standards and generate an informed political debate and democratic involvement in political processes (Ball and Larsson, 1989). Through restructuring these infra-structures are being exposed to market forces and successive waves of privatisation (Beach, 2005b), firstly in the ancillary service sections and increasingly in terms of the privatisation of education supply.

This (re-)privatisation follows on from the development of welfare systems in Sweden as well as elsewhere in Europe and other parts of the world (see also Rosskam, Ed, 2006; Beach, 2005a, b) and is at times referred to also as (re-)commodification. For education and care in the wealthier sections of the national populations this (re-)commodification means really very little, in the senses that to greater or lesser extents these sections of the populace have constantly exploited private facilities anyway. But with respect to education and care as projects within a service economy for the mass of the population it means a great deal, as a significant step in a process of conversion of the initially domestic (socially useful) labour (of women in the home) to firstly socialised labour in the public services of the State and then to an objectified form of labour in privatised, commercialised services on a service market (Beach, 2004a). Also significant is that this restructuring of production relations has taken place in a relatively short time period (Beach, 2005a, b). Teaching and education, from being practices and sites of useful labour (in the home) have been quickly transformed into practices and sites of firstly socially useful and publicly available (socialised) labour and then economically productive labour. Education is expanding rapidly as a direct factor of economic production that is carried out in private economic interests and arrangements.

The terms *productive and useful labour*, as discussed for instance in Marxist literature, are important concepts. In Marxist use these concepts differ from the understanding generally employed in bourgeois economic theory, as in Marxism productive labour is a concept very distinct from that of useful labour. Useful labour is an activity which meets a human need other than the accumulation of capital. Productive labour is labour that is *productive principally in the economic sense* by creating a profit for someone. It is the antithesis of useful labour in this sense and is the unpaid part of labour measured in proportion to the capital invested in and acquired from production that is expropriated from workers and distributed by various means among the capitalist class. The two concepts of useful labour (and its concomitant value form of *use value*) and productive labour (and its value form of *accumulated economic value*), although not always openly referenced on every page of the present book, are important to just about every last word that is written on education, teaching and learning in it. The book is in this sense an ethnographic study of the cultural production of education value inside local school communities. The book is essentially Marxian in its analyses. As Sayers (1990) points out, one of the key tenets of Marxist dialectics is that in order for us to understand things as they concretely exist as part of material reality, it is vital to see them in the context of their interconnections (p. 143).

Changing Swedish schools

A lot is happening in education in Europe at the present time, and most of it is related to the above pointers regarding (first) the socialisation of useful labour and (then) the habituation, (re-)privatisation and commercialisation (or commoditisation) of that socially useful labour as a form of economically productive labour. This is seen not the least in the strong common currency of restructuring in education in Europe at the present time (Beach, 2005b), where despite always being a potential variable (Dale, 1997; Whitty et al, 1998), education re-structuring almost always seems to share common characteristics of a transformation of education supply through the introduction of a market model of delivery in which services are deliberately altered so that a market concept and envisaged practices of competition can become the arbiters of provision (Beach, 2004a, 2005a, b). Zambeta (2004) speaks here of a concept of education as part of a Schumpeterian State, in which liberal ideas about markets are exploited in an attempt to reconstruct education supply in line with certain preconceived economic interests (Hill, 2006).

The present book ethnographically names, identifies, describes and discusses numerous grounded issues connected with the development of Schumpeterian State education policies and politics in Sweden's schools. It highlights and discusses some of the political decisions that have been made and the changes that have been introduced through education policy in areas such as the curriculum, teachers' work conditions, rights and duties, job stability, student learning, the creation of education markets and grading and assessment practices. The book looks both at 'common schools' and adult education. It closes with a discussion of the meaning and significance of the developments highlighted as a characterisation of globalisation processes and the de-regulation of State intervention.

Lindblad et al (2005) have described changes in education in Sweden as related to the development of new forms of discoursing. The following table summarises some of the main developments in State discourses:

Table 2: Some significant changes in schooling and education since 1980

Decentralisation and deregulation
In 1980 the national school curriculum for the compulsory school (Lgr 80) was introduced to replace the curriculum from 1969 (Lgr 69). From 1980 each school was obliged to present a work plan for how it aimed to achieve centrally formulated national education goals. Each school was to be organised in work units or teams,

and the teachers were expected to meet regularly in these teams. Local management of school and local development became the new model for controlling school. Emphases on contructivist and socio-cultural concepts of learning, personal flexibility, creativity and responsibility for learning were clarified further in the curriculum reforms of the 1990s and were developed and promoted in government discourse, as was a suggestion about a need for new understandings of quality in learning. Individual responsibility and freedom of choice were to become the means to help produce creative, motivated, alert, inquiring, self-governing and flexible learners and discerning producers and consumers of knowledge for Sweden in the present and future European knowledge economy.

Devolution
Devolution means the transfer of rights and responsibility by a central government to local authorities. It has been part of Swedish education policies since the 1980s. For instance, employer responsibilities were transferred from the State to local authorities in 1989, when teachers became municipal (local State) rather than (central) State employees, via the Municipal Education Act. The MEA was strongly contested by the teachers. It divided the central and the local level, delegated more decision making to the local arena and thereby weakened the relationship between the national State government and the teachers. Previous national policies prescribed how the teachers were expected to do their job, now the State only set the goals and the frameworks of education (through funding). Teachers and school management were to find the ways to fulfil these goals. This move towards an enhanced local management of schools was common in Europe at the time.

Economic control and refurbishment
State payments to the municipalities for education were altered in 1993 when State support became a lump sum, together with support for other aspects of the public services (health, education, social services, child-welfare). The municipal council distributed these resources to the various services in terms of their interpretations of local requirements, needs and fluctuations.

Individualisation and the new curricula
New curriculum guidelines were established in 1994 based on recommendations from a 1991 government committee. These recommendations, published in SOU 1992:94, gave rise to new curricula for the compulsory comprehensive (Lpo 94) and upper-secondary school (Lpf –94). The new curricula enhanced the devolution of education power and control from the centre to the peripheries and comprised national goals rather than detailed prescriptions about teacher work. Distinctions between school aims—as 'targets' to give direction and ambition (strävansmål) and 'attainments' (uppnåelsemål)—were introduced. Individualisation of teaching was emphasised. A new grading system with a new marking scale was also introduced in 1994 and the new curriculum was also extended into the preschool years. The pre-school obtained increased pedagogical responsibilities in 1994 and its own

curriculum in 1998 (Lpfö 98). The curriculum of the compulsory school also comprises the preschool class and the school-time leisure-centres.

Life-long learning
Education consumption has been extended in national and international education policy across the life-cycle from early childhood to late adulthood for ever broader cross-sections of the population and ever larger numbers of people in relation to ever increasing areas and aspects of life (including love, labour and recreation). And discourses have been appropriated and engineered to encourage and perhaps even terrorise people and groups (including even governments themselves) to consume this education. In the present moment education has become discoursed not only as a stepping stone into the knowledge-based society. It is also a medium for life-long learning and a ticket (voucher/qualification) of access to valuable psychological tools (Proposition 200%1:73; OECD, 2002).

Marketisation
In 1992 the almost complete State monopoly on school education was broken by the new conservative-coalition government when independent schools, defined as schools that are accountable to authorities other than municipalities, county councils or the national State on primary and secondary levels, were established through tax money. This introduced a system of competition between schools on a quasi market. Only 2 or 3 elite private schools had existed before 1992. The independent schools were meant to be open for all pupils and there were no fees. A voucher system was introduced to allow pupils and their parents to choose between different schools. This did not eliminate distinctive class and geographic markings involved in school availability and selection.

New Public Management
Demands for consumerism, value for money and accountability gathered pace in education during the 1980s and became one of the main planks of the new conservative coalition government in the early 1990s. Education became increasingly described as a sub-system of the economy by this government rather than a component of the welfare system, and parents (on behalf of their children) became described as consumers in an education market with the power to increase efficiency, effectiveness and productivity. Marketisation was to be used as a means to create 'the best school system in Europe', as the then Minister of Schooling (Beatrice Ask) phrased it. Put simply, education was to be governed according to criteria of cost-effectiveness and efficiency through a system of public choice that was claimed to stimulate rationalisation in accordance with individual needs in the allocation of scarce resources. A system of quality auditing for schools was introduced in 2003 via the Swedish National Agency for Education (Rgr 2001/02: 188). The audits were intended to stimulate teachers to change their dispositions to act and think in relation to the performance indicators, steering technologies and evaluations of NPM.

New ways of discoursing teacher and learner roles and identities
New policy discourses constitute a major portion of the discursive order of the 'renewal' of education in Sweden. They address three things in particular. First the need for teachers to become co-creative and interactive knowledge workers, who are 'instrumental' in the production of the conditions of production for new kinds of learner subjectivity and new consumerist learner identities, together with learners. These things are obviously conducive with the new (commodity) concept of life-long learning. Second a new ideology about the learners' inner power to learn and awakening a 'lust for learning' has developed as a bandwagon for the new commodity form of flexible, renewable, changeable education on expanding education markets. Third statements about the need and values of helping students learn how to become responsible individuals who can identify their own needs, and who can make 'the right choices' in their education now and in the future is also extensively evidenced.

Researching the restructuring of schools and the re-culturing of teachers

As suggested in table 2, the organisational framework and concepts for teaching and learning in Sweden's schools have been successively changed in the past fifteen to twenty years through national school policies, from pre-school levels to the compulsory comprehensive school and the upper secondary school. These suggested changes were stated as having specific purposes. Most often mentioned was the intention to increase the flexibility of the system (Lindblad, et al., 2005) and to stimulate creativity and the development of life-long learning and new learner identities (Gustafsson, 2003; Beach, 2006a; Båth, 2006). Not included in the table, but no less apparent though, are similar changes in the discoursing of adult and higher education (Beach, 1997, 2004a, 2006b; Carlén, 1999; Wass, 2004; Fejes, 2006; Henning-Loeb, 2006). Wass (2004) made a critical discourse analysis of the renewal of Swedish adult education. She identified several discourses at play within the discursive order of that part of the educational field. These were a discourse of marketisation, a discourse of co-operation, a discourse of individualisation and a discourse of learning. 'Flexibility' and 'validation' were other key words. As she suggested there are parallel developments in school and higher education.

The suggested changes to the education system have had significant implications for the work, responsibilities and roles of teachers and schools (Lindqvist, 2002; Nordanger, 2002; Dovemark, 2004a; Wass, 2004; Båth, 2006; Henning-Loeb, 2006). Marianne Dovemark's (2004a) thesis examined these issues in some detail in a comprehensive school. Dovemark studied discourses about a new concept of schooling, learning and teacher professionalism. Aspects such as what the image of school, education and its claims look like and how they are talked about and materialised in everyday work and interaction by pupils, teachers and school managers were the ethnographically researched central themes.

Dovemark pointed to contradictory structures and discourses as what was most characteristic for schooling at the time. Solidarity and equality as targets of the new school, she wrote, were implemented in a school where competition and exclusion were the main driving forces. Schools and their teachers were to provide extended possibilities of freedom of choice for students and to produce creative, motivated, alert, inquiring, self-governing and flexible users and developers as opposed to just recipient reproducers of knowledge. However, according to Dovemark, a field of tension existed in schools between this new idealism and a practical realism of standards-based-assessment and performance-based control and selection with both deep historical roots and new forms of support from the new-right. The present book has been developed from ethnographic research projects which have focussed on what this tension may mean for Sweden's schools, their pupils and teachers, and their respective commitments and identities. It is based on cooperation between two researchers, Dennis Beach and Marianne Dovemark, aided by national and international collaborators in five ethnographic research projects.[1]

These five projects are very much related ones. They are concerned with making ethnographic sense of issues of education change in late capitalism, from early childhood education up to upper-secondary schools and adult education, in terms of what the noted education changes involve, mean and lead to for the people involved and the societies they are part of. The projects are part of a larger project series that started with PhD research in teacher and other forms of higher education in the mid 1980s (Beach, 1995, 1996, 1997, 2000) and that is still ongoing in relation to two current research projects.

The first of the five research projects involved in the book was an ethnographic investigation based on participant observation over one full school year on a half-time basis in one specifically selected Swedish upper-secondary school in 1998 and 1999, after the 1994 Curriculum Reform (Proposition 1990/91: 18;

1   One of these researchers, Marie Carlson from Göteborg University has been particularly involved as joint project holder, together with Dennis Beach, on one of the ethnographic research projects on which the book is heavily based. This project was funded by a grant from the Swedish Research Council (VR) section for Research in the Educational Sciences (UVK: Competing Ideas in the renewal of SFI - An Investigation of Discursive Practices in an SFI-education during Restructuring: Swedish Research Council Section for Research in Educational Sciences: 2001-5181).

SOU, 1996: 1; 1997: 1; Beach 2003a, b, 2004). This project included interviews with teachers and students on strategies, experiences and ideas about how to work within a context where schooling is on the one hand described in terms of new, shared responsibilities for local development, self-determination and freedom of choice, through a reduction in central regulation, but is also, on the other, carried out in a formal context that has traditionally supported other value positions regarding the need of hard standards and performance assessment, and is now also emphasising the need for more tightly economically managed systems (in terms of both the proximity, invasiveness and detail of management). Conversations with teachers, head-teachers and students at the school and from four other sites in 1999, 2000 and 2003 were important in the research. The upper secondary school Natural Science and Trade and Commerce programmes were given particular attention. The research was supported economically by grants from the Swedish National School Agency and the European SOCRATES programme.

The second project was a PhD study at the Department of Education and Education Research at Göteborg University, sponsored by a grant from the University College of Borås (Dovemark, 2004a). This research was concentrated on the development of responsibility for learning, on learner creativity and on learner self-determination in the compulsory comprehensive (6-16) school. The research was conducted in one particular school in Western Sweden (Dovemark, 2004a, b; Dovemark and Beach, 2004; Beach and Dovemark, 2005b, c) and involved participant observation in one class on an *intermittent basis* (Jeffrey and Troman, 2004) over a two year period between 2001 and 2003. The students/pupils were in grades 7 and 8 of the school at the time.

The third project is a recently completed European Union SOCRATES initiative termed the CLASP (Creative Learning and Student's Perspectives) project (Jeffrey, 2006). This project used ethnographies of school creativity (Jeffrey and Woods, 2003) as a common research platform and had 9 European partners and three main aims. These were: (i) to identify the strategies teachers and students use to develop creative learning in educational contexts, (ii) to examine the effectiveness of incorporating student perspectives into the evaluation and development of creativity in teaching and learning and (iii) to highlight the advantages in this process of examining cross European practices. Within the Swedish CLASP component data and analyses emanating from the two previous projects were reanalysed and re-examined in a new case study upper-secondary school called New School. Research in this school involved intermittent visits spread out over a twelve month period and comprising 120 hours of participant observation, together with a number of formal interviews and informal field conversations.

The fourth project is a Swedish Research Council project concerned with the complexities of steering and control within restructured adult education. SFI education (literally Swedish as a Foreign Language for Immigrants) within a particular Municipal Region in Sweden that we have termed Hillfield formed the main case study context. Research was conducted in two particular organisations (also Beach 2006b) and has primarily been concerned with the consequences of education restructuring for teacher values and practices, learner identities, commitments and constraints, education discourses and the value practices of humanist education and creativity in adult SFI-education contexts (Beach, 2004a, 2006b; Beach and Carlson, 2004; Carlson, 2004, 2005).

These four projects and other earlier ethnographic investigations have identified what Ball (1994, 1998) describes as a new policy context for education and education work (Gustafsson, 2003; Beach, 1995, 1996, 1997, 2000, 2003a, b, c, 2005a, b; Dovemark, 2004a, b; Beach and Dovemark, 2005a, b; Lindblad et al, 2005). National policy documents such as the new school curricula (e.g. Lpo, 94; Lpf, 94; Lpfö, 98), the 1995 collective agreement for teachers in the public education system (The School Development Agreement, termed 'en satsning till 2000') and its commentary materials from the two teacher unions and the employer organisation (The Association of Swedish Municipalities; TASM), the *Municipal Education Act*, and the Commission Reports these documents and developments have been based on (e.g. SOU 1990: 20), form one corner of this policy context.

This 'corner' of policy development is present in vernacular forms across Europe at the present time (Beach, 2005a). It emphasises decentralisation, diversity and the need of change in the education system, toward greater flexibility and freedom of choice (Lundahl, 2001; Lindblad et al, 2005).[2] However, in order to result in anticipated and hoped for changes, this policy corner needs accompanying policy technologies that can stabilise necessary *social relations* by providing *material environments* to help co-ordinate the activities of agents in arenas of implementation (also Fullan and Hargreaves, 1992; Ball, 1994; Jeffrey and Woods, 2003; Wass, 2004; Henning-Loeb, 2006).

---

2   What is described is a neo-liberal shift toward loose procedural control, tight substantial control and a belief service-system composed by regulated quasi markets (Beach, 2003a, 2004a; Beach & Dovemark, 2005a). This shift in governance is also occurring in European higher education according to for instance Lazzeretti and Tavoletti (2006).

One such policy technology was developed as an amendment to the 1991 *Sector Funding* for schools, when the earmarked money provided by the State to municipalities was transformed from a specific to a general purse for the welfare sector (i.e. child-care, education, elderly care and health care combined) more broadly. Local municipalities decided on distributions. Also significant was the abolition of the School Boards in 1991, which were replaced by the National School Agency. The shifting of curriculum control from steering by rules and directives to steering by objectives and results is a further example.

Despite these new policy technologies the realisation arenas provided by modern schools may still not always provide comfortable spaces for the new policy ideas, and both policy colapse and contradictory practices can often be identified (Beach, 2003, a, b; Dovemark, 2004a, b; Beach and Dovemark, 2005a; Loxely and Thomas, 2001). This has been accounted for in previous research on at least three foundations. One is the unwillingness of agents to engage wholeheartedly in teaching and learning experiences in line with new idealism. This is sometimes referred to as teacher conservatism. Another is comprised by the social and material conditions of the education context and a third relates to forms of policy interference (Beach, 1997).

The ideas about policy tensions from previous research have been re-interrogated and re-explored in a new project called the *Hybrid Classrooms* project. This project is financed by the Swedish Research Council for the Humanities and Social Sciences[3] and is the fifth component project in the present book. The project interrogates the current discourses of creativity and performativity in education and asks on what (empirical, philosophical and linguistic) grounds and by what methods they are made convincing. As well as critical ethnography, critical discourse analysis is used (Chouliarki and Fairclough, 1999) and the learner identities, professional identities and subjectivities involved in managing education policy ideas in actual education circumstances are given space. Dennis Beach and Marianne Dovemark are involved in this project together with Dr. Jan Gustafsson and Professor Elisabet Öhrn from Göteborg University and Borås University College respectively.

The disposition of the book

The book comprises eleven chapters in addition to the introduction. The first of these, *Labs and the Quality of Learning*, comes from research on the upper-secondary school curriculum reform from the mid-nineties onwards. This project

3 Creativity and performativity in teaching and learning. VR-Project 2004-7024.

was concerned with what happens to student learning in education when the main education objective that guides this is caught between contrasting policy rhetoric involving the new self-reliance and creativity discourses on the one hand and performitivity on the other. The aim of learning in the context of the creativity discourse was said be about self-directed studies and valorising personal and subjective education desires and initiatives as objective education capital. But as the chapter shows, under influence from the performativity discourse within a restraining material context and conservative education tradition of a banking form of education (Allman, 1999), this main goal 'transmutates' and becomes instead to arrive at pre-set answers within an exchange-based educational economy, for the purposes of passing a course and obtaining a good education qualification (also Beach, 2003a, b, 2006a). The chapter considers two different classifications of laboratory work in science education as arenas for the issues discussed. Both of these forms of lab-work were identified from ethnographic data and analyses.

The second chapter, *School as a Market*, has been developed from an analysis of school mathematics. It is based on a specific case study in mathematics courses from the project described above. Talk and behaviour inside mathematics classrooms are examined and a specific correspondence between school value practices and foundational societal values (specifically a market value relationship) is identified and critiqued. What is suggested is that the ideological elements of neo-liberalism and market capitalism have begun to infiltrate the discoursing and social practices of education in classrooms through processes of the *liquidation* of education subjects (*both* learners *and* content) in social discourse and (other) social practices. Also suggested is that there is broad hegemonic support for neo-liberalisation even from groups who are clearly disadvantaged by its principles in practice.

The third chapter, *Creativity as a Cultural Commodity*, is about the concepts of individual responsibility, self-regulated learning and life-long learning from the new education policy discourses of the late-nineteen nineties and early 21st century. In this chapter we discuss these 'new' ideas against data produced from participant observation and student interviews in a critical ethnographic investigation with three classes of students. These are a mixed ability class of 15 year-olds from an urban comprehensive school in West Sweden and two classes of upper-secondary pupils.

This investigation has been primarily concerned with what it means to learn according to the verbal expressions and social and physical practices of the learners themselves. It suggests again that a tension exists between new curriculum aims for creativity and self-regulation in learning and the demands stabilised by an education discourse of performativity. Moreover, the chapter suggests that the discourse of performativity is more deeply engrained in (and resonant with the social and material demands of) formal school culture than is the creativity discourse and that there is very little evidence of a positive relationship between the two discourses in practice.

The fourth chapter, *Pupil Responsibility*, is more openly Marxian in its points of departure than the first three, which are somewhat more interactionist. It is concerned with issues of value mediation in relation to what Ainley (2000), Allman (1999) and Brosio (1994) all describe as the two fundamental present day roles for modern-day schools within capitalist States. These are the ideological and material roles (Althusser 1971), where schools produce ideologically compliant workers and consumers for a new corporatist economy on the one hand, and form part of a corporate business plan for the accumulation of private capital in the welfare sector on the other (Hill, 2006). However, the chapter also suggests that the existing nation-State also has a declared and even sometimes materially supported democratic mission within education that can make the execution of these two roles difficult (Brosio, 1994). A further point is that the neo-liberal State does not fulfil this mission, because it's policies of welfare restructuring support the corporatisation of welfare not its social improvement (Beach, 2005b).

Neo-liberal support for the corporatisation of the welfare is apparent in education in at least two ways according to the chapter, which is based on ethnographic studies and student interviews. These data help suggest that whilst rituals that previously indoctrinated individuals into submissive behaviour in school, through forms of subordination and the mechanical memorisation of other's facts, have been replaced by outwardly self-monitored activities and self-determined learning, some things remain the same. Students are still graded, separated and characterised by teachers in terms of being weak or superior products and students still adopt these labels in their self-understanding, with negative effects on school performances and self-concept (Jost, Kruglanski and Nelson, 1998; Maki, 1998; Yates, Lee and Shinotsuka, 1996; Jonsson, 2004; Dovemark, 2004a, b). The curriculum that is meant to stimulate creativity and inclusiveness dampens creativity and positive involvement (Beach, 2003a, b; Jonsson, 2004). There is also a tendency toward social reproduction.

The fifth chapter, *Re-structuring Adult Education: A Local Case Study*, is about the marketisation of adult education in Sweden as seen through an ethnographic case study and is also openly Marxist. The chapter takes up a concrete example, the rise and fall of an adult education company called Studium Ltd.[4] This company was created in 2001 from the municipal adult education service (Komvux) and was the largest deliverer of adult education in 2001, until it lost its contracts during tendering in 2003 and effectively went into bankruptcy in 2004. The local tax-based economy footed the bill of the conversion processes and salary costs of under employed Studium employees, who all had tenure as public service officials due to previous labour agreements. This kind of situation, where public funds are used in order to pay for the conversion of public services to private is a consistent element of education restructuring according to international research (e.g. Sharpe, 2003; Whitty et al., 1997, 1998; Whitty and Power, 2003; Dale, 1997; Beach, 2004a, 2005a; Beach and Carlson, 2004). The chapter provides a bottom-up account of restructuring in a particular space-time location; adult SFI education in a particular local education authority.

The next two chapters, *Myths of Change in Adult Education* and *Creativity and Performativity in Adult Education*, respectively; are also taken from the adult education SFI project. The first is concerned with issues of adult education as a discourse and its discursive practices. It uses ethnographic data based mainly on field interviews and conversations to suggest that there are clear differences both within and between the talk and thought developed by differently positioned agents in processes of education restructuring, as well as consistencies. One dominant pattern concerns the need for a flexible workforce in the new work order *not a specifically educated one*. This way of discoursing represents the interests of employment and production. It is the discourse that is developing most in adult education today, according to our analyses, where these words obtained material consequences that challenged and overpowered the previous *comprehensive and humanistic* education discourse (Wass, 2004; Beach and Carlson, 2005; Fejes, 2006; Henning-Loeb, 2006). 'Flexibility' and the short term needs of trade, industry and employment are primary (Beach and Carlson, 2004, 2005; Carlson, 2005; Carlén, 1999).

---

4 The restructuring of adult education is the subject of three successive chapters. This restructuring was initiated on the basis of local decisions in 1999 to tender out adult education in order, formally, to reduce costs and make adult education more responsive to a new service economy, new employment needs and the needs of individuals. These decisions came into full force in 2002, after the completion of the National Adult Education Initiative (the AEI). They followed guidelines for franchise in the public sector, as per the 1992 Purchasing Act, and had consequences for all education suppliers, but in particular one of them.

The third SFI-chapter is supported by three of the ethnographic research projects named earlier: *the adult SFI project*, the SOCRATES CLASP project and the *Hybrid Classrooms* project. Most of the research was done in the first project at two sites called by the pseudonyms SWALL and StudiumF (also Beach, 2006b). Two levels of analysis have been important: (i) a surface level of analysis of everyday interaction and negotiation processes relating to oral, visual or written proposals for action and material resources in use and (ii) a deeper level of analysis concerning the structural orthography of learning and the rules, regulations and cultural interpellations of social technologies, social relations and social practices of communication. The two levels helped identify and name two distinct metaphors for creativity (novelty and change) and four pillars of humanism in education (thoughtfulness, reciprocity, authenticity, negotiation). The chapter suggests that the dividing line between creativity and routine are blurred, but that intuition and embodied experience always played a major role in educational decision making when humanism and creative teaching and learning was involved.

The next ethnographic example provided in the book, *Accommodations of Creativity Discourses*, is based on collective work in the *Hybrid Classrooms* project by Dennis Beach and Marianne Dovemark in relation to the above discussed theme of teacher professional identities, but this time with a cross section of working professionals from the secondary and upper-secondary school portions of the education system (grades 7-9 and 10-13 respectively, comprising pupils of 13 to 16 and 16 to 19 years of age). Extracts from interviews with teachers who have worked within the new policy context at these respective school levels are considered in particular. A tension is identified between the new *idealism* of the creativity discourse and a new realist discourse of managerialism and performativity. The research again suggests that there is little evidence of a positive relationship between the two discourses.

The final ethnographic chapter, *Teachers and New Education Aim*, again uses interview and conversation materials from the *Hybrid Classrooms* project. These have been produced during ethnographic engagements in three schools to provide a more bottom-up account of what the new forms of discoursing education in Sweden mean for teacher identities and teacher work. The extracts are supplemented by conversation materials and contextualising participant observations and have helped identify a number of different ways in which teachers express their subjective understanding with regard to things like the role of the teacher and new teacher and student identities. The chapter concerns in this sense the workings of ideology and discourse in education in relation to creativity and performativity policies in practice arenas and is about the conditions of development for the new forms of expression regarding professional practice artistry and professional identity. It identifies issues of repression and reproduction and also shows evidence of some subjective deconstruction of the contradictions embedded in education policy. A possibility for creative (resistant) agency is suggested.

The final substantive chapter, *New Schools and New Pedagogy*, sums up the restructuring of the Swedish education system as constructed by our ethnographic work. The main theme is that of whether what we can see in current school reform is new schools and new pedagogy, and if so what kind of schools and pedagogy, or new ways of continuing social reproduction, or perhaps in some way a hybrid comprising elements of both. A main policy/reform vector is identified. This concerns political expressions in formal policy about the need to reconstruct schools in line with neo-liberal ideas where concepts of freedom of choice and individual responsibility in the curriculum, deregulation and decentralisation are emphasised. However, the contradictions of these ideas in practice are considered and the chapter actually points at contradiction as the current main characteristic of the condition of education in welfarist society. It suggests that this applies throughout the education system in Sweden and is also pretty characteristic of education in general in many European countries today (Beach, 2005a). This chapter is followed by the final chapter in the book, which is a short chapter on the ethnographic methods we have used in our research. We describe our work as a serial form of critical ethnography of education.

Chapter 1

Labs and the quality of learning

The research for the present chapter has been conducted in two of the projects mentioned in the introduction. The first is the Swedish National Schools Agency project that attempted to research change in the Swedish Upper-Secondary School after the 1994 Curriculum Reform Act and the 1995 School Development Agreement (see also Beach, 1999a, b, d, 2001, 2003a, b, c). The second is the SOCRATES CLASP (Creative Learning and Student's Perspectives) project. The research has involved participant observation and conversational interviews with teachers and students from the upper-secondary school natural sciences programme concerning learning in laboratory science. In all, some 50 hours of participant observation has been done in upper-secondary school chemistry and physics labs. The data produced forms one specific part of a larger corpus of data and is brought together with interview data and materials from a PhD project on science teacher education (Beach, 1995) and an investigation of Medical Laboratory Science Education (MLSE) from a post-doctoral thesis (Beach, 1997). In these investigations creative and self-determined learning were in focus as key aspects of the development of critical and independent thinking in the science curriculum, for a more authentic understanding of the science disciplines (also Beach, 1999c). The chapter has been developed from an earlier publication (Beach, 2004b). Gratitude is acknowledged to JAI Press (Elsevier Ltd) for permission to use and further develop extensive parts of this publication.

Key characteristics of the observed labs

Both significant variations and certain strong consistencies have been identified in the ways lab activities develop in school (according to students) and are intended to work (according to teachers) through the ethnographic analyses conducted for this chapter. For instance, in just over half of the lab sessions observed consistent temporal patterns in the social regionalisation of space and the use of talk have been noted. Typically these labs have begun with an opening talk by the teacher from the front region of the room that included a presentation of aims, materials to be used, safety features to be considered and relevant theory.

Even demonstrations of the experiments to be done by students were given, as was a description of what was to be tested by these methods. Examples of the calculations to be made were also given.

During these engagements students sat in the bench region of the room, watching, listening to what was said and making notes, before doing the activities asked of them. These things have been noted previously in investigations of school science by Millar (1989) and in contributions to Hazel, (1990) as well as by Beach (1999c, 2004b), where the aim of the laboratory work was demonstrated as being the verification of assumed factual knowledge or established derivative theories. A field-note extract gives some insight:

> Liz was talking and writing on the white-board ... She wrote names and concepts in blue and formula describing chemical reactions in red ... She was talking about redox reactions ... She went through what these were and did a dummy run of the example to be tested ... After she had finished talking ... the students ... moved around ... gathering up various objects and powders ... Some of these were placed in a round-bottom crucible and taken to a glass fume-cupboard. A Bunsen burner was lit ... The substance was placed in the hot part of the flame ... The students were dressed in smocks and protective goggles. Some of them wrote things down on paper whilst others stood round and watched ... talking of the things they were asked to gaze at and write about ... When they had finished they cleared away, washed up, took off their smocks and goggles and sat down to start to write in their lab-report book about the things they had done and seen ...

These notes focus on the classroom order of a formalised activity that the students and the teacher involved are very familiar with. But they ignore informal issues and they avoid chance happenings, such as when a pen or a piece of paper falls to the floor and what patterns of physical movement there are in the room. Such is made uninteresting by the notes and their focus.

What is particularly characteristic for the formal activities of the school lab, according to the notes, is that they are tightly specified and that there is a specific and anticipatable outcome that can be easily approximated if students recognise and carry out the procedures described and follow the instructions they are given to the letter (Beach, 1999c, 2004b). And indeed, the lab activities in effect test the students' abilities to accomplish this and are thus also a means for the students to show whether they are able to recognise the classifications of science they are confronted by and do the manipulative tasks asked of them: i.e. 'whether they are of the right material ... for this (demanding) programme' (Brian: Sci High). Moreover, the students are also well aware of this performance dimension and this awareness significantly structures much of their behaviour. The following field-note journal extract from a physics lesson at Sci High provides a further example (also Beach, 2004b):

> Today's activities involved ... three laboratory tests ... Demonstrations, a verbal presentation and a written sheet of instructions were included ... Together this outlined specific knowledge connected to ongoing theory instruction ... and gave students familiarity with the equipment to be used ... The following written instructions were also available:
>
> Lab task 1:   Calculating amounts of work done in lifting and pulling a block.
> Material: Block, Newton-metre and ruler.
> Method: a) Lift the block from the floor to the table.
>   b) Pull the block one metre along the table.
> Calculation: How much work is done in each case?
>   How far do you need to pull the block so that the amount of work done in each case is the same?
>
> Lab task 2:   Calculating amounts of work done in lifting a cylinder from water to air.
> Material: Metal cylinder, beaker of water, thread, Newton-metre and ruler.
> Method: The cylinder is resting on the bottom of the beaker. Lift it up until it just leaves the water surface.
> Calculation: How much work is done?
>
> Lab task 3:   Calculating amounts of work done in drawing a trolley up an inclined plain.
> Material: Trolley, Newton-metre and ruler.
> Method: Measure the force (F) and the distance moved (s) at different angles of inclination. Look at the figure before making your measurements.
> Calculation: How is work influenced by the angle of inclination?

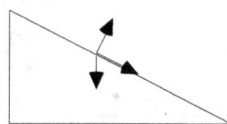

> Calculate the work required for a flat surface when the trolley moves through a distance h.
> ... After having watched the ... demonstration ... the groups ... collected equipment, moved to different parts of the room and set up the experiments ... They didn't do the tests in the same order ... but they did do the same tests and they obtained the same kind of results ... Some of the students compared their results with each other and could have shared results if they had wanted to ...

The presence of demonstration materials and instructions guided the development of activities in the above lesson. Three features were prominent. These were that the instructions provide a sense of the *rule following* that was going on, a sense of the *reproduction of knowledge* that was taking place and a sense of *how procedures always seem to finish up in a mathematical calculation that can be graded* according to approximations to known and therefore also predictable answers. These things suggest a *linear characteristic* to the work, where using a skill or technique with accuracy, making observations, and transforming data without having to make any deeper reflection or discussion about the meanings and implications of the social practices involved, is important for student success (also Millar, 1989; contributions to Hazel, 1990; Beach, 1999c, 2004b). The main summarising characteristics of these (verification) activities are given in the table below (also Beach, 2004b):

Table 1.1: The characteristics of verification activities according to ethnographic analyses of observation and interview data from upper-secondary school laboratory work:

Teacher activities	Student activities
Defining objectives	Accepting objectives without question
Identifying materials and equipment for the activities to be carried out	Collecting the materials and equipment to be used in the various activities
Describing procedures to be followed	Recognising and following procedures
Specifying tests and observations and describing how to make them	Doing tests and making observations and recordings as instructed
Stating the calculations to be made	Doing calculations as required
Describing the nature of the report and marking and grading this report	Completing the report according to set standards

These kinds of activities are strongly classified and framed in Bernstein's (1975, 1990) terms. And no matter how much we might claim that there are personalised and creative activities involved, the table suggests that in order to be successful the students normally need only to follow rules of procedure and do what they are told. This is also expressed by students themselves at times. As one of them put it in an interview, 'it is only if *something goes wrong* that we need to deviate from these rules' (Dean). Thus, instead of developing around personalised forms of learning in which students valorise their personal class-cultural capital and interests in the creation of education knowledge, the activities of the labs form a strongly individuated curriculum that involves teachers controlling the content, pacing and direction of student activities and making evaluative comparisons of them on the basis of how they perform. This reinforces a hierarchy of superiority that is also simultaneously acted out in the classroom in a way that links education as culturally produced in situ to the main characteristics of a particular form of hierarchic culture (Millar, 1989; Beach, 1999c). Activities are described in examples such as the following:

> Liz is dressed in her white-coat ... She shows a piece of marble chipping ... to the students who are gathered before her. She speaks ... about *decomposition ... combustion* and a bright glow ... She asked them to take a piece ... and examine its properties ... The students took on their robes and eye-attire ... They gathered pieces of stone ... took them to the fume cupboard and lit the Bunsen ... They passed the stone into a roaring blue flame as instructed and held it there (and) then placed the stone in a crucible and heated it strongly. They lay the ashes that were made in a flat white dish and examined them ... They dropped water on them as instructed ... and made them hiss and spit ... Then they cleared away ... washed up, disrobed, de-goggled (and) returned to the benches ... Liz asked them to describe their observations ... She wrote the things they said down on the whiteboard in ... chemistry short hand ... She also corrected some things ... The students copied down what she wrote. They wrote a lab-report (which Liz marked and graded) and were later heard chanting from it ... in another place ... prior to their exams ...
>
> (Field-notes)

Activities such as the ones described here are problematic with regard to creativity in learning according to researchers such as Jeffrey and Woods (2003), as the targets of learning are set by institutional determinants and representatives and precise replication is encouraged rather than critical reflection and invention. Things like *appropriation* (where rules of procedure are not simply made and accepted but are also negotiated and adapted) and *self-determined learning* are seriously troubled. Repetition and replication are the main elements. The accumulation of grades and qualifications has become the main recognised purpose of science and an essential reflection over the cognitive content and the social characteristics of learning are not only surplus to, but also perhaps problematic for, formal success in it. A student who was at the top of his chemistry class commented:

> It is pretty straightforward ... providing you have a hum about the theory ... This is the key. Recognising what it's actually about ... In the end what we really do is make measurements and put them into formulae to get the right answer ... It's only when you don't recognise the theory involved and what the answers should be about that it can get tricky ...
>
> (Tom, Student)

This comment suggests three things in particular we think. The first is that in order to be successful in verification activities, students seem to be aided if they see the point of what they are doing in terms of it testing their ability to reach an accepted conclusion and a measurably correct result for grading purposes. The second is that they are then further aided if they avoid challenging this as a normal state of affairs. In these circumstances a routine character replaces critical reflection and self-determined learning is reduced to identifying what to do to satisfy someone else's demands, what the answers to someone else's problem design are expected to be, how to go about reproducing these answers effectively and how to present them in ways that are likely to be appreciated by teachers. However, there is a third point that is a little more problematic, as Tom (above) actually suggests that 'sometimes rules are broken' as the lab experiment gives the wrong answer. In the investigation students have expressed these things as follows:

> *Kim*: (It's) about getting the right answer and we always check with him before the write up ... It is not always difficult but it (can be) boring ... It feels as though it's more about controlling ... that you can do something,

than it is about learning something ... We often know the things in principle beforehand ...
DB: What are your goals with the activity ...
Eric: (It's) about getting the right answer by applying the right procedures ... The right maths ... and the correct formula ...
DB: So how does this relate to ... reflection and understanding ...
Kim: (It's) about getting the ... answer (that) grades are given on and on the correct write up ... This shows reflection and understanding ... But sometimes you don't understand ... so I guess understanding is secondary, although it feels wrong to say so ... In a way I think we are supposed to tie things back to prior knowledge and maybe the idea of learning to work together too is important ... But it's not this that is assessed ... The lab report is ... It is about writing down the right answer and describing the right approach ... Not exactly what you've done (more) what you probably should have ...

Laboratory activities seem to be rather inauthentic practices according to the above. They involve students in the development of the technical, communication and co-operation skills needed to both protect and project a *positive image of themselves as good students* (Eric). However, they also have problematic consequences for the attainment of many of the 'new' creativity aims of science education. This applies particularly with respect to the creation of the new forms of human subjectivity that are expressed as central to creative and self-determined learning (Jeffrey and Woods, 2003; Jeffrey, 2006). Because rather than developing a creative, responsible and challenging subject position, in lab-work an enthroned science is simply accepted as a superior kind of knowledge to be reproduced and learned from by forms of reproduction that represent and generate a kind of mimetic isomorphism (Beach, 2004b).

Alternative laboratory activities

Laboratory activities with the above classification and framing relations were not the only form of lab-work at the research schools. There were other examples. These were called *constructivist* labs (Beach, 1997, 2004b, 2006a).

In constructivist lab-work classification and framing relations were far weaker. For instance, instructions about how to do lab-activities and tests were more meagre and were openly negotiated rather than top down enforced, and there was some freedom of choice about what to do, when, where and how. Moreover,

theory was not explicitly taught prior to the lab, but was to be derived from
it and discussed afterwards. Students were not meant to just 'apply existing
knowledge and theory in the calculation activities of conventional lab-work'
(Jen, biology/Sci High). The aim was that they *should use their own knowledge
... in the identification of what a given problem was an example of and in the design
of a way of investigating that problem further* (Liz, Sci High).

Constructivist labs were particularly preponderant at the main investigation
site (Sci High), particularly in the general science A course. In this course the
students chose both how many and which labs they were going to do (between 4
and 8 from a choice of 10, ranging from hay-infusion tests to quadrant sampling,
soil and water sample testing, and a squid dissection) as well as (at least to a
degree) how to present their findings to others:

> (I)t is your thinking and your results that are important ... You must
> use your own reflections about ... scientific processes and thinking (and)
> devise your own approach. It's not about replicating known results ... It
> is about thinking and acting ... creatively ...   (Jen)

The aims of constructivist labs differ from those of verification activities.
However, observations have revealed that in the same sense as there was some
creativity involved in relation to replication activities—at least 'when things went
wrong'—there was also some replication involved in the creativity context of
the constructivist lab work. Some kind of hybrid seemed to develop between
creativity and performance based assessment. The characteristics of lab-reports
provide one example.

Two processes were identified as important in conditioning the representation
of student lab work in the lab-report (Beach, 2004b, 2006a). One is reflected
in teachers' descriptions of what they look for when they assess work (i.e.
demonstrations of a good *understanding of science concepts by students and an
ability to employ the skills and procedures of scientific enquiry.* (Brian, Teacher). This
definition was never challenged by a definition that valorised creativity and is
reflected in the second process, which is the ways students describe how they
'suss out ... the criteria teachers use for a high pass', which they read as being
an ability to produce a *correct reproduction of science facts* and to identify, use
and describe the *right answers and the right methods for getting* them in their lab
reports (Tom, Student). Jen's definition of acting and thinking independently
lacks purchase in actual practice it seems.

A couple of chunks of talk from tapes in the most recent interviews with upper-secondary students reflect the things aired above, but they also illustrate that the changes represented in constructivist work perhaps mainly reflect changes in processes of collecting knowledge (Beach, 1997), not mind-changes in terms of what scientific knowledge is. Students have developed a degree of independence. They will go to libraries, electronic databases and other sources to find things out, and don't just rely on teachers and the course textbook to give them a right answer. But this answer is still taken as *reflecting things as they really are* (Tom, Student) and represents in this way an epistemological realism similar to that engendered in verification activities. Furthermore, school knowledge is still seen to have its primary use value in terms of the way it can be exchanged for course grades. So whilst constructivist lab-work is meant to be a creative project where students *develop their thinking skills ... by reflecting about what a problem and its investigation entails and including this in a write up* (Jen, Teacher), this constructivist meta-cognitive interest does not have the effects intended. The following fieldwork diary extract from CLASP interviews reflects on this:

> ... The students are sometimes asked to devise work themselves ... but each project leads to an answer that can be easily judged correct or incorrect, and is marked accordingly. Also, they are called upon to apply their knowledge ... to design an experiment and determine what its suitable results are (but) this is again assessed and graded in relation to the approach that is known to produce a measurably correct result. (Teachers) are asking students to work without direct supervision, without constant correction, without guiding models and without instructions (but) their practices still reinforce the belief that there is a single right answer and a correct way of finding and evaluating this, and that science has the answer to both already ... Furthermore, students are still graded and positioned in relation to ... how they perform ... These things reinforce a fetishist education relation ... Whilst the constructivist approach applies a theoretically defined model of student learning to the development of education (in principle), the model should not be but is applied regardless of the ... conditions and traditions of education and culture and regardless of student ... commitments toward the demands placed on them ...

The following field-journal extract exemplifies further:

... There are a number of students missing ... Liz said that we were to do an experiment with sodium hydrogen carbonate, which was 'an unusual ionic compound ... in that when heated it does not melt but decomposes ...' The experiment today is about determining what the decomposition products are (and designing) an experiment to do this.

... The students were to speak to Liz about their design before getting started ... There were side-arm test tubes at the front of the room and limewater. The students were given a printed sheet to work from that described the problem ... and also contained (formulae for) six ... decomposition possibilities ... This was meant as a guide to the students, *who were to ... describe and also use a process of experimentation ... to arrive at the correct equation ...* The six alternative decomposition equations were:

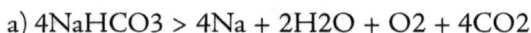

a) $4NaHCO_3 > 4Na + 2H_2O + O_2 + 4CO_2$

b) $NaHCO_3 > NaOH + CO_2$

c) $2NaHCO_3 > Na_2O + H_2O + 2CO_2$

d) $2NaHCO_3 > Na_2CO_3 + H_2O + CO_2$

e) $2NaHCO_3 > 2Na + H_2 + 2C + 3O_2$

f) $4NaHCO_3 > 2Na_2O + 2H_2 + O_2 + 4CO_2$

... The students set about the experiment fairly quickly and were ... heating the compound soon after the ... introduction ... Some of them had weighed the compound beforehand, others hadn't. The students I was with soon had their substance in a side arm test tube. They held it in a hand-clamp and heated it strongly inside a fume cupboard ...

One student made written observations of things like colour changes and so on ... I spoke with the students about what they were doing and looking for ... The answer from one of them, John, illustrates a common point. This was that the main aim, which by the teacher had been described in process terms of thinking about, arriving at, testing and describing a method to identify a chemical product, had been reduced primarily to finding the right equation. [In the context of science education the emphasis on process in discourse became one on product in practice]:

John: I'm not sure what's going to happen but I'm pretty sure down to a couple of alternatives what the answer should be ... Oh look, see

here there's water forming ... It would eliminate a, sorry b, e and f ...
DB: Is that what you're trying to do, eliminate alternatives?
John: That's the main aim, to get the correct solution ...
DB: OK ... There's water, that eliminates some ... and there are a couple that are unreasonable ... But what if the powder was damp ...
John: Mmm yes, it seems to be disappearing ... maybe ...

As is noted in the above, keen observation is needed at the beginning of the reaction in order not to miss a key product, water. Further, some knowledge of how long the reaction is likely to take is also useful, as is trust or knowledge that sodium bicarb doesn't hold water of crystallisation ...

That the sample was dry with no water of crystallisation might have been valuable to ascertain first by the students and could have also been discussed by them. But the ones I was with didn't do this. Instead they tended to rush into the work of identifying the right equation based on observations that would be inconclusive unless this prior knowledge was known. Getting to the right equation from the alternatives a-f was what students focussed on ... and they also became quite stressed in their approach to the work:

Julie: What is it do you think? I was sure it was d but there is no water vapour so now I don't know. We can't just weigh the samples and compare them ...
Kathy: I was sure it should be but ... there is no water vapour ...
DB: Well let's see ... maybe you missed the water but I can't see any ... Supposing there is no water ... What should we do now?
Kathy: ... Let's check the other products ... Well there's no Na there because that would react with air, it's very reactive, and H2 and O2 would also react very heavily and explosively so we can't have that ... Where does that leave us?
Kathy: Like I said. ... b ... We can test for acidity ... NaOH is basic ... .

Missing an observation caused problems for Kathy and her group ... and they became quite irritated about the loss of time, even though by getting onto the wrong track they were forced to rethink parts of an experiment instead of just weighing the final product and guessing what it was (and) they were thus prompted to do some creative thinking and some mental experimentation. But the main focus (still) fell solely on what the right solution to the equation puzzle given by the teacher was and difficulties in getting to this end product produced a stress reaction:

Angela: ... It's basic so it's got to be b, because even if we couldn't eliminate f by weighing and comparing, the NaO_2 is neutral ...

DB: Could there be any problems here ... On the evidence, I could put my money on b, like you Kathy, but something might have gone wrong ... Maybe there was water in the products but you couldn't see it or missed it ...

Julie: Yes the start product is also basic ... I checked ... so if there was some left at the end that would show up even if we had the oxide or the carbonate ... .Isn't bi-carbonate basic too ...

Kathy: Let's do it again ... or ask ...

The students asked the teacher about whether the little vapour they saw could have been water as a product of the decomposition. She said that was the conclusion others had drawn, and that therefore it could be correct (allowing them) to eliminate b as the correct answer:

Kathy: It can't be b then ... it has to be one of the others ...

Julie: (sarcastically) That was smart ... It'd have to be eh?

Kathy: ... So it's a, c, d then ...

Angela: ... But it's not a cos there was no Na ... It has to be c or d ...

Kathy: (triumphantly) That's what I said to start with ... it has to be d

Julie: ... We can't say that yet ... We have to weigh it ... Did you weigh it to start with ... (yes but lime water got in and contaminated the residue) Shit ... we'll have to do it again then ...

DB: (feeling a bit sorry for them) ... Maybe you don't need so much and you can speed it up in the crucible and begin your write up and final chat at the same time ... .Take a couple of grams or so and heat it strongly for about five minutes and then weigh the product ...

The students did as I suggested and, finally, *by working out the equivalent weights of the two possibilities were able to compare these to the obtained weight, to get the right answer* (Angie; my emphasis). Even so, elimination was still a bit sticky because *the alternatives were both equally close to what the actual measurement was (Julie) and the students had to eliminate the wrong one by comparing their results with those of two other groups* (ibid.) and then shifting their actual measurement slightly closer to this value. This way of resolving the dilemma of elimination was not included in the student write up ... In fact not one written lab report from any of the student groups included any reference to collaborations or adjustments of results of these kinds, even though I know there were several such instances that could have been reported ...

There are similarities between constructivist labs and other 'creative' education forms such as PBL (Problem Based Learning), if we compare the aims of constructivist work described with PBL as described by people like Barrows (Barrows, 1980; Barrows and Tamblyn, 1988). These similarities concern the development and reward of student interest and responsibility for education decision-making and learning, and the intention to encourage a liberated view of knowledge. But the question is whether this is what can be seen in practice. The example above would suggest not as in this example the students are apparently trapped in a banking orientation towards their education. This is partly because of their views of knowledge and ideas about the purpose of learning in locally established rules of procedure. But it is also because of the historically given way education qualifications work within the broader relations of education and production in society and the way students may be rewarded for accepting things within an education that offer the greatest exchange value to them (also Dovemark, 2004a, b; Beach, 2006b; Beach and Dovemark, 2005b). Products rather than processes seem to be what is most important.

If we take this as a reasonable representation then even specifically devised labs like the above still did not fulfil constructivist aims. For instance, as can be seen in the example, students did not generate a more liberated view of knowledge. Quite the opposite, they continued to perform in a way that subordinated their own first hand experience and personal knowledge and awareness to the authoritative knowledge, power relations and hierarchies of an established scientific discipline in an attempt to reproduce its particular knowledge products. The use of the teacher as an authority, the use of book facts (in tables) to correct personally made measurements and the avoidance of a discussion of both this fact and its implications in lab write ups emphasise this. Constructivist labs seem to be as problematic with respect to new education aims as the verification activities are. Perhaps more problematic! In constructivist labs reproduction is hidden behind the veneer of a seductive creativity discourse!

Discussion

There is now a strong policy emphasis in Swedish education on the value of creativity across the curriculum for developing new forms of expression in the use of new media in institutional learning environments and for developing new kinds of learning subjects (Lpo 94/98; Lindström, 2002; SOU 1999: 63; Gustafsson, 2003; Dovemark, 2004). This applies even though systematic research about the restraints and value of creativity in learning are still fairly restricted. The present chapter has to a small extent (hopefully) redressed the imbalance, by researching the role, scope and possibilities of creativity in learning in the institutional learning context of the school laboratory, where a general understanding is that truly creative processes of learning in (and of) science can occur (Beach, 1999c, 2004b). We hope this contextual knowledge will be of use for education planners, practitioners and researchers. It gives a critical view of lab science however, not as a process of creativity, but as one of reproduction and exchange.

Creativity in learning involves thinking and behaving in an imaginative and yet purposeful way in order to generate something new or some new knowledge (Seltzer and Bentley, 1999; Craft, 2002; Jeffrey and Craft, 2001; Paulsen, 1996; Lindström, 2002; Persson and Thavenius, 2003; Lindgren, 2001; Leach, 2001; Beach and Dovemark, 2005a, b; Beach, 2006a, b; Jeffrey, 2006). This is suggested also by the synonyms of creativity, such as imagination, ingeniousness, innovation, inventiveness and originality, and its essence of having skills and imagination enough to be genuinely productive in ones learning (Beach, 2006a). Words such as inspired, talented, resourceful, fecund, fertile and fruitful spring to mind, as opposed to their opposites, mimetic, uninspired, infertile and unimaginative. The present chapter would suggest that little obvious creativity exists in lab science in the sense of these terms.

The chapter has concentrated in its empirical analysis on two kinds of lab-work in connection to this issue. These have been identified from analyses of ethnographic data and are termed verification labs and constructivist labs. From the perspective of creativity in education, at first glance the latter seems to be interesting. However, a substantial amount of conflict between the constructivist intentions and what comes to pass in actual classrooms has emerged, and three points that have been attributed great significance throughout the history of curriculum theory as a sub-discipline of education research stride forth from the analysis as particularly interesting. The first of these is that education outcomes are not straightforward reproductions in practice of the ideas expressed in written (formal) curricula or teacher thinking. Indeed what is indicated is that something intervenes in the enactment of ideas in praxis and encourages certain kinds of practices to ensue within the educational context whilst others are effectively opposed (Allman, 1999; Beach, 2000, 2004b, 2006a; Cole, 2003). A hybrid practice emerges, as do hybrid texts. This is not unsuspected. As Barker and Galasinski suggest, the instability of meaning in language implies that culture, identities and identifications are places of hybridity rather than fixed, stable entities. Cultures are zones of shifting boundaries and hybridization (Barker and Galasinski, 2001, p. 11).

This 'expression' has something to say about agency in the contexts we are considering, and it is the kernel of the second main point, which also has two main dimensions. The first is that, as is very often seen to be the case in ethnographic work, the agents whose perspectives are taken and activities documented in investigations are in a sense clearly possible to describe as the makers of their own identities, meanings, understandings and histories. The second is that they make these histories and identities under historical and material conditions—through the use of artefacts, in traditions and through rituals—that they do not directly create, that are not directly under their control and that may not necessarily have been formed in their best interests and that this has a significant impact on what comes to pass and on which understandings are formed of the experiences people have of these events. The third point is linked to this suggestion. It is that active *curriculum agency is* thus a *situational* and *contingent* condition to be *struggled for*, not a universal, historically and materially independent fact of education life for education participants (Beach, 2003b, c; Gustafsson, 2003). It is a question of hegemony in other words. An additional point is that this has perhaps not been adequately factored into the calculations of what is needed in order for a constructivist science curriculum to result in authentically creative forms of learning. Inovative learning ensued in lab activities, but not as anticipated.

Conclusions

What happens to creativity in an exchange based, fetishist education relationship characterised by the presence of a pervasive performativity has been focussed on in the present chapter. What it suggests is that under such circumstances individuals can rarely summon up the force to carry out self-reflection as they live in dispersal as alienated subjects that are not only determined by objects that are external to them, but are themselves also made into things, even as a consequence of their own actions. Under these conditions possibilities for the development of creative learning have been severely curtailed through a commoditisation of the subjects of science education and the subsequent corruption and objectification of knowledge and self-knowledge. These developments counteract expressed curriculum intentions for creative learning but resonate better with the characteristic conditions of a performativity culture. However, further, and to reiterate, the argument is also that they do not ensue solely or even primarily because of the local views and education values of teachers and students or the laws of nature. More important are the stronger hegemonic forces that transform local resistances and alternatives into general forms of cohesion with an authoritarian past, present and future. Local practices are characterised by both reproduction and change in this sense, as the examples discussed in the chapter also hopefully demonstrate, including the example of rule-bending within rule following in verificationist work in what was initially intended to be a constructivist lab activity. Hybrid practices ensued between the discourses of creativity and performativity in the education contexts of laboratory science observed.

Chapter 2

School as a market

As Peters et al. (2000) have written, power in education is mediated through work processes and language, as a modern politics of governmentality through which organisational identities are created (Fejes, 2006). The present chapter is concerned with these issues of mediation in relation to what we described in the introduction as two fundamental present day roles for modern-day schools, through which ideologically compliant workers and consumers for a new corporatist economy are produced, at the same time as schools as institutions also become part of a corporate business plan for the accumulation of private capital in the welfare sector (Beach, 2005a, b; Hill 2006). However, as also Brosio has suggested (1994), the existing nation-State has also a democratic education mission that can make the execution of these two roles difficult.

The *corporatisation* of the welfare State is apparent in education in at least two ways according to e.g. Beach (2003a, 2005a) and Zambeta (2004). It is apparent firstly in education policies. Education policies suggest that there is no gaping hole between market logic and good education and that the two can be 'run together' (also Beach, 2004a; Beach and Dovemark, 2005b), as in the Blairite social compromise in the stakeholder welfare society (Loxley and Thomas, 2001; Goodson and Norrie, 2005). It is apparent secondly in the curriculum, where even though this fact may be disguised, a form of investment logic dominates daily talk and practices in school classrooms and staffrooms (Beach 1999a, b, 2001, 2003a). This was touched on already in the previous chapter, but even the present chapter is concerned with such curriculum issues.

The chapter is based on an ethnographic investigation of upper-secondary schooling in Sweden at the end of the 1990s, in a specific case comprised by the first two mathematics courses on an upper-secondary school natural sciences programme at one upper-secondary school (Beach, 2003a). It draws on a previously published text (Beach, 2003a) Mathematics Goes to Market, from the book *Democratic education: Ethnographic challenges* edited by Dennis Beach, Tuula Gordon and Elina Lahelma.

Two main aspects of the infusion and disguise of neo-liberal interests in education are identified and discussed in the chapter: one concerning discursive practices, another concerning social and material ones. Talk and behaviour inside mathematics classrooms is examined and a correspondence between school and society (specifically a market value relationship, as expressed through a form of *banking education*) is identified and problematised (Freire, 1970; Brosio, 1994; Allman, 1999; Beach, 2004b).

Freire (1970, ch2) described banking education as a form of *education that maintains and stimulates contradiction* through attitudes and practices, which mirror oppressive society as a whole. These include relationships such as (a) the teacher teaches and the students are taught; (b) the teacher knows everything and the students know nothing; (c) the teacher thinks and the students are thought about; (d) the teacher talks and the students listen; (e) the teacher disciplines and the students are disciplined; (f) the teacher chooses and enforces choice, and the students comply; (g) the teacher acts and the students have the illusion of acting through the action of the teacher; (h) the teacher chooses the program content, and the students adapt to it; (i) the teacher confuses the authority of knowledge with his or her own professional authority, which is set in opposition to the freedom of the students; (j) the teacher is the Subject of the learning process, *while the pupils are mere objects.*

Within a banking concept of education learners become adaptable, manageable beings. But as Freire (op cit.) also put it, the more students *work at storing the deposits entrusted to them, the less they develop a critical consciousness* from their intervention in the world as transformers of that world. That is, the more completely they accept the passive role imposed on them, the more they tend simply to adapt to the world as it is, and 'adhere' to the fragmented view of reality deposited in them. *This minimises or annuls creative power and stimulates a credulity that serves the interests of oppressors, who care neither to have the world revealed nor to see it transformed*, according to Freire. The banking concept of education is thus heterodoxical with and antagonistic toward humanistic and transformational education values. It encourages the value practices of education to become fetishised within processes of *value liquidation* (Allman 1999; McMurtry 1999; Brosio 1994).

One year of participant observation that combined conventional ethnography with critical theory and critical discourse analysis (cf. Fairclough 1989, 1993, 1995) formed the theoretical, empirical and analytical foundations of the research behind the present chapter. This has led to a strong concentration on the language of classroom interaction and a strong contextualisation of this linguistic dimension. Three developments in the use of language are focussed on in particular. These are the ways in which text and talk are oriented, vary with social context and are used for controlling, monitoring and naming social interaction in education and education products.

Education from civil commons to commodity form

As described already in the introduction, but see also Beach (2003a), since the mid-1980s, the civil commons of the Nordic welfare States that emerged in the 1940s and 1950s from the taxation of surplus value to support Social-Democratic concepts of the 'folk-home' (the welfare State as the home of all citizens) have come increasingly under fire from the political right, for undermining cost effective services and individual responsibility, and a new welfare discourse has emerged (as a form of 'stakeholder' or 'public choice' welfarism) that is now in ascendancy (Beach, 2003a, 2005a, b; Lindblad et al., 2005). This discourse describes a new form of welfare that celebrates a decentralised, entrepreneurial welfare concept resonant with the GATS agreement. It positions welfare as a commodity that can be selected for consumption, with a price that can be set for profitability (Beach, 2004a, 2005a; Dovemark, 2004a). Market ideas and economic incentives become the new structuring principles for a welfare provision controlled by welfare agencies and economic relations in a welfare society (Dale 1997; Lindblad 1994).

The replacement of the folk-home concept of welfare at the level of discursive practice by a commodity form has had consequences for education provision according to Beach (2005b) and Goodson and Norrie (2005). Some of these are already visible in the Nordic countries, even though they are less preponderant there than elsewhere (Gordon et al., 2003; Beach, 2005a), where instead of a collectively owned and supported single national education system for all, what is developing is an emphatic privatisation of the means of education production (Beach, 2004a), the provision of a market for private sector involvement in education (Broady and Börjesson, 2005; Beach, 2006c) and an introduction of management based on an economic rationalist model (called new public management). These are the external factors. There are however also internal changes as well. These include, according to Broady and Börjesson (2005) and Beach (2003a), an exodus of middle class students from schools in poorer areas and an increase in the competitiveness and privatisation of learning, where people and organisations are becoming inauthentic toward their own values and experiences so as to be successful in the new 'education-as-market' situation (Dovemark, 2004a; Beach and Dovemark, 2004, 2005b). The educational market relation in Nordic countries is thus not yet so much about direct takeovers by external corporate agents. It is more about issues of habituation and how the manner by which modern formal education is being influenced by the prevailing societal economic system is being updated through forms of self-governance (Beach, 2003a; Rose, 1995; Fejes, 2006).

Education restructuring and a new school vision

Several government policies and propositions have been instrumental in establishing the new education context (Lindblad et al., 2005). One of these is Government Proposition 1990/91: 18, regarding decentralisation (Dovemark, 2004a). This proposition expressed that the traditional way of controlling education by State regulation should end, and that control should be exercised instead by Parliament stating education objectives and frameworks centrally and handing over the responsibility for their execution to the municipalities (Proposition 1990/91, p. 17). The expressed aim here was to create new schools that emphasised self-regulation and life-long learning for tomorrow's knowledge society. New national curricula with national objectives reflecting these ambitions were introduced in 1994 (Lindblad 1994, Lundahl 2001; Zackari 2001; Lindblad et al., 2005) and the result was expressed as follows by a head-teacher at one of our research sites:

> We have ... the opportunity to live out pedagogical ambitions for (more) individual responsibility and freedom of choice for students and teachers (as) the key to school improvement ... We have moved from governing by rules to goals. Our aim is to help students to be motivated, alert, inquiring, self-governing and flexible users ... of knowledge. It is in their best interests but demands their responsibility ... We need self-motivated learners in the knowledge society (and) must organise situations to reinforce these qualities ... in order to identify and overcome obstacles in the drive toward ... creativity and self-discipline ... This can be done if we learn to recognise that all students can be active and creative and that successful learning is accomplished actively and creatively ...

Decentralisation and the new curriculum reform worked in tandem with the School Development Agreement (SDA) of 1995 (Lindblad et al., 2005), where individual salary setting and de-regulated work time were introduced in an attempt to give greater autonomy to local schools. Team teaching, collaborative planning and co-operation were extended and professional reflection, it was claimed, was to replace steering by regulations. Municipal districts, local schools, and teachers, at least theoretically obtained possibilities for defining learning, stipulating education goals, selecting content and methods, and for formulating grading criteria and the basic format of evaluation (Sundkvist 2000, Carlgren 2000; Dovemark, 2004a). However, these changes can also be seen in economic terms. They were initiated after the sale of State owned enterprises by a former right-centre coalition government in the aftermath of a national economic crisis brought about by a massive growth in the national debt incurred by that same government. Furthermore, the changes can also be seen in terms of their effects. What changed and what remained the same? Did, for instance, the formality of key subjects decrease after the reform and did self-determined learning increase (see also chapter 1)? Were formal accountability measures, examinations, homework, spot-tests, National equivalence examinations and university entry requirements still appropriated for grading and evaluating student performances and for separating students for differential treatments on the basis of their performances (Korp, 2006)? The present chapter aims to try to answer these questions. Upper-secondary maths is looked at in particular.

Upper-secondary school mathematics

Upper-secondary school mathematics is normally described in terms of its relations to the parent discipline of mathematics, as concerned with complex formulae, difficult theories and demanding cognitive activities (Beach, 2003a), such as analytical thinking, quantitative analysis, applied logic, syllogism and analytical philosophy. However, in the present study maths did not comprise any of these things in any obvious way. It comprised mundane algorithms to be completed under time-pressure and, rather than reflecting over abstract knowledge and complex formulae, getting right answers to concrete algorithms and completing work in time to get good grades was stressed (Dahland 1998; Beach 1999a, b, c, 2001, 2003a, b).[5] The importance of these practices is suggested in the following fieldwork diary extract:

> Most students had at least a distinction (but) are (still) worried about grades and are blaming Liz for them not getting a top grade (which) they need ... to be competitive toward university entrance ... They need to do

5 These things very often typify school maths from early years all the way through the compulsory school in Sweden, if we read with for instance Gustafsson (2003) and Bentley (2003) and into the upper-secondary school (Dahland 1998; Beach 1999a,b, 2001, 2003a).

the work to be competitive and get the results ... Pre-set problems are developed and swapped in examinations to obtain good school grades and university places. These are major forces conditioning the social practices of the education ...

What is described above is related to a 'banking concept of education' (Freire, 1970; Allman, 1999), by which a potentially educative relationship is transformed into a relationship that reflects the characteristics of capital conversion, accumulation and exchange in a competitive and privatised learning processes (Beach and Dovemark, 2005b). In the Communist Manifesto of 1848, Marx and Engels' describe this kind of development as commodification, the reification of aspects of social life as natural objects with a fetishised economic value form. Such fetishisations help to constitute the market value relationship spoken on earlier and were visible in field-notes and interview data in comments like the following from four different maths teachers at the research sites:

This job is about helping students recognise their abilities and ... make the best of what they have ... Joint abilities to maximise output sets limits on any return that can be made from education for those involved in it.

If only there was more time ... we could give them the attention they need ... All of them have ability. I have to help them ... find ways of being effective and make the best of their abilities and what they have to offer as learners ...

There is an amount of ability, time, available resources and a set of demands. It is a simple equation of optimising availability and effort to get a good result ... These students are all potentially capable ones ... I have to help them become effective learners as well ... They bring what they can to the work. I do what I can to help them get a good return on their ability and effort ...

We have created a new school environment and organise resources to help students take charge of their own learning ... They can all be successful ... but there is an ideal and then there is reality ... They don't all have the ability or motivation needed to be successful ... given the competition ...

They don't all recognise the need to invest. This shows in the end ... The sooner the better really ...

The working form and discourse of banking education is apparent above as standing against the vision of the new school curriculum, where maths is said to be about 'helping participants to develop understandings of themselves, their subject and their situation, so they may be able to take more responsibility for their learning' (Liz), as it objectifies the students working relationships within the education in relation to standardised performance criteria (Beach, 2003a). Differentiation is normalised and aims like free choice and understanding are claimed but contradicted and abandoned, whilst aims like covering the syllabus or textbook in time so selections of individuals for further investment processes in economically rationalist cycles of education can be made, are upheld. Differentiating practices are created. Students are separated out for different kinds of treatment.

> Different problems (exist) with different groups ... The weaker students need less frustrating work to occupy them ... The clever students need to be convinced to tell us about their problems so we can help them with them ... Some have problems but don't want to say so ...
> (Ken: Teacher)

> We are to help students ... find their own levels and spaces ... to make use of resources ... to the best of their abilities ... Some are worth an extra effort because of their extra-ordinary abilities and interests ... We can help them go far ... Others, not science students ... need to be occupied with something ... so we can get on with helping those who ... have the ability to do well. ...
> (Brian: Teacher)

As expressed in Beach (2003a), it would be easy to blame teachers for the objectification of students and the differentiating outcomes of education. But before we do this, we must remember that although teachers compare and grade student performances and treat students as investment objects on the basis of how they use the resources and consume the mathematical activities that are given to them, this is not only a decision made by individual teachers themselves (Bowles and Gintis 1976, 1988a, b; Brosio 1994). It is also part of a global and historical school practice. In this sense teacher understandings of the distribution of student ability and their acceptance of the liberal attainment ethic are culpable factors in the accommodation of new principles to old ideas. But teachers did not invent the differentiation they employ, nor do they fully control the procedures by which it is reproduced in school. Beach (2003a, p. 122) wrote:

> It is true that economic principles of investment that teachers condone and support resonate better with education practices than formal aims do, in that students do the same things at the same time and are then compared and graded according to their performances against a given standard. And it is true that teachers do make students into objects in an education market place whose intrinsic worth is based on calculations of an objectified investment value. But neither of these things are things that individual teachers alone are responsible for. Maths education involves students in privatised and repetitive calculations and the attainment of measurably correct answers to identical problems with set answers that are exchanged for school grades and it sets them up to be assessed, graded and selected in practices that reproduce and inscribe the capitalist hallmark of domination and subordination (through) performance standards over which they have little control. But this 'commoditised ideal' of banking education is stabilised by its external relations to long-standing production relations in wider society and is internalised and accepted as normal by both students and teachers alike. Students internalise performativity and investment values ... as resistance correlates with counter productive tendencies.

What is described here are the outcomes of new ideas within the specific context of the upper-secondary school mathematics programme observed, but what is also suggested is that these outcomes, although they are both obvious and logical, aren't inevitable. They are cultural and contingent. They represent the formation of objective forms of education capital (such as described in Bourdieu's work: e.g. Bourdieu 1997). They are culturally produced as key aspects of education and ideology and are coherent with social and cultural reproduction through education in a class-based capitalist society.

Hegemony and opposition

In Beach (2003a) ethnographic descriptions and discussions were analysed in relation to a particular concept of hegemony, as a potential to constitute the world in line with the interests of a specific group through the common and unquestioned adoption of a logic that determines what is generally understood to be true. This is a question of hegemony according to Gramsci (1967/1988) as it relates to the alliances by means of which a leading class assumes a position of leadership over others by 'guaranteeing' them certain benefits (Gramsci 1967, 1988; Beach 1995, 1997, 1999b, d, 2000; Bernstein 1990). However, as the guarantee is usually false, hegemony also becomes a question of an articulation of interests, not just through a guarantee of reward, but also through a fusion of economic, political, intellectual and moral leadership brought about by groups that have the ability to articulate the interests of others to their own by means of ideological struggle.

Hegemony means that education institutions are not monolithic entities. There is always a degree of incompleteness and contradiction about them. For instance, in the present investigation the idealised needs of abstract individuals as articulated in school policy texts like the national curricula are always negated by the material educational needs of concrete classes and the individual members of these classes and can be recognised and responded to by them. The educational needs of the working class and its individuals (and their teachers) are not the same as are those of the upper- and upper-middle classes (and their teachers). Moreover, some of the agents inside the education contexts we have done research in recognise this. Several teachers for instance tried actively to break the concept of banking education in mathematics and some students openly expressed, albeit in their own ways, the view that the maths they experienced represented a boring, repetitive, crypto-capitalist, money-to-money investment logic that was played out in everyday life, with negative effects on the majority of those exposed to it (Beach, 2003a, b). A good question to ask therefore is what happened to this opposition? This was framed as follows in Beach (2003a):

> There was teacher opposition to banking education ... However, this resistance was often restricted, localised and even essentially reproductive. Alternative maths was either used simply 'as a motivational device and soft option for weaker groups' (Brian: Teacher) or it was used first after differentiation had been accomplished ... Student opposition obtained an even worse fate. Either it was ignored as 'an inconsistency that everyone goes through' (Liz), or it was turned back on students as a means of suggesting that they, not the maths, were the learning

problem. For instance, 'Jon simply didn't have the metal for maths' ...
(Beach, 2003a, p. 123)

On closer observation there were two different levels of criticism from students to consider. The most common one had a basic symmetry with the working hegemony. Typical here was a criticism that maths was 'high pace and repetitive, tough, but if you have a head for numbers and are set on a good career you'll get by' (student). This symmetry is visible also with respect to teachers' understandings of the demands of maths. In maths 'students have to accommodate to demands to find the best solution to a problem. Maths can be experienced as repetitive and boring (but) there is no other way. They simply have to buckle down to it' (Brian: Teacher). As one student, Jon, put it: *there is no time for opposition and debate ... only time to learn the (facts) for solving the problems ... If you stop to question what ... or why ... you fall behind. Once you get behind ... catching up is never ending ...* There is a normalisation tendency here, in that the criticism is absorbed into a dominant discourse of limited supply and dominant ideas about the need of effort and ability to achieve. Common concepts about maths being a special subject that requires special ability and a commitment to work are reproduced, as is a normative understanding that student performances will always reflect these qualities. A pathological view of oppositional students also often becomes apparent. Such a view is expressed by Ken, a teacher at one of the sites:

> There is a syllabus ... I can do so much (the rest) is up to them ... I explain (things) in the time that we can give (after that) you just have to move on ... Some of them can't keep pace. They lack ability or effort usually. The good ones are aware of their goals ... and buckle down to the job of learning ... Interest, commitment and ability ... separate good (from) mediocre performers ... and science students ... from most others ...
>
> (Ken)

Described above is how, inside education as an internal, symbolic market, individuals are graded according to their choices and performances with respect to contents and ideas that are acted towards as fixed and ready made (Lundahl, 2001; Beach and Dovemark, 2005b). However, also suggested is that they accept this subjection as freedom and flexibility and in so doing become supporters of an ideological practice that works against the development of common values by reducing effective agency to a reactionary form. This is very evident in mathematics education in the examples given, as within it education control and selection is accomplished in discursive, ideological and material practices, through consensus rather than overt force. Rituals are deployed that indoctrinate individuals to submit to a market ideology.

The concept of maximisation of self-interests, suggested by the examples, is important within the liberalist concept of the market. And what we are trying to suggest is that this notion of the 'selfish individual' is consistently reproduced and reinforced within the present educational arrangements and discourses of upper-secondary schooling (Båth, 2006; Korp, 2006). As illustrated in relation to mathematics in the present chapter, education is, despite new policy rhetoric, not about freedom to learn, and nor is it about authentic learning or fair rights of negotiation, broadened involvement, the realisation of an intrinsic value as a learner and the promotion of life-long learning (Beach, 2003a)! It is a fetishistic and commoditised system of relations where competitive exclusion and ideological reproduction prevail.

Put in plainer language, maths is a competitive subject that makes the procedures of performance related differentiation seem fair; even to those who have their educational life chances damaged through these procedures. Maths education is in this sense seen in a very different way to the common one, as a distinctive part of a *hegemonic bloc* of forces and practices that provide a structural and cultural *correspondence with the ideological and confirmatory needs of a capitalist investment logic* (Bowles and Gintis 1988a, b; Brosio 1994).

Discussion

The suggestions made in the present chapter are consistent in several respects with those of the previous one, regarding the structure versus agency debate in educational research, where what is being suggested should now be quite obvious. This is that there are formations of power operating in relation to maths education that have a common ancestry in, structural similarity with and a common moral foundation inside a market value programme (Beach, 2003a), and that this limited the development of the upper-secondary school curriculum reform in particular ways, because even though agency existed more than just hypothetically within the researched contexts, active agency has still reproduced rather than opposed commoditisation inside everyday education practices. This means that although it is currently assumed that teachers and students have extensive agency to develop education practices, this agency is severely limited.

Banking concepts of education have developed and or been maintained within the current attempts to reform education, even against the interests (both materially expressed and implicit) of those working within it.

Banking concepts of education are antithetical to the concepts of education expressed in the new school vision, as they contribute both materially and ideologically to the suppression of autonomous, oppositional thought, and also set foundations for the development of a capitalist structure of inter-subjectivity (both through inter-discursive articulations and incentives of control) that enables a regular interpellation (Althusser, 1969) of market discourses at individual levels that allows a market value programme to be actively supported even by those who are oppressed by and would otherwise only be made subject to it. Moreover, structuring education according to the logic of the market means structuring it against values of equity, social inclusion, social justice and critical reflection. These things are materially repressed in the world of the market. As Brosio (1994), Ainley (2000), Hill (2001, 2006), Allman (1999) and McMurtry (1998) point out, the values of a good education and market values are antithetical because of a logical contradiction concerning what it means to positively attain within them.

The antithesis signalled by McMurtry (1998 p. 188) regarding the respective logics of the market and (good) education is an important point. In good education, practices of autonomous co-determination predominate, where people become creative, critical thinkers and doers. In markets dependency relations and the possibilities of exploitation prevail, as people pay to consume and come to depend on the products, services and (good) judgements of others. Inside a market programme the value-practices of education are not about living out progressive democratic principles or helping students develop understanding (Beach, 2003a). They are about reproducing the conditions of reproduction for a market discourse within local forms of work (Beach, 2001, 2003b).

As written in Beach (2003a), the market in the sense that it is used here is not just a device for the allocation and distribution of goods, it is also a system for producing and ordering preferences that in turn become embedded in culture (Peters et al., 2000). It is a form of govern-mentality (Fejes, 2006), where the governing of schooling becomes the inscription of political rationalities in the sensitivities, dispositions and wariness of individuals. It is a system of reason that shapes and fashions not only schools themselves and their curricula, but also the individuals within them. The reform of the State and the individual become joined as a social project through changing both practices and the inner capabilities of people as individuals (Popkewitz, 2000).

The reproductive tendencies of the economic system within education do not stop at this however according to other research connected to the present chapter. According to this research, in the same sense as within economic privatisation more broadly, inside the new education system, when market interests override issues concerned with equity and equality, the children of the culturally rich (in terms of social and cultural capital) may tend to get educationally rich (in terms of qualifications) whilst the children of the people 'at the bottom' of the socio-economic ladder (with less social- and cultural capital) may tend to end up also at the bottom of the ladder of educational attainment (Beach, 1999a, b, 2001, 2003b; Svensson 2001, 2002, 2006; Ball, 2003; Eriksson and Jonsson 2003; Korp, 2006). This will lead to a further accentuation of inequalities and a growth of distress. It is an element of the links between cultural production in school and the broader aspects of cultural-, and ultimately even social reproduction and is an issue that is explored further in the next two chapters of the book.

Conclusions

The present chapter has very much been about the identity possibilities and subject positions produced through student-teacher actions and interactions in part of the formal school. It is about how, although produced within the school context, the social and discursive practices and ideas that are expressed by the students and teachers are also resonant with dominant cultural understandings of the distribution of ability, individual limitation and investment thinking and the cultural requirements for the reproduction of a hierarchic social order. These culturally reproductive beliefs support a view of good education as involving effective accommodation to subtly imposed external demands that become internally self-regulating. They concern 'governmentality' in the sense of Foucault or, perhaps more accurately the working of hegemony in the senses expressed by Gramsci.

On the other hand, the chapter is also about material forms of control. Successful students have to do certain things to be successful; such as repetitive calculations and exams to accumulate education capital; and have to act towards this situation as if it was a natural one where ability, genuine commitment, solid directions and practice make the perfect student, and where success is taken to confirm the value of the learner as an investment object (Beach, 2003a). And it is also about denial! Whilst what is normal to maths, as a form of the banking concept of education, is sitting still, doing what you are told and engaging in repetitive activities toward the determined ends of being assessed and selected by an external power in relation to an ability-discourse over which one has little control, the importance of this *as a form of partially self-imposed and therefore also avoidable compliance* is often denied.

Finally the chapter is about the development of market ideas inside education practices in the modern curriculum. Just specifically an emphatic competitiveness and privatisation of learning seems to be developing in the education investigated and people and organisations are also becoming inauthentic in their practices toward their own values and experiences so as to be successful. Although the current education to market relationship in recent school reforms in Sweden is thus not yet about direct takeovers by external corporate agents, it is about reproducing the conditions necessary for a prevailing societal economic value system to take hold (Beach, 2003a). This is the issue of habituation spoken on as a pan-European (even global) educational development in Beach (2005a, b).

What the chapter has not fully taken up but could have is issues of class, class inequality and class antagonism. Education in Sweden is still formally a part of the public commons of the welfare state, at least in the main and on paper. But both the concept of the welfare state and the content of education are changing (Gordon et al., 2003; Beach and Dovemark, 2005a; Lindblad et al., 2005), and in the name of solidarity we should always ask who is being included in the concept of community as it changes and who is being left out. The former folk-home form for the welfare state created obstacles for inclusion through its notions of identity based on ethnicity, religion and sexuality. But as other research has suggested the market is expanding not reducing inequalities (Ball, 2003; Broady and Börjesson, 2005). Class differences have expanded significantly in Sweden since the introduction of market principles of control, be this in education, health, transport or dental hygene, as they have elsewhere (Beach, 2005a, b).

Chapter 3

Creativity as a cultural commodity

The ethnography in the present chapter is an example of what we term educational policy ethnography, by which we mean the investigation of living processes of policy interaction from inside educational contexts in the wake of specifically formulated and targeted educational principles, practices and projects that are intended to have direct and foreseen consequences for defined education cultures (also Gustafsson, 2003; Dovemark, 2004a; Troman et al., 2006). The educational policies in focus are recent policies of creativity, responsibility and self-determination in education in Swedish schools (SOU 1990:20; School Minister Ask in the Skolverk report, 1992: 2, p. 46; Skolverket, 1992; Kommunförbundet, 1996; SOU 2000: 39; Lindensjö and Lundgren, 2000; Dovemark, 2004a). They have been researched in three education sites, through intermittent site visits over seven years from 1998 to 2004. These visits have involved slightly different approaches to the time factor in ethnography.

Jeffrey and Troman (2004) have identified three different ways of organising and 'using time' in ethnographic fieldwork. One of these was a compressed mode. This mode involves an intensive period of continual work in the field of say two or three days to up to a week or two, to provide intensive descriptions of events under that time period and to allow for and facilitate the comparison and interrogation of existing theoretical ideas. This period is not intended to be an isolated and independent piece of research however. It comprises just one part of a more encompassing investigation.

The second time mode was termed the discriminating intermittent mode by Jeffrey and Troman. In this mode the length of time spent doing the research can be anything from two or three months to several years, but with a very flexible approach to the frequency of site visits. Adopting this approach means spreading several days of observation (in full or half day packages) over an extended time period, with the exact frequency depending on the researcher selecting particular foci as the research develops.

The compressed and discriminating intermittent modes are very often combined in actual ethnographic field research practices with the third mode described by Jeffrey and Troman, which they termed the recurrent research mode.

In this mode specifically identified and pre-named temporal phases formalise the research methodology in terms of sampling decisions and the aim is to research the same temporal phases, e.g. beginning or end of term, school celebratory periods (e.g. Christmas party, sports-day and prize-giving), exam periods or things like external inspections, student council meetings, meetings of the Board of Governors, teacher-team-meetings and so forth on a pre-determined basis.

In the research reported on here we have combined all three modes within long term fieldwork at three different sites; each of which has been visited over different periods, ranging from about 18 months to three years in total span, just before the turn of the millennium in one instance and between 2001 and 2004 in the other two. The research aimed to develop insight into the ways in which differently positioned groups and individuals became actively tied to local processes and institutional relations. The intention was to identify and analyse the processes through which actors carve out and stabilise particular forms of behaviour in school and to disclose something of the interests they may be operating in and how they work. In Willis (2000) terms we are speaking here of a project of showing ambiguous, irreducible, complex and often ironic, collective and cultural forms of knowledge that engender codes of understanding and embrace particular forms of action potential (Beach, 2006c).

Students talking about going to school and about learning

We have focused on a number of issues in our investigations of school policy projects. These included the reasons pupils gave for why they went to school in the first place, what they did there, and why. Did they go to school in order to make and develop their own knowledge through creative interactions in the curriculum, in line with the new constructivism inspired creativity agenda and the new curricula, or do other issues prevail?[6]

The students/pupils we have spoken with gave many different accounts of why they went to school. However, almost all of them, but particularly those who were amongst the most successful individuals at each site, emphasised school as ideally being about helping them to plan and prepare for their future

---

6   Research in three classes has been extensively focussed. These are a mixed ability class of fifteen year-olds (Alpha) from an urban comprehensive school in West Sweden and two classes of upper-secondary science pupils, one from an upper-secondary school called Sci High and one from a school called New School. However, even other upper-secondary students have been involved in the investigation, mainly from other (usually practical/vocational) programmes of study at the schools. All in all we have collectively spent about 1,500 hours engaged in participant observation in the schools. Subsidiary observations have also been carried out in three other classes and over 50 formal interviews and a large number of field conversations have been done with students and their teachers.

and as ideally being for helping them to get a good job (or in some cases a job at all), or a desirable further or higher education (also Giota, 2001). In this sense they discursively position school as an institution that is about developing 'positive' social relations, possibilities and practices in one context that have their orientation and rewards in a later one (Dovemark, 2004b). Particularly science students at New School (where we deliberately focussed on this issue extensively) talked about school in this way, as a 'preparation for something to come ... rather (than) as something worth living for actually in the here and now' (Tom). This has also been identified previously as a common middle-class strategy (even Ball, 2003).

Many students spoke of distinctions between what could be called the formal/official, the informal and the physical/material parts of the school (also Gordon et al., 2000). The formal school was the one spoken about most, which doesn't necessarily mean that it was the most important in all situations for most students. This part of the school was often described in relation to future aims, where it was either described as a place of ruin and broken dreams, by formally unsuccessful students, or of valorisation and a stepping stone into a positive future, for successful ones. There were also ambivalent positions of tolerance and colonisation somewhere between. In the case of positive valorisations, the formal school tended to appear as 'an obvious place for learning facts for the future' (Klara) and for 'preparing for the future' (Pete).

Most students talked about 'success or failure in the future', as being in some way related to 'success in the official part of school' (Pete) and expressed that 'success at learning (facts and skills) was of paramount importance to them as individuals' (Tom) as these 'facts ... were the answers ... to tests and questions ... that gave good marks (and) influenced grading' (Klara). Magnus, a pupil who was described as 'outstanding' (Carole) by his teachers, put things as follows: 'the formal school (is) a place for learning new things that will be important later', whilst Rita, another successful student in the formal school, suggested that it 'was the part of school that was important for learning things that are necessary ... for work and the future'. As she put it, 'you go to school ... to get a good education (and) job ... in the future' (Rita).

The formal school was however spoken about differently by different student categories. Some, usually but not only younger pupils, appeared to fear it, others to revere it, and there were clear patterns in how often it was referred to by different student groups. Formally successful students talked more, more often and in more varied ways about the formal school than did the formally less successful ones, particularly older ones. Moreover, when the latter did talk about the formal or official school it was, as our later examples show, often in less than positive terms. It was often described as an uncomfortable place (cf. Gordon et al., 2000) that was (usually) tolerated at best but definitely not often enjoyed.

The informal school was also addressed differently by different individuals. And again there were some patterns in respect of the categories of belonging to formally successful or formally less successful parts of the student cohort. According to our data dressing smart, having the right (trendy, popular, attractive, fun, 'dangerous') clothes and friends were important to most students some of the time (regardless of issues of formal success and/or lack of it, social class, gender, or ethnicity). But for some of them these things were the most important issues almost all of the time. 'Being daring and challenging toward authority' (Andy) also counted highly for some. Furthermore, there were also status hierarchies in the informal school, although these were based on the accumulation of different kinds of 'credits' and from different sources than in the formal. It was mainly the informal school that was regarded as a place for socialising, although some students did colonise the spaces of the formal school for informal projects. Actual material and also 'virtual' card-playing during unsupervised but still 'formal' periods was the most common.

Success in the official school

The formal school as a site for compliance and reproductive learning styles and strategies is something that according to research from the seventies and eighties has a long history in the Swedish school system (see e.g. Marton, Hounsell and Enwistle, 1986; Svensson, 1986; Säljö, 1975, 1982, 1986). However, this 'attitude' towards learning is also also reflected today in over 70% of our interview comments on learning in the formal school, which asserts just how highly valorised learning things with a tangible exchange rate within education and between education and the job market still is; at least at a subjective level. All formally successful students express this (Beach, 1999a, b, 2001, 2003a, b; Dovemark, 2004; Dovemark and Beach, 2004b). The following fieldnote extract relates to this issue:

> For formally successful students there is an obvious parallel between learning at school and getting a good qualification and a good job to follow. And working hard at 'being good at school' (Marcus) as well as then also actually 'being good in school' (Klara) was expressed as

important in a double sense. As Klara and several other successful students put it, the aim was not only to 'work hard so as to get good grades ... to get into the upper-secondary science programme and then after that a university course with good career prospects' (Klara, Carole and others in similar terms), but also 'to be seen to be good at school (and) interested in school work by teachers' (Marcus). As Carole (student) put it. 'doing well at school is important to my future and I want to get as good grades as possible in all subjects ... I need these to get into medical school ... I want to be a doctor and you need high points to get in there ... Through performances in school it is possible ... to identify and select the right people for valuable university places and positions ... as these performances serve as measures of ... quality or value (and) help us show our abilities' (Carole) ... 'The school system helps to find the right people for the right course in university ... or the right job' (Pete) ...

The students' comments are clear with regards to the operation of an investment logic within the formal school. However, their comments are also mirrored and matched evenly at this level by many teacher voices. As one of them put it:

> We have to put demands on them and need to make these as clear as possible to be fair to all of them so the right students get the right rewards for the correct attitude and performance ... Setting grades and evaluating their knowledge is the main professional duty for us ...
> (Brian: Teacher, Sci High)

Learning seems to have particular characteristics according to these field-notes that align well with an education akin to Willis' notion of fetishised cultural commodities (1999) and Freire's (1970) 'banking education', as a form of accumulated labour that is predominantly seen as important in terms of exchange values and cultural and symbolic capital that is anticipated to influence education, life and career chances positively (Allman, 1999; Dovemark, 2004; Beach and Dovemark, 2004a, b, 2005b). Students holding such views are the antithesis of Willis's Lads (Willis, 1977, 2000). Teachers holding them liken Mac An Ghail's (1988) old disciplinarians. Compliance and hard work are highlighted as investment objects that can be exchanged for qualifications that give the promise of a valuable education future and a good job to follow (Beach, 1999a, b, 2003a, b). The demands of performativity rather than creativity predominate here and supply the main priorities that influence personal dispositions toward learning (Beach and Dovemark, 2005c). This was important to the material history and culture of schools as many students perceive them:

> You go to school ... to learn things you don't know ... and teachers should ... help us get the good grades ... they know we will need in order to get on ... We are here to get help in correcting things we don't understand (so) we can pass exams ... and get on in life   (Carole)

Thus the data and analysis here suggest that with certain pupils and teachers in particularly the highly formalised singularities in the official school, the predominant form for the organisation of teaching and learning is equitable with an objectified form where teaching is highly classified and framed, where subject knowledge is valorised and objective and where learning becomes a form of accumulated labour. Performativty has a positive cultural value from this perspective. However, there is a problem with respect to this normative view of school and the ideological and material compliances it encourages, because if and when the main aim for students becomes finding and reproducing other people's answers to other people's questions, they may be ordered, graded and selected according to categories over which they have little control in a manner contradictory to creativity and self-determination. Students become dependent and objectified rather than creative and active.

A different orientation

Not every student had the performativity orientation to school described above. Indeed some students, like Willis's Lads in *Learning to Labour* (Willis, 1977), openly ridiculed it. For them other things than formal learning formed the main purpose of going to school and they saw compliance to the performativity requirements of the formal school as a sign of weakness not strength (Gordon et al., 2000; Beach and Dovemark, 2004b, 2005b). However, another important point to note is that using school spaces for socialising and having fun was in the majority predisposed to students who, according to our data, were rebelling against or had rejected, been rejected from, or were for some other reason outside the formal school ambition of high levels of individual success and a long academic education career (also Beach, 2001, 2003a, b). There was evidence of an anti-school subculture.

> I come to school to mix, sober up, play pool ... It is a place to be in the day ... It's free ... it's usually open ... you know there's girls and you can have a laugh ... It's easy to get round the attendance thing ... You turn up (first) and then bunk off ... I meet friends in the Cafe, listen to music, play pool ... Sometimes school is like a prison ... But you can bunk off and clown about sometimes (to break) the boredom of it all ... You can more or less do what you want here. (Faton)

Using the school first and foremost for socialising purposes is in a sense a *colonising response* (Beach, 2003a, b; Beach and Dovemark, 2004b, 2005b) toward the formal territory of the school in that schools are not being used in line with what the major institutional power brokers (teachers and head teachers mainly) understand them as existing for. However, it is still teachers and school leaders (such as head teachers) who have formal power and in their voices it is the 'pupils (not) the school that is at fault and to blame' (Ulla), as such uses also 'mark a distinction between good and bad students' (Brian). Good students 'use school (properly) for proper study procedures ... not to oaf around in' (Ulla). Pupils have a different view. Or at least some of them do:

> We do crazy things sometimes (or even) just keep our heads down so as not to draw attention to ourselves if we are carrying on with things we don't want others to know about ... We do things for ourselves ... for a laugh (or) a challenge ... What we don't usually do ... is 'swot' and bother too much about what teachers want us to do ... (Eric)

> It's a good thing you have your friends ... We go to school to meet ... show off new clothes (and) arrange what to do outside of school, like going to the city or the local mall, meeting for a coffee, going to a friend's house to hang after school ... or during school time even, just hanging and talking even, anything ... (Karen)

Students from the practical/vocational programmes tended to represent the 'alternative' school subcultures the most in our data (also Beach, 1999b, 2001; Beach and Dovemark, 2004b, 2005b). These students tend more often to just 'come to school when they feel like it' (Eric) and more or less 'do what they want when they are there' (ibid.). And they emphasise therefore, in contrast to 'mainstream' academic students, that they are able to exercise some genuine freedom of choice within their education now that their differentiation out of the streams of intense academic learning and competition of the 'normal school culture' has been completed (Beach and Dovemark, 2004a, b). It is first here, according to the students themselves, that they have been 'really able to feel free' (Faton) of the fetishist relations of production of a 'banking form' of education (Beach and Dovemark, 2005b, c), 'because they no longer care about winning over teachers (and) getting qualifications and credentials' (Les). They 'have other priorities than (performing like) *good* pupils' (Gail) and they find 'very little of positive value in the formal school anyway' (Lynne). Andersson (1999) and Giota (2001) have suggested that this is the way the official school is experienced by all students—except the most conformist of them—if and when they take a more authentic position in respect to how school reflects (and deals with) their own class-cultural values and life-outlook (also Willis, 1977).

The conformist student outlook is not exclusively located in the 'successful' academic quarters of the mainstream school, but it is predominant there because it is here that the exchange value of education is primary (Dovemark, 2004a, b; Dovemark and Beach, 2004a, b; 2005b; Korp, 2006; Tholin, 2006). Students have put this in their own terms, *you try to do whatever you can to get good grades so you can get into the education you desire and need ... and later a good job or career* (Toby).

School as commodity culture and schooling as fetishist practice

A main characteristic of the conformist outlook described above is a tendency to express a distinct compliance with a hegemonic understanding of the formal school functions of grading, where an accumulation of grades with a high exchange value is expressed as the main point of learning and where selection based on learning performances becomes the main accepted aim of education (Korp, 2006). This is what we mean by education as a cultural commodity and learning as accumulated labour; by which we mean an objectified form of learning in which correct (kinds of) performances are what count.

Performativity is predominant in the formal school. And it even becomes a principle of governance as it enables functional relationships to develop between education and selection through the institutionalisation of objective regulations of the self (Jeffrey, 2002, 2003, 2006; Beach, 2001, 2003a, b). Formal school is basically an extreme form of performativity culture that employs judgements, comparisons and displays of ability as a means of incentive, control and exchange based on material and symbolic rewards and sanctions that students have to, if not accept, at least seem to accept and respond to as quite normal (Beach, 2003a; see also Mac An Ghail, 1988). Student comments from both Sci High and New School are used below to illustrate this:

> There are standards to measure up to ... That's how things are ... You do what you have to and perform according to requirements ... You sometimes try to influence teachers in setting and marking tests (and) try to get your grade up if its not as good as you want it to be ... (Gemma)

> It's very repetitive work sometimes and a lot of studying outside of school hours. You have to learn how to get to the right answers ... That's all there is to it ... There's not much negotiating space or invention involved. 2 + 2 is 4, unless you're working in base 3 ... Some things you need to know by heart so you can use them when you need to ... It helps to instinctively recognise the answers to some algorithms ... Things go more quickly and that is important when there's a lot to do ...   (John)

> There are right ways and wrong ways with little between ... Freedom to determine what you will study actually gets in the way ... because we waste time experimenting ... Direct recognition is important ... such as being able to recognise potentials ... without thinking ... We need good grades ... and that's mostly about hard work and ability ...
>   (Gemma)

These statements do not fit well with the aims of creative learning and the recent constructivist reframing of knowledge and learning in the new school curricula (Lpo 94; Lpf, 94). In creative learning learners must become free from external determinations so they can fabricate their own knowledge from their own first hand experiences and they must be able to determine the course of their learning themselves, based on a valorisation of their own personal class-cultural capital and values as learning outcomes (Beach and Dovemark, 2005b). This is exactly and specifically what formally successful students in our samples were not doing according to statements like the ones above. As they put it:

> Studying successfully is about knowing what ... is important ... Good
> learning means being self-disciplined and (making) sacrifices in order
> to learn what the teachers say is important ... (Tess and Joan)

> You plan ... and scheme out how to get those good grades ... What things
> they will ask ... how and what the most economic way of answering is ...
> You might even stay home from a test if you ... don't feel prepared ... if
> you think you'd be better waiting ... Mainly it is about working hard to
> answer questions teachers give you and (finding) out about things they
> say are important (to) be successful ...   (Trev)

The above type of statements represented by far the majority of comments
from science students from Sci High and New School, as well as comments by
the self- and teacher identified 'best students' at Dovemark's sites, all of whom
agreed on some main principles of education when asked. These were 'that it was
imperative for high quality in their learning that the teacher had control, knew
their subject and made them accountable by setting high targets for them to
attain' (e.g. Pete and Andy) and that the teachers should not 'leave the students
to make ... decisions about what to learn and how' (e.g. Janet and Kate). However,
one further dimension of the student perspective on creativity also emerged.
This was that creativity could even become fetishised (Willis, 1999; Beach,
1999c, 2003a; Lundahl, 2001; Dovemark, 2004a; Beach and Dovemark, 2004a,
b, 2005b). One student, Klara, gave a common kind of expression along these
lines when she described freedom in learning as presenting *a great opportunity*
for you to show what you (can do). Those who don't take this chance ... only have
themselves to blame ... In these situations taking active responsibilities or not
becomes a new feature in the differentiation of students in school (Lundahl,
2001). Formally successful students seem to know this and they also seem to
know how to exploit it to a competitive advantage.

Discussion: Learning and alienation

According to the present chapter, but see also Beach and Dovemark (2004b,
2005b), students are formally successful in the official school primarily through
conforming to requirements that are diametrically opposed to the development
of creativity, critical reflection, self-determination and learner-independence, for
two basic reasons. The first is that formal success requires something other than
creativity, critical reflection and self-determination most of the time. The second

is that it is dependent on a fetishisation of creativity and self-determination. *Learning* becomes an activity concerned with the private acquisition of education goods as education capital (Beach, 2003a, b). Alienation characterises this kind of learning culture well.

As we described in Beach and Dovemark (2005b), Marx described alienation in his economic and philosophical manuscripts, when he expressed how, due to the existence of private property and the division of labour and capital, workers experience the external expression of creative power through labour in a negative as opposed to what would be more natural, a positive sense, as they become estranged from their own labour, the labour process itself, fellow humans and their own species being, because they are no longer in control of their own productive life (Beach, 1999c, d, 2000). Engels (1969) wrote concerning alienation that whilst voluntary productive activity is the highest enjoyment known, so too is compulsory toil a cruel punishment, as nothing is more terrible than being constrained everyday from morning to night to work for something that actually has nothing whatsoever to do with the work itself.

Alienation, as expressed above, seems able to characterise the learning as accumulated labour of *formally successful students* in the present chapter, as the chapter describes exactly the conditions of external pressure or coercion to learn, in a situation where there is no actual significance or value attached to the process and content of the learning itself. Learning has primarily an instrumental exchange value. It lacks genuinely creative, practical, subjective value in its own right, as it is not intrinsically satisfying, but merely a means to another end. Learning is essentially meaningless in itself. It *offers little beyond a qualification, grade or credit* as a means to engage the emotions and the imagination (Beach, 1999d; Allman, 1999). It is consumed as a form of labour power that is converted into a form of objective capital (i.e. qualifications).

Several propositions can be developed from the above. One of these is that new formal education policies about creativity only have a very slight impact on the learning of successful students in the predominantly performativity sutured subculture of education in the formal/official school. Another is that this shouldn't really be surprising to us, as in competitive and consumerist (capitalist) school forms, what students think they 'want', need and are materially rewarded by, are things like knowledge about *how to get a good grade*, and what *amount of effort* represents a balanced *optimisation of the qualification-work load variable* for doing well in school. Here education becomes a fetishised commodity involving primarily three things. These are (i) the conversion of all other value forms of education labour to an economic value form (e.g. marks, grades and qualifications) that can be counted and accumulated, (ii) the unequal accumulation of these economic forms (as marks, grades, qualifications and 'distinctions') by some individuals at the expense of others to both create and uphold a concept of 'the successful student' and (iii) the production and interpellation of a normalising ideology for these practices. These are again aspects of cultural production in school and its relations to cultural reproduction. When the unequal accumulation of grades and qualifications correlate with class, ethnicity and gender, the practices of cultural production and reproduction also become elements of social reproduction.

The above three points form the primary constituents of formal success in formal school culture according to the present chapter, as they form what Bourdieu (1996) has termed a repertory of actual and virtual possibilities in the spaces of recognition that are offered to agents through available cultural positions, social relations and the use of the symbolic force (Beach, 1999c, d, 2000; Gustafsson, 2003). In this sense education agents are not restrained only by their 'individual', intellectual possibilities and skills, as in liberalist understandings of agency. They also inherit and are objectified by, rather than create or deconstruct, both the dominant operational discources as well as what is immediately available as cultural resources in the social-cultural contexts they are part of (Beach, 2003c).

Conclusions

'New' ideas for creativity in learning (see also Kommunförbundet, 1996; Skolverket, 1992; School Minister Ask in the Skolverk report, 1992: 2, p. 46; SOU 2000: 39; Lindensjö and Lundgren, 2000; SOU 1990:20; Dovemark, 2004a) are reflected in National Curricula and in other formal policy statements relating to such things as students developing capacities to take personal responsibility for learning by taking part in education planning and assessment and choosing and evaluating courses, subjects, themes and activities for themselves for their own satisfaction. In this sense schools are described as more and more needing to create conditions for the development of new capacities amongst students (Lundahl, 2001; Dovemark, 2004). However, whilst this 'new school idealism' describes an increase in delegated responsibilities to the learner (and the local arena more generally) and symbolically ascribes value to self-determination, learner creativity, independence and freedom of choice, the empirical evidence here suggests that there is a tension between this *idealism* and a second discourse (of performativity), which is deeply engrained in the formal culture of the official school. Also suggested is that there is little evidence of a positive relationship between these two educational discourses and that objectified forms of learning (as e.g. accumulated labour) and performativity predominate in the formal school, particularly amongst the most successful student groups.

Chapter 4

Pupil responsibility

As described already in previous chapters, Sweden's present school curricula emphasise personal flexibility, creativity, responsibility for learning and suggest new understandings of quality in learning, where individual freedom of choice is meant to help produce creative, motivated, alert, inquiring, self-governing and flexible users and developers of knowledge. These curriculum changes relate to similar changes in the relationships between the State, professional agencies and market interests in education planning and delivery and previous chapters have suggested something of the difficulty of realising the new education vision implied by policy changes in current education circumstances. In the present chapter; which is largely based on two previous works (Dovemark, 2004a, b and Beach and Dovemark, 2004a) we discuss these new developments and their effects from the perspective of different students in school in relation to ethnographic descriptions and student interviews.

The analysis suggests some changes to the ways schools work. The mechanical memorisation of facts has to a degree been replaced by outwardly self-monitored activities and self-determined learning. But some things remain the same. Students are still graded, separated and characterised by teachers in terms of being weak or superior products and students still adopt the labels ascribed to them in their own self-understanding. Furthermore, the curriculum that is meant to stimulate creativity and inclusiveness dampens creativity and positive involvement for many students.

The new school vision as a general vista

An important point of departure for the present chapter is comprised by new education policy discourses that call for increased flexibility, individual responsibility and for the mobilisation of local and self- regulation in education in Sweden's schools (Lindblad et al., 2005). Amongst these are the following documents: the national school curriculum (Lpo 94/98), local school development plans from our research sites and official national reports and propositions (such as SOU 1997: 21, 1992: 94; 1999: 63; Skolverket, 2001 and Government Propositions 1988/89:4 and 1990/91:18). According to these texts education is now supposed to proceed from the motivation and interest of the pupils, through self-regulation, responsibility and an ability to find their own knowledge (Zackari, 2001; Lundahl, 2001). What it means to be a good learner has been 'shifted' in/by these texts (Gustafsson, 2003) as a part of what is described as a 'new school vision' in the schools we have investigated. Key dimensions of this 'vision' were presented as follows by one headmaster:

> We want to create ... freedom of choice for students and teachers, who will take responsibility for the curriculum by controlling content from within a system of choice options. Students can determine where and when they learn ... We will guarantee that everything is of value ... for a new future where flexibility is important ... Our aim is to help students to be motivated, alert, inquiring, self-governing and flexible users as opposed to just recipients of knowledge.

However, the 'new school vision' is not an isololated phenomenon, but rather something that reflects a new kind of educational planet-speak (Frejes, 2006) within a globalised educational discourse (Dovemark, 2004a, b) as one example of the way in which these global discourses become locally embedded and spoken in the vernacular. Dovemark (2004a) says it is a local response to supranational (e.g. OECD 1996, 2000a, b) and national policy declarations and a form of appropriation that emphasises a reduction in central and rules regulation and an increase in delegated responsibilities, goal-rationality, self-determination and freedom of choice for students, within a broad intention to develop new forms of creativity in learning where control features have been shifted to management by objectives and results (Wahlström, 2002) and where—in line with a new politically expressed interest for what learners should become (creative, self-reliant and discerning consumers and producers of knowledge) rather than what they should know—the development of new forms of human subjectivity are expressed as central (Lundahl, 2001; Zackari, 2001; Lindblad et al., 2001; Lindblad and Popkewitz, 2003; Sundberg, 2003; Beach, 2001).

The new school vision: four empirical cases

In the present chapter we will use four case-study students (Kyjtim, Britta, Klara and Rita) from one and the same class, which Dovemark followed during one school year, two to three times a week (Dovemark, 2004a, b), to illustrate some of the points we have made in the previous three chapters concerning how the school and its classrooms offer different conditions of experience to different learners that serve as opportunities for some to develop psychologically valuable tools and become flexible and creative enough to take responsibility for their work and form obstacles for others. The following fieldwork journal text about interviews with pupils comments on how they experience, recognise and respond differently to the school situation.

> Pupils make different experiences out of the discourse of flexibility and responsibility and ... make different choices ... This strategy works quite well for some of them but not others ... Also, the teachers expect the pupils to work at home in order to finish different tasks. Many pupils think this is a good idea, because they can get peace and quiet and the opportunity to get help as well. But if you don't have these possibilities then things can be difficult ... One thing that then becomes obvious is that basic cultural and even social capital helps in the extraction of educational capital ... Upper- and upper-middle class children should be expected to extract more value from education than working class children ... Working class children could be expected instead to be devalued in their meetings with school ... This also seems to happen in practice ...

Kyjtim was one of the key informants who helped us identify the above difference in relation to home circumstances and resources such as space, quietness and support. He was born in Bosnia and moved to Sweden some years into his school career. He sometimes seemed to challenge and upset his teachers, by his attitude and by walking around in the classroom and corridor talking to everybody he met. He also had, not surprisingly given his fairly recent arrival in the country, some difficulties with Swedish and expressed that he often found it difficult to concentrate on his reading.

The following field-note extract suggests something of the characteristics of Kyjtim's situation. It is from the first morning period (08.30-09.00), where the teachers have a shared agreement that all pupils should read for thirty minutes at the start of every school day:

> 08.45   In the corridor by Gunnar's (the teacher) group several of the pupils start talking. Kyjtim says: 'It is nearly 9 o'clock. School is starting'. Doesn't he understand morning reading as schoolwork?

08.58   Several of the pupils are still reading. I am sitting quietly writing. Sven wants to see what I am writing. I let him read the first notes of the day. He quickly gets fed up. Rita, Sara and Anna are sitting at 'their table' talking.

09.00   Most of the pupils stop reading and start talking or playing with their books ... Kyjtim is just sat looking at his book. Turning a few pages now and then.

All the classes in the corridor adhered to the same principle for the morning session and the teachers generally succeeded in getting most pupils to accept, understand and, for some of them at least, even value this principle in practice. However, as suggested above, some pupils may fare less than well than others. The following fieldwork journal extract addresses this:

The corridor is quiet and most of the pupils are reading from their books ... Kyjtim is quiet, but he's doing nothing, just looking down at the pages of the book. The question is if Kyjtim can take responsibility for his work when he has difficulties with Swedish. He doesn't seem to realise that the reading period is a part of the school day ... Sometimes he just keeps in the background, dawdling, as when he pretends to read. Sometimes he just walks around talking to his schoolmates. However, he also challenges and defies the teachers, which often results in him calling negative attention to himself ...

Kyjtim seems to realise what is expected of him at school and that he needs to work quite hard. And when talking to him about which programme he wants to follow at the upper-secondary school (gymnasium), he says he really wants to start the media programme, even though he realises 'that it will be very hard because of the high marks you need'. Also, he says that he understands his situation but gets frustrated because of a lack of help at school and at home.

Kyjtim: Sometimes ... you have to take (work) home (but) my Mum and the others cannot do English and stuff like that ... and even if the books explain ... it's so difficult and I don't always understand ... If there isn't a teacher to explain it I can't do the work ... Mum goes to school as well and we have to help her sometimes.

Marianne: OK, but what about your situation in school ... Is it possible for you to ask for help if you can't get it at home?
Kyjtim: No, there is no one to help me ... if I put up my hand and I'm talking (the teacher) goes to the one who is quiet ... But it's hard not to talk when you are just ... waiting doing nothing.

Kyjtim introduces some of the difficulties some students can end up in when they are given tasks to interpret by themselves or with friends. Kyjtim stresses this with words like, 'the books explain ... but it is difficult and I don't understand'. His problems are compounded by the way homework is anticipated and by the fact that many students socialise more in school than study, and prefer to take their work home with them. Teachers accept this. But it adds to the problems of students like Kyjtim, who cannot get help at home.

Kyjtim, is a student with a non-Swedish background and with restricted resources for language support in Swedish at home. He is not the only type of student to 'suffer' in the new school context however. A girl called Britta provides another example.

Britta is a girl who is often seen alone in school. She seems always to be strolling around in the corridor, in the classroom and even on the schoolyard during lessons. And she also seems to have difficulty concentrating on her tasks. When she isn't 'strolling around' she can seem to just sit and do nothing. The field-note extract below describes this:

> 11.00 Every time you see Britta she is either alone doing nothing or she is talking to pupils from another class. You seldom see her talking to any classmate. She is walking up and down in the corridor. She is wearing her rucksack, which strengthens the impression that she is always on the move ... The teacher said that Britta has given up and doesn't try to make contact with her any more now ... 12.45 Back in the corridor Britta is back at the same table doing nothing. She's wearing her rucksack. She walks up to two boys from another class ...

Britta seems to be anything but 'at home' in the school environment. She has few obvious close friends and when she works, she works alone. She moves constantly from place to place and doesn't get much schoolwork done according to her teachers. Nevertheless, she seldom asks for help from her teachers or classmates and seldom takes an initiative to speak to teachers and other pupils about schoolwork. She keeps quiet and hardly shows any interest in what goes on during lessons. In fact, in this milieu where everybody is supposed to take an initiative she seems to get the opportunity time after time to just slip away. However, there are exceptions to this rule. As Britta has shown through her lesson behaviour and comments, in one or two lessons a week she wants to 'stay in the classroom and try to get things done'. This takes place when the class has one certain teacher who Britta likes. Britta means that this teacher takes her seriously and she is keen to do the tasks given.

> 09.15 Britta arrives at the classroom. She looks worried (as she) looks at the blackboard and exclaims 'Oh ... no!' Gunnar (the teacher) turns round to B: 'Yes, but this could be good for you as well. You need this.' Britta sits down on the edge of the chair. She sits down diagonally because of her rucksack ... She puts one of her elbows on the table and lets her head rest in her hands. 09.23 Britta puts the rucksack on the floor and talks to Lisa who is opposite her. B bends down to get her rucksack, opens it and gets a paper out of it. She shows the paper to Lisa. Lisa puts up one hand in the air and moves it like she is bouncing a ball.

Britta seldom takes an initiative and hardly ever calls for help. And if she does she gives up quickly if the teacher doesn't come almost straight away.

> Britta is sitting on her chair writing on her hand. Jens walks up to Klara. 09.47. Klara: 'Gunnar!' Gunnar (the teacher): 'Yes' Gunnar turns round and walks up to Klara. They are talking about a mathematical task together. Britta lifts her hands into the air, puts her elbows on the desk and sprawls out her fingers. She starts talking to Lisa ... 09.50 Britta loudly: 'Gunnar!' Gunnar is still talking to Klara. Britta pulls one of her knees up to her cheek and puts one of her feet on the seat, calls once again: 'Gunnar!' No visible reaction ... Britta picks up her rucksack, opens it and takes something out. Shuts the rucksack again and puts it back on the floor. Gunnar walks across the classroom. He passes Britta and walks out into the corridor. No visible reaction from Britta.
>
> (Fieldnotes)

Another thing we have noticed in the data about Britta is that she is often physically outside the classroom during formal lessons, but that even when she is present, she can still signify distance in other ways, such as through the use of gestures and posture. For instance, in an art lesson when the pupils were supposed to make sculptures by 'plastering' papier maché over a ballon, Britta just blew up her balloon and then sat, rocking back and forth on her chair with the balloon in her knee. The teacher went to her once or twice but then gave up.

> *Marianne*: You don't need to do it then?
> *Britta*: No, they don't care ... I could have walked out of that room ... They wouldn't even notice ...

There is a difference between Kyjtim (who is excluded because of resources and language) and Britta (who is socially and emotionally distant in the new school) and the two following examples, illustrated by Klara and Rita. The clearest difference is the way of acting in the classroom shown by Klara and Rita. Both Klara and Rita have positive associations and personal projects in school, even though there are some important differences between them.

Klara is an outwardly well adapted girl with university educated parents from the upper-middle classes and is also a girl who seems to know what she wants from both school and life. She was very conscious about school. For instance, when trying to get time to interview her it was important, contrary to the other pupils, to do so during break time, as Klara 'didn't want to miss any school work that might be important'. According to field-notes she is a pupil who works hard in lessons and who also gets worried if it looks like she won't finish a job in time. Time after time she asks the teachers what will happen if she hasn't finished and whenever you meet her in school she seems to be working. She almost always leaves the classroom last and is one of those pupils who always seems to do most homework.

Klara seems to realise that it is up to her to take an initiative. She demands and calls for the teacher when she needs help and she even follows the teacher sometimes when she thinks she does not get help quickly enough. Moreover, she also takes an initiative to sit with school mates who are 'on the same level' as her. She knows who is at what point in every subject and is therefore very aware of where she can get help if she needs it. She both seeks and even sometimes demands help at these times from teachers and others.

> 09.25   Klara sits down at Jens' and Mats' desk (and) takes out a calculator. She is sitting talking to Jens (about) a mathematical task.

09.36   The teacher walks up to Klara, Jens and Mats. He sits down and they are talking about a mathematical problem ... 09.56 Klara beckons and the teacher walks up to her and starts to discuss the problem with her again. He sits down beside her.   (Field-notes)

Taking an initiative to get (and then getting attention) seems to be distinctly different for different students and, in contrast to what they probably really need, teachers seem to give more attention to capable, conscious and demanding students like Klara than they do students like Britta (Beach, 1999a, 2001). Also the content of the interactions are different. When talking to students like Klara, teachers often talk about strongly classified content, as in the above situation. When talking to students like Britta they do not. The content of interactions there, where they exist at all, are often concentrated around behavioural issues (see also Beach, 1999a; Tickle, 1983; Dovemark, 2004a, b). But most of the time Britta is actually just ignored.

Klara is very conscious of her opportunities in a system built upon the idea of freedom of choice, yet in another very naïve about the conditions in which her choices are made and of the effects of her demands on the learning possibilities for others. That is, she seems very conscious of her opportunities and she knows what is expected of her to 'make the best out of things'. But whilst she also realises that there are others in her class who don't take this opportunity', she expresses that they 'can only blame themselves' and that 'it is their problem'. The material effects of Klara's demands of time and attention in an environment where these are available in limited supply is just ignored:

Marianne: You get many possibilities to choose ... are there problems?
Klara: ... that it is more ... up to you ... I know there are some who don't care ... but ... I think it is ... their problem (and) their own fault ... You get the opportunity ... and it's up to you ... You can make demands on your self ... and those, those who do take responsibility ... they are really all right ... but those who don't (laugh) ... It doesn't work out for them ...
Marianne: What happens with them?
Klara: I don't know (laugh) ... I suppose it will show up in the marks because we do work a lot on our own ... and it will show up in the marks I think.

When we look closely at statements like the above from demanding, competent students like Klara, we can see how schooling in Sweden is trapped between a vision of a school that exhibits freedom of choice in a concept of democracy and collective good on the one hand, but that can be troubled by the material practices of selfish individual projects in conditions of limited resource availability on the other. The school vision is naïve in this sense. It allows conscious, aware, well equipped and selfish students to become successful students, by using a greater portion of the time, resources and materials that should be made available to all. However, although when expressed in this way, it is easy to see the demands of students like Klara as unreasonable and unfair on the chances of others, in the mainstream school her demands are expressed differently, as 'her reward for hard work and endeavour' (Gunnar). Her 'success' is expressed as well deserved, fair and just. Moreover, Klara has excellent support systems at home and the materials needed, such as a new computer, books and quiet spaces to work in:

> I often take work home ... Sometimes it's too noisy in lessons and then you can't really concentrate on what you are doing ... and I write a lot on the computer at home ... I never get to one here at school (laugh) ... I really haven't used the computers here (laugh) ...

Klara is very focussed on how to succeed in school. She wants to join the Natural Science programme at upper-secondary school and will sacrifice almost anything, including friendships, to do this. She made this clear not just through her appropriation of resources, but also through the ways she both creates and uses social relations to improve her school performance. To her 'it didn't matter if she hadn't so many friends in class now', because when she gets onto the Natural Science programme, 'she will get the friends she wants'. Klara is future oriented and focuses strategically on how to succeed at getting the best marks for a desired education in the future.

Rita was another student who fared well in the new school vision. She was one of a group of four close friends who had created their own personal space in school. This was a special room between two doors in the corridor outside the classroom where they had put some chairs and a little table. This was 'their little space' as they put it, and the four girls went to this little room whenever they had the opportunity. However, although they all performed at an average or better than average level in school tests and on homework, they rarely worked on school work when they were together. When they were in their 'little room ... they rarely work with the school work' (Rita) but rather spend their time 'socialising ... and talking about other things than schoolwork' (Rita). This is also suggested in the following field-note extract:

> 09.17 Three boys are still in the classroom ... A voice from the corridor says 'No, I don't want to sit in the classroom.' Some girls are walking up and down in the corridor. They are carrying their handbags. The four girls are sitting in their little space between the two doors ... One of them has got earphones. It is quite dark ...

Rita doesn't work excessively during formal lesson time. She isn't one of the class swots. But she still hands over the work the teachers expect the pupils to have done, fully completed, and on time. Rita explained how she manages this during an interview:

> *Marianne*: Is it hard to plan your time ... or do you think that the time you get in school is enough to do your work?
> *Rita*: Yes ... it is enough for me anyway ... I do most of it at home ... There isn't any equipment any way ... If you sit here in school working on the computer somebody can switch it off before you have finished ... and then ... you have to sit there and rewrite it ... So I never use the computer here ...
> *Marianne*: How much work do you do at home? Is it every day?
> *Rita*: No, not every day ... I haven't got so much time. I've got my horse (and) sports ... I do as much as I can ... Sometimes I have to sit up late working ... I work more at home ... I haven't got time to do a lot here any way ...
> *Marianne*: When you tell me that you haven't got time here in school to do the job ... or it is hard to do it ... I suppose ... well ... sometimes you are sitting with friends talking instead of doing the work ...
> *Rita*: Yes ... that can be a reason ... but I work better at home any way ... because at home I've got the equipment I need ...

Rita doesn't seem at first glance to take school particularly seriously, but she is actually very clear about what is expected of her. She also delivers good work to the teachers when she is supposed to and knows she can do it at the last minute

the evening before it is supposed to be handed in. She does formal schoolwork at
home not in school and the choice seems to be easy for her to make. She makes
the best out of school without letting it interfere with her main interests. She
sees friends as important and indeed stated that it is friends that make it OK
to come to school day after day. As she put it, 'you come to be with your friends
... The boring things you can do at home'. In this sense Rita makes something
of her own out of her school possibilities, together with her friends in informal
social relations projects (also Bliding, 2004). She makes her own choices and
decides what she wants to do.

> We are supposed to work in groups now ... but I will work on my own
> ... We are supposed to find facts about different countries ... in English ...
> We are supposed to work in groups but I am going to work on my own
> at home. Nobody but me wanted to work with Australia ...

Where as Klara associates clearly with the aims of the formal school and
will groom social relationships to serve the ends of formal schooling, Rita's
associations are distinctly tilted toward the informal as well, without this
undermining her achievement or aims and thoughts about a positive future
career and so on. She is social and popular with other pupils and the teachers
and is also keen on 'handing good work'. But she also expresses that friends are
important and she invests a lot of time in social relations projects with them. Rita
seems to have the ability to make her own choices without this having adverse
effects on her performances and her teachers' evaluations of her.

Rita's adaptations to school illustrate how the idea of free choice presumes
several things, if you want to have a reasonable social life and still want to appear
successful within the formal school. One of them is that you have recognised
the need to be seen as productive, so you can be left on your own when you
want to be, and that you have enough self-discipline to be able to work on your
own when you need to. Another is that if you have made the choice not to work
during school time you have the space and facilities to be able to work at home.
Some pupils succeed. Others have difficulties.

Discussion

In the materials presented and discussed in this chapter education is clearly a
commodity with two sources of value; common use value and exchange value.
But making use of this double edged commodity in an appropriate way is a

complex issue tied to both student consciousness of their education situation and the material social reality of that situation and their private life.

Klara is an interesting student in this context, as both the demands and the effects of the demands she makes on her surroundings when developing her own private education project illustrate the case in point. 'Ideologically' (in terms of the new dominant discourses of self-determination, individual choice and initiative taking) Klara is an ideal student who is aware of what education means materially in our society and who 'gets on'. She knows where help is available, she seeks help when she needs it and she uses all the resources available to her to, in a sense, work hard and produce her own future. However, in another sense she is very different to this, as a parasite on her environment who typifies the extractionist tendencies of the social class she comes from. She takes and consumes more of the limited resources of the classroom than she should and in her use of these resources, which she consumes and converts into educational capital for her own private accumulation (grades and qualifications). She often denies space to others who may need it more.[7]

How school pupils take responsibility is in this scenario a product of an active social process, in which students can no longer straightforwardly be seen as the passive bearers of ideologies that determine their actions, or as steered by social structures beyond their comprehension and means of influence. Students are instead seen as active in the production of ideology, structure and an educational class position. This is in line with for instance Willis (2000) notion, that the creativity of the individual and the group is always operating, even when it is restrained by material conditions. Student perceptions of the curriculum and its utility, their perceptions of the demands of institutional life and the creativity of their responses are forged in a class cultural context that they then act back upon.

This is rendered quite clear by the examples we have provided, as the empirical examples we have given in the chapter show how four students have handled the aims of the 'new school' differently, but they also show in particular, how being seen as a responsible and flexible student in the 'new school' is mainly about

---

7   As stated in Beach and Dovemark (2005b), the processes of the accumulation of common goods (time and resources) and their conversion into an economic form (education capital) is homologous with the processes of accumulation and conversion described in capitalist society more broadly, in works from Marx's *Das Capital* volume 1 onwards (see also e.g. McMurtry, 1998). However, their invocation here and the suggestions from this invocation are not made solely in order to reaffirm this singular point. We aim also to demonstrate the importance when trying to understand an institution like the school, of emphasising the characteristics of the society and culture of which the school is a part, and assessing the impact of these practices and belief systems of each on the other.

'choosing to do *the right* things' in a context where not everyone is able to do this. The social and emotional distance of students to the aims and traditions of the school are important here and the outcomes contradict the modern *equity by choice* rhetoric of the stakeholder welfare services discourse (Loxley and Thomas, 2001). Inequality is enhanced!

According to the 'new' curricula and other policy documents; and also according to the local education management and teachers; in the 'new school' students are supposed to have the capacity to take an initiative, deal with tasks independently and hand completed work in on time. But these are things with both a use-value and an exchange value in a context where the means of production of exchange value is always in limited supply. And in such contexts any one student's over-use of resources means shortages for others. Klara's success is in this scenario ultimately perhaps the most important feature of the failure of students like Britta and Kyjtim and, at the same time, Britta's reluctance and Kyjtim's limitations to consume educational resources makes it easier for Klara to be successful.

Conclusion

The four cases show that the 'responsible and flexible' student is the one who does not challenge, defy or critique the system, but instead *effectively* decodes it and then exploits it for private gain. Rita and Klara succeed in this kind of organisation, but in quite different ways. They both focus on individual success, but for Klara there also seems to be efforts made in which social relations are developed and broken in line with a desire to accumulate educational capital, regardless of the consequences of this for others. Some people would call Klara a highly motivated and 'ideal student'. Indeed this is what most of her teachers call her. Others might describe her in the same sense that they might describe the upper-middle class she emanates from, as ruthless, egocentric and a danger to those around her. However, lest it be forgotten, Klara didn't create the competitive circumstances of capitalist schooling or its most recent neo-liberal forms. She, her teachers and her peers, are simply responding to these things in the best way they can. Success and failure is not only an individual issue here.

When studying the materialisation of the official discourse of flexibility and responsibility of the individual in the school context, the intention of the official discourse points at a practical solution of the practical problems of schooling rather than at changes to the foundations of education philosophy. In relation to the issue of education change and the currently expressed aims of curriculum reform, the key question for things like 'flexibility and responsibility' in this sense is not so much based on individual creativity and capability, but on the recognition of possibilities and an access to the resources required to use them. This means that whilst the experiences of young people may have changed quite radically over the last two decades the materialisation of 'flexibility and responsibility' through 'free choice' in school still suggests that in the age of high modernity life chances and processes of social reproduction may still remain highly structured (Furlong and Cartnel, 1999; Dovemark, 2004b; Beach and Dovemark, 2004b, 2005b).

Chapter 5

Re-structuring adult education

Three interacting activity systems of the *production* of goods, *identity/ies* and *ideology* figure consistently in Marxist and neo-Marxist (e.g. Althusserian) analyses of education (see e.g. Althusser, 1971; Allman, 1999; Hill, 2001; Cole, 2003; Sharpe, 2003; Beach and Dovemark, 2005b). They are central in the present chapter, which, originally published in a similar form in the *Journal of Critical Education Policy Studies* (Beach, 2004a), is concerned with education restructuring in adult education in recent years. Specifically it deals with the restructuring of municipal (i.e. local government owned and run) adult education (Komvux: an acronym for *Kommunal vuxenutbildning*: Trans. Communal Adult Education). It raises the questions: what the main *organisational concepts* within the restructuring process were; what importance was given to these; how restructuring influenced the work situation and the organisation of teaching and learning; which visions and prognoses were articulated with respect to restructuring; and in whose interests these have concretely operated.

Three things were particularly significant in the restructuring processes. First a decision to tender adult education in 1999, second the establishment of a municipally owned company (Studium Ltd, on May 16th, 2001) to take part in the tendering process and third, and also somewhat paradoxically, how under the subsequent eighteen-month period this company lost most of its adult education delivery on the basis of decisions made by the Municipal Adult Education Board, the franchising agency created within the local education authority for the tendering processes. Such were the contradictions of the situation in question, which seemed more intent on breaking down a pre-existing service than building something new. The situation evolved alongside policy changes in adult education, including the social construction of new forms of governance and new adult learner and educator identities (see also Wass, 2004; Frejes, 2006; Henning-Loeb, 2006).[8]

---

8 Similar changes to those focussed on in adult education have also developed in other parts of the public sector in Sweden and other European countries recently, for services like health and education (Beach, 2005a), as well as in the U.S.A., Australia and the U.K. (Ball, 1993, 1997, 2003; Gerwitz, 2002; Whitty et al., 1998; Whitty & Power, 2003; Hursh & Camille, 2003). Serious problems of economy and equality have occurred within these services post restructuring, as an aspect of private sector influence. It seems

Markets, citizens and services

A common way in which corporations and private interests take over the public sector is via the creation of a *quasi-market*. In this situation, rather than direct interactions between service deliverers and final consumers determining supply, politicians determine the level of consumer needs and bureaucrats allocate consumers to suppliers, who are then paid for their services by public money. Instead of direct consumer pressure controlling public services, in this case (local) governments establish agencies for mediating between the interests of individuals, the State and capital. This process is described in the 1992 Purchasing Act in Sweden (SFS 1992: 1528; see also SOU, 1991: 104) and has been referenced in Hillfield in documents such as 'Corporatisation' (Sw. *Bolagisering* Dnr 320/99, Hillfield City Office) and 'Suggestions for changes in the organisation of adult education' (Sw. *Förslag till förändrad organisation för utbildningsnämndens vuxenutbildningsverksamhet*, Rnr 54/01, Dnr 0879, Hillfield City Office). The concept of the market becomes a metaphor for public supply rather than a direct working model for it.

A quasi market such as this was the way in which adult education was opened up to market forces in Hillfield. It allowed politicians to maintain control of education delivery in two steps: (i) by imposing a restriction on the number of actors on the market by offering only a limited number of contracts to education suppliers and (ii) by setting up a student delivery and monitoring system to identify education recipients, allocate them to suppliers and gauge the quality of the education provided by the use of a standardised evaluation model.

Quasi markets are fairly typical for education restructuring in the current global context (Dale, 1997; Whitty et al., 1998; Beach, 2005a; SFS 1992: 1528; SOU, 1991: 104). But as an aspect of change between the State, private capital and customers, their constitution does not correspond to a direct takeover of education by corporate organisations on the basis of direct market relations, but to an updating of organisational principles and discourses in line with the interests of politically and economically dominant groups and the value programme of the prevailing economic system; which in the present global moment is predominantly a neo-liberalist one (Rosskam, Ed, 2006). The quasi market is a political tool in other words. It helps politicians wrest education

that the more the private sector becomes involved in delivering public services, the worse the level of general service has become in terms of broad availability and class differences in the use of services by citizens (McMurtry, 1998; Gustafsson, 2002; Beach, 2005a,b). This is very evident in basic (social, physical, mental and dental) health, education, water supply, energy supply and transport in particular (ibid.).

control from local bureaucracy and relocates this control within a politically controlled education-to-market agency.

Politics, education control and markets

Attempts by politicians to wrest control of adult education from the hands of bureaucrats in Hillfield has been mentioned by several informants in the present investigation, including a former chief regional adult education officer (Harry Boye). He claimed that politicians had been attempting to get increasing levels of control over adult education for years, through the introduction of a series of policies designed to curb the range of influence held by education bureaucrats and professionals' like himself. The national adult education initiative (Kunskapslyftet) was suggested to be particularly important:

> An attempt to gain control over adult education ... has been going on years but it ... reached a head in 1997 in the Adult Education Initiative (which) was dealt with very differently in Hillfield than other regions ... Since 1996 there's been a deconstruction ... and a definitive break in 1997, with the AEI, which the local politicians used in order to further tighten their control over bureaucrats like me ...

The Adult Education Initiative (AEI: Sw. Kunskapslyft) was a massive investment in adult education in Sweden (Wass, 2004; Henning-Loeb, 2004; Frejes, 2004) that was set up by the central government in 1997, as a five-year nationwide project that was officially for broadening adult involvement in education, for using education as a buffer against unemployment and for, at the same time, also boosting official employment levels and stimulating economic growth (SOU 1996: 27; SOU 1997: 158). But as Harry Boye implicates it, the AEI was also significant for the way adult education was later restructured. It acted as a bandwagon for the creation of a quasi market in adult education services with new forms of education governance (Wass, 2004; Fejes, 2006).

Harald Spanks, the AEB chairperson during the restructuring period, discussed the advantage of controlling a quasi-market for the local government in terms of the way 'this allowed some education control even during a capital shortage without the risks of ownership'. However, processes of conversion such as the ones implied have, as also Beach (2004a, 2005b) suggests, effects that go beyond the transfer of costs for education supply and impinge upon both professional identity, values and forms of governmentality as well. Because when a public service is transformed into a limited company to compete for the rights to deliver services, these services become privatised and competitive items with a commodity value and their workers, instead of being *public employees* providing guidance, care or education in a client interest according to a defined need and professional guidelines, take on the characteristics of the value form of labour of capitalist production (Beach, 2004a, 2005b). This is part of the logic of the capitalist labour process that enables surplus value to be accumulated through the capitalisation of labour power (Rikowski, 2003). Professional labour and the products of that labour are transformed into forms of objective capital (also Macdonald, 2003). These effects can also be recognised in comments by the majority of education leaders and politicians in Hillfield when they defend their decisions to restructure education delivery. We are talking about a transformation of production relations.

Betty, a former Dean of SFI at Studium, and Barbara and Greta, two former SFI teachers there, commented on the model of education development used for the AEI in Hillfield as follows:

> The model ... offers a system for politically controlling education delivery with pre-selected education suppliers with the Adult Education Board as the only legal customer ... Both the question of which education supplier is given a contract (and where) students are finally directed, lies in the hands of politicians, bureaucrats and labour market representatives not individuals ... This is a radical restriction of the norm of individual freedom of choice not an introduction of systems for making individual choices ... That was just a myth ... Despite constant claims to the opposite ... Learners (sic) do not make their own choices of where to study, this is decided by the Student Placement Agency (SPA) and even when they are invited to choose, their choices can't be rational because there is insufficient information back to them about the education available ...

Just about everyone spoken with in the investigation mentioned this issue that 'far from free choices being made, the reverse has been the case and students have simply been relocated to suppliers through placement agency decisions' (Greta). The idea was commented on as follows in recent interviews with former teachers and administrators at Studium:

None of the SFI pupils have really been able to influence where they were to study ... What happened was that the AEB agreed on a volume from different suppliers and tied up the system to contracts that determine where individuals will be placed ...   (Barbara)

The initial suggestions were that the individual should have the right to choose ... but that's not how things turned out, because the buyer has agreed on a volume from different suppliers and has in that way tied up the system ... Contracts determine where individuals are placed ... Choice has become very restricted ...   (Betty)

There's competition and the idea is that things will improve because of it ... But of course no one has been able to choose us because we don't exist anymore (and) as far as we are concerned the competition has not been on equal terms and has in fact been terribly misfortunate. I can understand that we shouldn't be the only game in town but the inclusion of more suppliers has been badly managed ... It's less a question of free competition and more one of political control ... Plus, the information out to students about what is available, particularly in SFI, has not really worked ... . Nor can it be expected to really ... They have just been placed with a supplier and told 'take it or leave it because there's a queue and if you don't use your place we'll give it to one of the six or eight hundred who are waiting in line ...'   (Barbara)

Freedom of choice has been ... discussed a lot ... but there has been ... disagreement about what kind of freedom and freedom for whom. Is it the individual who should choose or should someone choose for the individual? Who has the freedom? One of the things said at the time of the franchising process was that learners would have freedom of choice to study what they wanted where they wanted. But as far as I can see no SFI learner influenced where he or she studied ... Politicians have taken over ...   (Greta)

The tendency for education to be more and more conditioned by market speak and market thinking in Sweden has also been pointed out by other researchers, such as Wass (2004), Henning-Loeb (2006) and Frejes (2006) in respect of adult education organisational practices and discourse and teacher and learner indentities respectively. Moreover, this 'transition' to a market concept is not restricted to adult education. Lindblad et al. (2005) have discussed the issue in relation to primary education and health, whilst Beach (2003a) and Båth (2006) have noted the 'shift' in discourse in respect of upper-secondary schooling.

Talking about restructuring

Several specific discourses can be identified from interviews concerning the motivations for restructuring in Hillfield. These discourses vary from ones that reproduce a simple logic of capital provided by people who are defending decisions to restructure, to ones that are openly against it. Most common though is a discourse of bewilderment, as for instance comments discussing restructuring as a process concerning 'top-down ideas that seem to have to be implemented whatever the cost (that) was all very confusing to us and came as a great shock' (Betty). This bewilderment suggests that there may be a field of structurally tense relations that researchers have described and analysed previously in terms of idea world versus world of practice (Czarniawska-Joerges, 1990), level of reform versus level of reality and arena of formulation versus arena of realisation or arena of implementation (Lindensjö and Lundgren, 1986; Ball, 1994). The concepts relate to the complexity and contradictions that characterise different experiences of education renewal.

Teachers, almost exclusively, spoke about their experiences of restructuring in relation to what they termed 'as a destructive process ... with a lot of confusion and contradiction' (e.g. Barabara; see also Beach, 2004a; Carlson, 2005). However, there was also a frustration over how things that have been built up over many years 'are being torn down in the execution of an idea that seems necessary to push through whatever the ... costs may be' (Ken), a 'confusion regarding professional identities and roles' (Greta) and 'contradiction through a lack of democracy in what was officially motivated as a democracy project' (Barabara). As one informant put it, 'whilst the official rhetoric ... expresses democracy, teacher professionalism and autonomy, a new steering block within the local authority has developed that is in a strong conflict of interests with these ideals as it has to be primarily driven by economic thinking' (Greta). Finally some turbulence has also been talked about, as has an intensified sense of job insecurity (Beach and Carlson, 2005).

Stories from the 'bottom' of the organisation of adult education in Hillfield tended to speak in a very different tone, to voices from 'the top' (Beach, 2004a; Carlson, 2005). Top of the organisation stories were about economic need, flexibility requirements, individual responsibility and choice and new kinds of learning in new learning partnerships. Bottom stories were about confusion, frustration and loss of identity. Barbara and Ronny (a teacher in the upper-secondary school sector) put things in the following ways:

> Most of us have lost our old jobs and are currently involved in a readjustment project ... to find new workplaces or an education of some kind ... Many of the teachers were expected to move into the regular comprehensive or upper-secondary school sectors ... where there is a degree of teacher shortage. However, many of us ... have resisted the move ... and there have also been some heated exchanges ... with critical voices heard from teachers and union representatives ... Many teachers have protested against what they see as a view of professionalism in which the idea is that if you can teach one thing (to one group) you can teach anything (to anyone). And once a teacher always a teacher ... (Barbara)

> I have absolutely no idea what I'll be doing and term starts in two weeks ... I have previously taught philosophy and history on a temporary contract but there are now 450 surplus teachers ... Just now it looks as though I'll be working somewhere between 40 and 60 percent ... But there's a real shortage of money ... and the number of independent schools has increased ... Coupled to events in adult education the last few months it is creating great confusion about employment for teachers who lack a permanent contract ...   (Ronny)

It is not flexibility and efficiency that are expressed above, but feelings about a disposability and insecurity that has been brought about from an increasingly unregulated selling and buying of labour power in a new labour market, which apparently applies to all teachers (Beach, 2004a, 2006b). Moreover, although they see themselves as winners in the new situation, even currently fully employed teachers of adults in Hillfield expressed strong experiences of insecurity, as they 'don't know what will happen in the next round of negotiations ... or in the quality control attached to present delivery' (Betty). And even they are concerned about the flexibility fetish that has been introduced and is beginning to influence the curriculum through the development of 'flexi-courses', 'individual study plans' and 'learner workshops' (Ken). These things have, according to our ethnographic materials, begun to extensively replace more conventional classroom teaching (also Henning-Loeb, 2006). Employed adult educators have discussed such effects in the following ways:

> A lot of the criticism that you could hear was that we weren't flexible and (were) for people who were already educationally successful. There was a series of such criticisms (but) not much interest in trying to see how things really were ... There was an idea that the education would improve once it was exposed to competition because the view was that increased competition gives improved quality ... (Ken)

> Opening up for competition was a thing of the times and at the bottom line was the belief that things would become cheaper ... They didn't! They got more expensive and we'll be paying for it through the tax budget for the next five years ... Now it's form more than content that counts ... (Barry)

> I'm teaching flex courses (to) a mix of different students ... with different needs ... The intention is to mentor them ... so they can pass the course and study as far as possible when they can and where they can but I don't think it works out well ... Most of the time goes to making individual study plans and such like and hardly any goes to actually teaching ... We've been made into learning managers and coaches instead of teachers ... It's as if the personal trainer fad in the middle classes has struck home everywhere ... (Ken)

> The changes are said to be part of a natural progression in everyone's best interests ... But this is questionable. It all seems just political ... Costs have not been reduced, freedoms have not developed and education content is not all that new ... What has happened is that some of us are still employed and in work but most are employed without work (and) the ones who are in work never know how long they'll have it ... (Ingrid)

The above comments on lived experiences of restructuring from the chalk face of education suggest that the actual processes of restructuring haven't had (and perhaps they shouldn't have been expected to have had) the benefits that were openly associated with them by the top management portion of adult education (Beach, 2004a; Wass, 2004; Henning-Loeb, 2006). According to voices from the chalk face, 'things haven't become more flexible, money has not been saved and education processes have not involved more freedom of choice and self-determination' (e.g. Greta; Betty; Ken) and in the end, the turn of events seems only to have visibly been about *the proliferation of market interests and the moral justification of the further objectification of education work* through the introduction of a level of competition in the negotiation and allocation of contracts (Beach, 2004a). As expressed previously there has been a rise in economic thinking and decision making, an introduction of new managerial steering technologies and a development of an emphatic labour market influence (Carlson, 2004). Teachers have expressed this as an outcome of 'an increased emphasis on labour market thinking and an increased involvement of labour market representatives in adult education planning ... that has taken place since the Adult Education Initiative' (Ken):

> The connection with the labour market (started) with the AEI ... The dominant idea is that we should educate people so they can get work and that if they can't or don't get a job or qualification for a job then the education isn't worthwhile ... It's all part of an economic calculation and has been imported directly into the new framework for SFI where pupils become individuals who ... are seen as investment objects, worthy of investing in or not, as the case may be ... There is an obvious conflict between this and a humanistic perspective that is also visible in how we make up courses and programmes ... It's all about flex courses, workshops, individual study plans and the like ... so people can fit studying into life projects where work dominates, rather than building life projects around a desire for improvement through education ... But flex courses don't suit everyone, neither all students, nor all teachers or all situations ... Courses become very minimalist ... What is important for the moment dominates ... Learning becomes fragmented ...   (Barbara)

The new idea is that flexi courses will be used and that these will work in the interests of the 'needier groups' as politicians call them. But in SFI this is a total fallacy ... They demand ... study skills and students who are able to manage and plan their own learning ... Most of our students lack necessary study routines (so) what happens is that we pilot them through the courses and ignore the content of what they actually understand so

they can fit their learning in with their employment and job-seeking ...
It becomes very fragmented ... Learning difficulties are passed on all the
time ...   (Ingrid)

The economic, managerial, labour market perspective that is suggested above
to have begun to condition talk about and practices within adult education
(Beach and Carlson, 2004, Carlson, 2004, 2005) within municipal adult
education now doesn't mean that such perspectives were absent in the past
(Henning-Loeb, 2006). What it does seem to mean though is that this flexible
kind of labour-market-needs-related education is being given openly now, in new
forms, and as a clear rule, paid for by public money rather than being delivered
through a hidden curriculum or as a subsidiary part of education supply (Carlén,
1999; Beach, 2004a). The situation was different previously. Komvux (at least
officially) provided a humanist education for adults who wanted to fulfil the
demands of upper-secondary qualification and companies commissioned and
then paid for (admittedly against tax relief) specialist courses for their employees
when they felt they needed or could benefit from them (Beach and Carlson,
2004; Carlén, 1999). An informant put this as follows:

Companies used to buy education from us ... for their employees ... We
pushed things pretty hard ... to fit their requests because our (school)
economy ... pulled in a lot of money ... that we could then use for ...
conferences and so on ... It was a great situation ... Now education in 'flex
courses' that cater to individual needs and the labour market is what we
do almost all the time ... On the one hand we give a quick fix to get people
into work or we are flexible and bend enough to allow them to combine
work and study so that they can at least appear to get an education ...
There is very little else left ... What companies were paying for before
... they are getting now, paid for by the tax budget ... It's clear who gains
from this ...   (Ken)

Popular discourses about a new work order suggest that we are living in a
free world where human advancement, self-reliance, flexibility, independence
and autonomy are catered for through markets. However, the material
developments from restructuring and the bottom up experiences of informants
'in education markets' stand against this idea. They suggest that our brave new
world can be more suitably characterised in another way, where instead of the

idealism of flexibility, variety, choice, freedom and the creation of new spaces for the development of individual responsibility, creativity and new skills and personalities there are the *material conditions* of workers (teachers, managers, bureaucrats, administrators, ancillary labourers and students) in a new economy, where what people say they want and need more than anything else is a 'stability and security that they are presently being denied' (Ronny)!

In contrast to ideal images of restructuring and the education market, voices from the material experiences at the bottom end of restructured 'enterprises' make little or no concrete mention of freedom of choice for the majority of people, except of course when they talk about its absence, but speak instead to the 'costs (sometimes personal) of conversions of public wealth to private' (Ronny) and the negative effects of 'the closing down of public arenas for aesthetic, cultural and intellectual expression and absorption ... to make way for private *for-profit* ones to replace them' (Ken). Moreover, rather than being free, people express that they are 'becoming increasingly steered by contractual arrangements that have been negotiated and cemented into place by others' (Betty; Barbara) in working conditions where learning 'has become fetishised as a commodity in schools as new sites for the extraction of surplus value' (Greta).

These forms of 'alienation' in the new free market era are a side of restructuring that challenges the validity of dominant discourses. They signal that in order for restructuring to be grasped allowances have to be made for the diversity of human experience and the foundations for these diverse experiences. Market and quasi-market solutions are expressed as experienced as being of far from equal value to everyone according to our data and analyses. We suspect there are clear material reasons for this diversity.

We are looking here at changed relations between the State, civil society and the market in the discoursing and organisation of education supply (Lindblad et al., 2005; Fejes, 2006; Båth, 2006). This represents a changed culture of adult education (Wass, 2004; Henning-Loeb, 2006; Fejes, 2006). In this changed culture teachers, students and administrators are entering into labour relations in ever increasing numbers as objective factors of production in processes that are owned and controlled by people other than themselves but are discoursed in very different ways, through a propagation of myths that help promote a witchcraft of change (Beach and Carlson, 2004). This witchcraft of change combines myths about shortcomings of the past and strengths of a brave new world of the future. What has been ignored is that there was variety in the past and that the new flexi courses lead to fragmented learning and change education work in the process from a professional to a mechanical and managerial activity.

Discussion

The present chapter describes some of the experiences of education subjects after the introduction of a quasi-market for adult education that extended the capitalisation of the public sector within a key public service. In this situation 'customer needs', employability, flexibility, individual freedom of choice and reduced costs were central concepts for motivating changes, but these things have not been lived out and experienced in the senses one might assume. There is a chasm between the idealist rhetoric of restructuring and experiences in terms of what *neo-liberal restructuring* has really meant for those affected by it. Some material outcomes are summarised below (see also Beach, 2004a).

Table 5.1: Outcomes of restructuring in adult education in Hillfield

Company formation: e.g. Lernia, ABF AB, Studium Ltd.
Conversion of public services to private
Business takeover of education supply
The creation of a quasi market for consolidating privatisation
Local authorities forming agencies for contracting out education
Public payment for the public supply of education in the interests of businesses
replacing business payment for the supply of this education
Costs of administration shifted from costs of public ownership and control to costs
of managing and monitoring outsourced delivery
Increased costs from franchise effects on public employment
Increased privatisation of the means of education production
The increased objectification of labour in adult education
A view of learners as economically rational, flexible consumers and selfinterested
individuals and the reconstruction of the curriculum in line with this vision
A redefinition of democracy in terms of consumer choice
An increased objectification of teachers, learners and curricula
The creation of a labour buffer in a readjustment project
Fear and insecurity
Senses of disposability
Fragmented professional identities
Stress and disillusionment

The features of restructuring expressed here suggest several important things, but include primarily a decline in public financing of welfare services and an increase in public financing of private interests, an increase in the surveillance of professionals, the furtherance of corporate management regimes through new accountability agendas and the production of significant changes in the labour process for public service professionals that have negative effects on self-reliance, self-confidence and self-esteem. These are similar changes to those noted by Rachael Sharpe (2003) in higher education in her charge that in each capitalist country where restructuring has occurred, the revolution in education policy that has been brought about has constantly produced such effects (also Whitty et al., 1998, Dale, 1997; Beach, 2004a, 2005a). However, what is perhaps interesting in this is that Sweden's welfare State (which has developed over a long period of political control by the social democratic labour party) has undergone restructuring with cultural effects not dissimilar from those apparent in countries like Britain, which have had long periods of conservative office. This may suggest that education restructuring shares fundamental elements in common and may possess a global characteristic and that the Hillfield case study may be able to suggest what at least some part of this global characteristic is like when viewed ethnographically from the bottom part of an organisation upwards. As expressed in Beach (2004a):[9]

> Adult education ... is (being) increasingly provided subject to cost (and therefore profitability) as opposed to professional judgements about good value practices and is in this sense ... objectified by developing through social relations that transform people into objects rather than subjects, and alienated, in the sense that work becomes successively and increasingly accommodated toward a value form of labour characteristic for competitive, privatised production. This has affected conditions of labour for teachers remaining in adult education (through reductions in paid trust time with new employers and the enforcement of individual salary setting to replace collective bargaining), teacher-union influence on education content and delivery and levels of professional involvement in education administration ... However, also important was that ... the local government (as a local implementer of State policy) was complicit in the processes of conversion and in this sense helped to stabilise a human conformity to the dehumanising (trans-human) labour process ... This has nothing to do with increased degrees of individual determination and freedom or the enablement of forms of self-determination, as is often claimed. It is not about freedom! It is about control and repression!

9   www.jceps.com/index.php?pageID=article&articleID=25 (June 8, 2006).

But it is also fully in line with recommendations for the conversion of public services in Sweden to private and the 1992 Purchasing Act and is therefore both legal and ideologically legitimated, so perhaps we should also question the values of our legal and legislative apparatuses and wonder about whose interests they actually operate in.

Several dimensions of restructuring in education emerge in the chapter. These concern firstly the principles of formation of interests in education restructuring and how political forces have channelled global ideas, principles and ideologies into a local arena to challenge existing education relationships and influence the formation of education policy and people's professional lives and identities. Political manipulation in ideological interests, the appropriation of media pressure, the deconstruction of bureaucracy to enable a faster and more direct form of political control and the replacement of the ideas of direct democracy in adult education (see e.g. Larsson, 1993) by a notion of a democracy served by an ideology of public choice offer examples as the spaces for oppositional activity are squeezed shut.

We could ask, who has expressed an experience of agency and in what ways has this experience of agency been expressed in the new context? And what becomes clear when we ask this question is that there are both winners and losers in the new situation. Two groups have suffered the most, or at least most directly. These are firstly the people who need an education but have been left without one and their teachers from the service sector of adult education who have lost the possibility of working with the jobs they desire, the right to seek the public service employment for which they are experienced and have been educated, and the possibility to exercise professional control over the curriculum. However, there has also been a forced adaptation of teachers to market requirements (Beach, 2004a). This can be described as a motor of re-culturalisation in adult education (Beach and Carlson, 2004, 2005; Carlson, 2005). It concerns processes of *liquidation* in the conversion of public wealth to private capital in a scenario where education is no longer even formally democratic and comprehensive, but is instead about the application of a global form of neo-liberal market discourse to a local education situation no matter what the individual costs and consequences might be.

Conclusions

Previously the values of municipal adult education in Sweden have been described as humanist, democratic and egalitarian (Fejes, 2006). And although the question as to whether or not these aims were fulfilled is moot (Wass, 2004), it is clear that such ambitions are now are being undermined when the actions of market designers dislocate students and workers from the public sector to the quasi-private through the objectification of education work, as the labour processes of education thereafter become increasingly conditioned toward value forms of labour and economic interests rather than the provision of education according to common, collective, solidaric and democratic needs and interests. According to informants in Hillfield this process began in the five-year nationwide project that started in 1997 and formed a part of a joint education and labour market effort for increasing employment levels and economic growth in Sweden (termed the Adult Educational Initiative; AEI-Sw Kunskapslyft) (Beach, 2006b). It was followed by the creation of a local company from the former Public (Community) Adult Education Service, the establishment of a local (quasi-) market for stimulating competition amongst suppliers and the impending bankruptcy of the municipally owned company due to its more favourable (but also more expensive) conditions of labour. In the long term what has changed are the value bases and philosophies of institutional practices and the nature of (professional) work; at least according to our informants. These things have changed primarily as a result of emphases on an operating core value (i.e. the need to calculate and cut costs to save resources in a capital availability crisis). However, within the new market context this operating value core easily turns from savings to profit and it will be clear then in whose interests adult education will have begun to operate.

Chapter 6

Myths of change in adult education

Adult education in Hillfield is the subject also of the present chapter, which again focuses on the restructuring initiated by Hillfield Municipal Council in 1999 that came into full force in 2002, after the completion of the National Adult Education Initiative (the AEI). And again we look at the situation of the company (Studium Ltd) that was established by the Metropolitan Council from the municipally owned and run adult education service, *Komvux*, to take part in tendering processes and to safeguard the provision of community owned adult education in the region. As stated in the previous chapter, restructuring did not follow a traditional market concept, but rather followed a quasi-market model that allowed politicians to control education by setting up a bureaucratically monitored system of competitive delivery. The chapter has been developed from a rewritten version of a previously published article from the European Educational Researcher Journal (Beach and Carlson, 2004).

The concept freedom of choice

Individual freedom of choice was one of the concepts that was used most frequently in local policy documents in the run in to the restructuring of SFI (Beach and Carlson, 2004, 2005; Carlson, 2004, 2005) and was also intensively discussed locally both prior to and during the major tendering of adult education. There were however, as suggested in the previous chapter, strong disagreements about what the concept actually stood for and in what way it was meant to work. This is not uncommon of course. As for instance also Ball and Bowe (1989) have put it, concepts in policy texts are often loosely defined and operate in practice at fairly high levels of abstraction to both open up and close down interpretive possibilities for the activities they are said to relate to (also Wass, 2004; Fejes, 2006).

Particularly concepts with strong positive connotations such as the just mentioned 'freedom of choice', 'variation', 'quality' and 'knowledge' have varied social meanings in different discourses and speech contexts and there are instances where people can quite prolifically change their meanings within the same argument (Smith 1993, Beach and Carlson, 2004; Fejes, 2006). This means that even though our interviewees generally articulated strong agreement with statements that suggested that 'there hasn't been any real freedom of choice provided by the reorganisation of adult education, at least not for course participants' (Barbara), and some informants have even declared that they even 'see an increased amount of organisational control in the new situation' (Betty), there are differences of interpretation. One SFI school leader asked if there were any SFI participants who had been given a chance to choose once the present set of agreements about delivery were put in place.

One of the things that was said at the time of the franchising process was that pupils would have freedom of choice to study what they wanted where they wanted. But things became very steered. As far as I can see there wasn't really any SFI pupil who was able to influence where they were to study. And that's really funny when you consider that even children in comprehensive school and upper-secondary school can do so ... There is probably less choice now than before ...

When reasoning further about the lack of 'freedom of choice' for individuals, many of the interviewees mention issues of political power and a desire from politicians to exert greater control over education. One of them is the following former Studium teacher:

> The idea was that things will improve because of competition ... But of course no one has been able to choose Komvux or Studium because they don't exist anymore ... I can understand that Komvux shouldn't be the only game in town but the inclusion of more suppliers has been badly managed ... Less a question of free competition than an odd form of control ... The information out to students about what is available has not really worked ... The agency has placed them with a supplier and has said take it or leave it ...   (Greta: Teacher, Studium)

Other former Komvux teachers have expressed things in similar terms. However, there are other benefits of restructuring that have to be weighed against restrictions in freedom of choice according to some informants. For instance, according to Harold Spanks, the former chairman of the regional adult education board, the expressed advantage of a quasi-market was that it limited the risks of ownership without any great losses being suffered by the people (teachers, learners, administrators) involved (see also City Auditor's Report, Stadsrevision 2003). But of course this depends on how 'losses' are calculated as well as on definitions of what counts as a loss. As is also suggested in the previous chapter, when a public service is legally and economically transformed into a limited company many losses are incurred that are often ignored. These losses are not only direct economic ones. Several other effects accrue with respect to professional identities.

Notions of the meaning of change

Within the discursive order of the benefits of change a lot of the argumentation is founded upon a play of opposites—'finding new pathways' versus 'old'—and the importance of 'breaking fixed patterns' is often stressed (Beach and Carlson, 2004, 2005; Carlson, 2005; Fejes, 2006; Henning-Loeb, 2006; Båth, 2006). Restructuring in Hillfield in this vein, as stated previously, was often described as just specifically 'renewal ... It was about making something new and different from the past' (Harald Spanks).

This kind of discourse of renewal was applied particularly by actors from the top of the organisation of adult education, and was usually accompanied by both implicit and explicit attacks on the former comprehensive adult education system; i.e. the former Komvux system; which was often denigrated as 'old and stayed' not 'new and vibrant', as 'wasteful' and not 'effective' and as 'traditional' and 'not flexible' (Wass 2004) in a play of opposites that may be an example of what Ball has stated as the way new policies often feed off and gain legitimacy from the deriding and demolition of previous ones (Ball, 1998: 125) and of the way (new) languages are used in order to support (or even perhaps constitute, Fejes, 2006) what can be called a new orthodoxy, as a form of governmentality where only some 'solutions' and not others are possible (Ball, 1998; Fairclough, 1993; Potter, 1996; Beach 2000; Beach and Carlson, 2004; Wass, 2004). Stronach (1993, p. 26) talks about repetitive circularities, the use of myths, the logics of witchcraft and the structures of ritual. A former Chief Adult Education Officer spoke as follows:

> There was a lot of talk about renewal ... new forms of pedagogy ... new recruitment ... enhanced effectivness and more flexibility and freedom of choice in the system ... But it's a myth to think that just because you form a company you'll get these things ... They're talked about and even believed to a degree, in most circles ... certainly in some ... and a lot of effort has been put in to make these ideas acceptable ... Not just believable but also de facto believed! What isn't always mentioned

is what is now at the bottom line ... The economy of the company (and that means profits for its shareholders) must come first ... no matter what (and) the well being of the education in other respects must suffer if it compromises profits ... The new aim was meant to be about new partnership, dynamism, new pathways and a more effective organisation ... This was the myth. Things haven't been like that ...

(Harry Boye: former Hillfield District CAEO)

This reasoning about myths and realisations can partly be compared with Ball's discussion (1998: 124) of the advocacy of the market or commercial form of educational reform as the 'solution' to educational problems; as a form of 'policy magic' (Stronach, 1993; Beach and Carlson, 2004, 2005; Carlson, 2004, 2005). Moreover, although desired changes are often presented as natural, they are still 'questionable' and are of course also questioned by teachers and others on the inside of policy cycles and on the soft underside of policy processes (Gustafsson, 2003). Barbara, a teacher, spoke as follows:

The claim is that the changes that are taking place are part of a natural progression ... that represents everyone's best interests ... But this is questionable. The changes are costing not saving money, and at such an extent that it will take years to recoup the losses ... Costs have not been reduced, freedoms have not developed and content is not renewed. The public purse will foot the costs ... thus subsidising the conversion of welfare from public supply to private interest ...

(Barbara former Studium teacher)

Teachers' voices are not usually privy to internal organisational details and most teachers did not put things in the way Barbara does above. What they more commonly expressed was, as discussed also in the previous chapter and in Beach (2004a), a frustration over how 'things are being torn down in the execution of an idea regardless of the personal and professional costs' (Betty). Barbara has put things in the following way:

We have a guaranteed income (but) have lost our jobs ... Many of us were expected to move into the regular school ... This is a loss of professional identity and we have resisted the move ... Many teachers feel they will be asked to teach in areas that they are not qualified in and they protest

against what they see as a view of professionalism in which the idea seems
to be that if you can teach one thing you can teach anything and once a
teacher always a teacher ... It has cost a lot of money and ... you have to
ask ... in what interests ...

The GMC motivated the tendering of adult education in two main ways.
Firstly in terms of reducing the size of the municipally owned service apparatus
as an economic necessity after the completion of the AEI programme, in the face
of a severely reduced budget, and secondly, as part of a movement from large scale,
regulated, comprehensive education, to a flexible education arrangement that
offered greater freedom of choice to individuals and was better able to respond to
the varied needs and lives of adult learners (Beach and Carlson, 2004). However,
in line with our suggestions above and in the previous chapter, we would suggest
that restructuring hasn't had these benefits. As also the Hillfield City Auditors
and teacher informants have expressed it, things haven't become more flexible,
money has not been saved and education processes have not involved more
freedom of choice and self-determination for individuals. In fact in the end,
the events we have seen and documented can all be expressed as being about
the moral justification of market interests and the further capitalisation of the
labour processes of education (Beach, 2004a).

Winners and losers in the cauldron of commoditisation

A notion of there clearly being both winners and losers in restructuring is
suggested by the volunteered and elicited statements presented in this and the
previous chapter. But this unevenness of outcomes is also apparent in more
material terms, in respect for instance of who has been tendered a major contract
and who hasn't (also Beach and Carlson, 2004; Beach, 2006b). Moreover,
there also seems to be one consistently promoted victor in the voices of most
informants. This being private enterprise, firstly through the introduction and
embedding of the rituals and ideologies of ... privatisation and market initiatives
for the buying and selling of education' (Ken) and secondly in terms of the
habituation of internal educational practices and processes with the languages,
symbols and inscriptions of market ideology and practices (Beach, 2003a, b, c
and chapters 2, 3 and 4 of the present volume). However, what in policy research
is called 'new managerialism'—i.e. the insertion of the theories and techniques of
business management and the 'cult of excellence' into public sector institutions
(Ball 1998: 123) is also apparent.

The inscription of market values and the rise of new managerialism are the main clear outcomes then, of the processes of neo-liberal transformation and seem to accompany the expanding areas of adult education as an enterprise 'connected to labour market initiatives' (Greta) that are 'the main growth areas' (Beach and Carlson, 2005; Carlson, 2005). As one informant, Barbara, put it, 'these organisations (actively) promote the ... usually short term (also) self-identified interests of trade and industry ... as these are represented and voiced within education committees by elected members of HBR (The Hillfield Business Region), who are also indirect sponsors of restructuring'. The growth areas can be compared to the 'shrinkers'. That is, the areas and organisations that have been replaced, such as the 'previously dominant ... humanist education of komvux ... that was badly copied in Studium'   (Ken).

There are consequnces of this transformation of adult education from a broad, humanist and comprehensive adult education service to a fractured, flexible form of adult education entrepreneurialism according to informants. One of these is that 'short-term reactionary planning has grown into the system ... replacing long-term stability' (Ken), as has the disposability of labour. Short term, job related skills and work related knowledge have become very much emphasised and students are allowed to 'flexibly' move in and out of their education in time with whether and how they are able to become employed within the labour market (Beach and Carlson, 2004):

> The connection with the labour market is very apparent. The dominant idea is that we should principally educate people so they can get work and a job or qualification for a job (otherwise) the education isn't worthwhile ...   (Harald Spanks)

> These days ... it's all about flex courses ... and the like ... so people can fit studying into life projects where work dominates ... Courses become very minimalist ... What is important for the moment dominates ... Learning becomes fragmented ...   (Ken)

New ways of speaking about the organisation of adult education have emerged (also Wass, 2004; Carlson, 2005; Beach and Carlson, 2005), together with a new discourse (Lindblad et al., 2005), with consequences for the subject positions available to and the identities developed by agents in adult education (Fejes, 2006; Henning-loeb, 2006). This new discourse embodies both an objectification and a distancing of the practices of education and its participants. Students become clients, customers, or even consumers, and education becomes a commodity like any other commodity: i.e. simply a product on a market. Individuals are treated as objects not subjects, despite all the rhetoric of the individual in focus. What Brown and Lauder (1996) called neo-Fordism is also strongly prevalent. Educational activities have been turned into saleable, sometimes even trademarked products as part of a national efficiency drive.

Good examples of the way the new discourse plays out in actual practices in Hillfield are in the meetings between the tracking organization, SPA, and the students who they place out and track at different education suppliers. The demands of getting a job on the one hand, which often for many economically poor immigrants, working class youngsters and short educated persons means any job, and the availability of short-term, short skilled labour in trade, industry and commerce on the other, now determines the space of education (Beach and Carlson, 2004), as the new education situation becomes increasingly dominated by a new labour market perspective (Carlson, 2004, 2005; Beach and Carlson, 2005). As suggested already in the previous chapter there is also a new ritual. Previously community adult education provided a 'humanistic education for adults who wanted to progress within the education system' (Betty) and fulfil the demands of upper-secondary qualification, whilst companies commissioned, 'bought and paid for specialist courses or programmes of study for their employees if they needed them and could benefit from them' (Ken). Things have changed:

> Before, although there were also courses in things like basic maths for people working at Ericsson Microwave and I also had courses with Swedish Telecom, Volvo and 'Manpower' ... Companies bought the education from us ... for their employees ... We pushed things pretty hard ... to fit their requests because this pulled in a lot of money ... that we could then use ... It was a great situation ... Now education in 'flex courses' that cater to individual needs and the labour market is what we do all the time ...   (Ken)

The idea of 'flexibility' versus 'fixed' is given a new turn above, as is the idea of new 'versus' old. The 'new' education is not new at all but rather a particular re-articulation of a previous arrangement. Education in private, economic interests, is being given as a rule in public organisations through public funds. Furthermore, flexibility is not flexibility as such, but more of an accommodation of education to short-term commercial needs as defined for the moment by business interests (Beach and Carlson, 2004, 2005). We can wonder, given this reversal of polarity, why the general popular understanding can be so easily seduced by the power of discourse as to see things in any other way. The former Managing Director of Studium explains this again by recourse to the power of discursive articulations under politically and ideologically saturated circumstances, partly by saying that 'novelty is always expressed as having its own attraction' and that the new ideals (in this case flexibility) are stressed as 'not to be found within the old school form', simply because these school forms are said to be the antithesis of flexibility. 'But no one bothers to see if this is really the case' (Ken). 'We are in the grip of an Orwellian machine: he who controls the past controls the future, he who controls the present controls the past' (Ken). Several of the teachers have expressed similar points. Others have contested the definition of the inflexibility of the old Komvux more directly:

> The suggestions have been that what characterised us in the past was that rigidity, and there was an idea that there would be greater flexibility in a system with several actors involved. There would be competition, new pedagogical methods and freedom of choice. And there has sort of been the idea of the beauty of newness and a sort of salvation aura as well. All periods have their trends and fancies ... The media has played on and promoted these ... What they have ignored is that there was great variety in the past and they have also ignored what the new flexi courses actually give rise to and lead to as a form of learning ... not to mention how education work is being changed in the process from a professional to a highly fragmented and almost mechanical activity ... (Harry Boye)

As suggested already in the previous chapter, popular discourses tie restructuring to ideas of renewal, refurbishment and improvement and suggest that we are living in a new free world where a whole array of human 'goods' (such as human advancement, self-reliance, flexibility, independence and autonomy) are catered for through markets and where, as well as this, money is saved in the process by tying service provision to market relations (Beach and Carlson, 2004, 2005; Beach, 2005a, b). However, the material developments from restructuring, as we have felt them through the words of our informants and have measured them in terms of actual developments in the local adult education arena, allow a more complex picture to develop. This picture suggests something very different to the suggestions of the dominant discourse. This suggestion is that our new situation (within the context of total flexibility and a market for everything) can be characterised in another way, where flexibility, variety, freedom of choice, new spaces for the development of new skills, economic savings and so on are myths that feed the psyche and stand in the way of and obscure our common grasp and understanding of the *material conditions* of a new education economy. The myths are interested in promoting a new governmentality in adult education; a new witchcraft or hegemony; if we read with Fejes (2006). This is about promoting one vision of education at the expense of others 'through ignorance or for ideological, political (or) private reasons' (Ronny).

Concluding remarks

In this chapter, which is based extensively on a previous work by Dennis Beach and Marie Carlson (Beach and Carlson, 2004), we have set out to analyse dominant discourses and alternative stories about education restructuring in respect of the organisation and delivery of adult education, so as to illuminate some sense of what has happened discursively, practically and ideologically in education renewal in a particular education authority, in terms of what the consequences were experienced and voiced as by teachers and education politicians, managers and leaders. The chapter in this sense has been concerned with the relationships between social and discursive practices. The issue of in whose best interests developments were sensed as working has been important.

The chapter suggests that there are clear differences in the discourses developed in adult education by differently positioned agents, but also consistencies. These often refer to the need for a flexible workforce in the new work order *not specifically an educated one*, which also seems to be what is developing in adult education in Hillfield today, where these words seem to have obtained material consequences inside interpretative, communicative and other social practices (Fairclough, 1993, 1995; Bourdieu, 1996; Hall, 1996). The rise to authority of a labour market and economic discourse trammelled by politicians and entrepreneurs is the most telling development. But it has not occurred in a common interest according to our interpretations of informants' voices. The interests served seem to be undeniably very private ones.

Chapter 7

Creativity and performativity in adult education

The present chapter is supported by three of the ethnographic research projects named in the introduction. The first is the Swedish Research Council (SRC) sponsored project concerned with the complexities of steering and control within adult SFI (literally Swedish for Immigrants— in direct translation from Swedish) within the Municipal Region in Sweden called by the pseudonym Hillforth. The second is the SOCRATES Creative Learning and Student's Perspectives (CLASP) project. The third is the more recent *Hybrid Classrooms* project, also economically supported by the SRC.

The research in all three projects has been concerned with the consequences of education restructuring for some aspect of education supply or learning quality; taken in line with Ball (1993) as changes in education through the introduction of a market model of delivery with roots in the world of business and the expressed intention of making education supply more economically effective. In the present chapter the concern is for the value practices of humanist education and creative learning in adult education contexts. Humanism and creativity are key issues in both old and new adult education in Sweden (also Larsson, 1993; Carlén, 1999; Carlson, 2002; Wass, 2004; Beach, 2004a, 2006b; Beach and Carlson, 2004). Most of the research was done at two sites, which we have called by the pseudonyms SWALL and StudiumF. The chapter has been developed from a fairly extensive rewrite of a previously published article in the international research journal *Ethnography and Education* (Beach, 2006b).

The research sites

Two research sites (SWALL and StudiumF) are focussed on. These were created through the recent processes of education restructuring for Adult Education in Hillforth. They have a common heritage in the former public service form of this education, called Komvux, which was the national educational flagship of the folk-home concept of social democracy. Komvux was concerned with balancing qualification deficits across generations and between social classes, ethnic groups and gender categories in Sweden, and with improving democratic participation and senses of 'belonging' in society based on humanist education principles (Larsson, 1993; Carlén, 1999; Carlson, 2002; Beach, 2004a; Fejes, 2006; Henning-Loeb, 2006). However, the two organisations are also different in some key ways. SWALL is a teacher collective specialising in SFI that broke away from Komvux in 2001 at the time of its conversion to a public limited company (Studium Ltd) and StudiumF is an education bureau (Sw: förvaltning) within Hillforth's local government that was formed after the economic collapse of this company two years later. Studium Ltd was the largest single provider of adult education in the region in 2001 and up until the signing of contracts after restructuring in 2003, at which time it effectively lost 80% of its delivery volume (Beach, 2004a, 2006b). This created a problem of redeployment in the company and eventually its bankruptcy. The creation of StudiumF was part of the local government response to this problem (Carlson, 2005).

StudiumF only existed for a little over a year (Beach, 2006b). It was a bureau within the public sector and therefore also part of Hillforth's local government organisation, for which reason it was also often regarded sceptically by other education delivers. Another part of the local government education organisation, the local adult education board (AEB), subcontracted StudiumF to deliver education in 2004 in vocational subjects and SFI, which it did in three separate city regions. These were North Eastern Hillforth, with high concentrations of council housing, unemployment and economic poverty; 'Downtown', on the outskirts of the upper-middle-class central region, close to the main shopping areas, universities and general city amenities; and 'North Bank', on the Hillport River close to former 'inner-basin' industrial shipping areas in one of the new *Knowledge Regions* (kunskapsregioner) in the city. The new Hillforth IT-University is situated here and high rent is contributing to the production of an upper class and commercial enclave.

One of the most consistently given reasons for the formation of the teacher collective we term *SWALL* 'was to ensure the continued supply of humanist education after decentralisation in the Swedish Adult Education Initiative (AEI)' and the introduction of new steering technologies from new public-management traditions (Wass, 2004; Beach, 2004; Beach and Carlson, 2004), according to the owner initiators of the organisation, five qualified SFI teachers and former Komvux colleagues (Sandra Hart, Sharon Pole, Sally Shaw, Sue Knights and Sam Shole). As they put it, restructuring 'allowed (them) to leave Komvux at the time of its reorganisation as a company and form their own organisation based on their own ideals' (Sue). However, one further thing that attention can be drawn to with regard to the formation of SWALL is something that also Dale (1999) has suggested. This is that the effects of restructuring are not easily painted as simply good or bad (also Carlson, 2002; Gustavsson, 2003). SWALL is an organisation that by being small and specialised fits common global expressions about the best means for attaining flexibility and effectiveness within the welfare sector in an era of neo-liberal (economic and managerialist) ascendancy (Green, 1999; Lindberg, 1999). But at the same time its owner-teachers have set up a practice which they hope will be able to stand for stability, humanist values and principles of extended professionalism, autonomy and control. These values often fall in conflict with issues of economic effectiveness and managerial expediency (Rose, 1995; Gordon et al., 2003). Such issues, together with the collaboration that was openly offered toward the project by the SWALL owner-teachers, formed the main reasons for including this organisation in the investigation.

Two levels of analysis have been important when teasing out the characteristics of practice of the education investigated at the two sites (Beach, 2005c). These are (i) a surface level of analysis of everyday interaction relating to oral, visual or written proposals for action and material resources in use and (ii) a deeper level of analysis concerning the structural orthography of learning, focusing on the institutional rules, regulations and cultural interpellations of social technologies, social relations and social practices of communication.

The two levels of analysis have helped identify and name two distinct metaphors for creativity (novelty and change) and four pillars of humanism in education (thoughtfulness, reciprocity, authenticity, negotiation). Field-notes and Fieldwork Diaries have been particularly important in these identification and naming processes, as they usually are in ethnography (Beach, 2006b) and these have indicated that in practice, humanist education was a central aim for all teachers at the sites researched, which could also be visibly seen in terms of the practices that were noted. Creative learning was also present at both sites according to our interpretations of the data produced, where it was usually accompanied by creative teaching as part of small-scale, *crafted and grafted* (Jeffrey and Woods, 2003) activities that were said to be part of 'relatively long processes of development and trial and error (intuitive) work' (Ingrid, teacher). According to the data analysis, the dividing line between creativity and routine was often blurred, but intuition and embodied experience always played a major role in educational decision making, when humanism and creative teaching and learning was involved (Beach, 2006b).

The *crafting* of new practices and their *grafting* into everyday routines suggests several things in particular of value to the investigation. Firstly, how teachers at both sites used professional skills, knowledge and freedom to 'array the learning environment in line with particular pedagogical traditions (to) promote creative learning' (Ingrid). This required 'professional autonomy and an authenticity to negotiate curriculum interactions with learners' (Sally) as a form of genuinely meaningful labour (also Jeffrey, 2006). Secondly, that this was done in order to 'enhance student commitment ... broaden sensory bases for learning and extend platforms of communication' (Maude) by 'introducing and supporting *collaboration* and encouraging the kinds of *questioning, discussion and motivation* (that help shift) the onus in learning from individual ... learning to social interaction' (Maude). Creative learning and humanist commitments are integrated here as work is done in ways that show respect for students and their values and knowledge and 'at the same time (aim to) assist creativity in learning' (Ingrid). The four elements of interrogation, negotiation, collaboration and motivation are all important according to our informants. Their combination is dependent on 'accumulated knowledge from (theoretical) studies and practical experience' (Maude). Success demands 'experience and training' (Sharon) in other words. Some examples are provided in the following section of the chapter.

About creative learning at the sites

An illustrative example of creative learning was the use of different colour-cards for verbs, adjectives, adverbs and nouns in word order games at Studium. These cards had been introduced by staff, to help students grasp 'how ... subject, predicate and ... adverbs ...' (Ingrid, teacher) 'move (together) within a choreography of grammar as I like to call it ... even when they actually have difficulty at first recognising, reading or even understanding the meaning of the word' (Maud, teacher). It was about a creative and stimulating use of colour 'to support word order pattern recognition ... in standard Swedish (and) a way of broadening the sensory bases and activity formats of second language learning' (Ingrid) as a form of socio-culturally inspired, constructivist language work (McGee, 1999; Berhanu, 2001; Carlson, 2002). These things were described as follows in field-notes:

> I watched the students ... They said the cards made things easier ... The teachers said they had initially been used 'as a novel way to solve a problem (but) had become part of (established) practices (that) had also been evaluated and proven to work' (Ingrid) ... In this sense they 'are not just new ideas (but rather) tried and tested approaches based on such

ideas' (Maude) ... They represent outcomes of ... professional wisdom and represent accumulated (embodied) knowledge (about) 'a tested and evaluated practice ...'   (Ingrid) ...

The teachers' work with 'the new creativity curriculum' (Kath, teacher) was a very *deliberate and planned* activity then that incorporated both 'practical and theoretical knowledge, as well as the collective experience and individual skills of both teachers and learners' (e.g. Sue). It was based on knowledge developed from praxis and wasn't something that just anyone would be likely (or should simply be expected) to be able to do. As Maude put it: 'Being creative in teaching (is done) to help creativity in learning', with this ... being about 'making new use of something or creating something ... or bringing about something that wouldn't otherwise have occurred' (Ingrid). But this 'is not only about being novel in your work as a teacher ... by having a good idea and creating something that is different ... It is not about just going to a museum or art gallery' (Maude). There is more to it 'than just being novel ... Novel teaching is not an aim in itself but a means of finding a way to 'help students see something they wouldn't otherwise' (Ingrid). Students have also described this in their own terms, usually in relation to things like how embodied experiences 'stimulate you' (Jone). They remind us of Merleau-Ponty's emphasis on the living body as an organic-existential unity for learning (Grundén, 2005; Beach, 2005d) and delineate what we feel is a common commitment at SWALL and Studium that has developed from teacher education and years of thought through and collectively discussed professional experience as a practical form of a phenomenological theory of learning (Beach, 2006b).

Theory, materiality and technique

As well as a particular underpinning organisational theory of learning, also different materials and technologies are used in classroom practices to stimulate creative learning. According to our fieldnotes they include cultural (and ethnic) art forms 'to stimulate thought and language' (Maude) ... 'the use (and naming) of colours, shapes and forms' (Kath) (and) the presence of 'creative writing, small plays, thematic dramatisation and forum theatre ... to support and encourage a more active (kind) of participation' (Ingrid).[10] According to student informants

10 All of the above points have been examined further in the ethnography, where it became clear that generally there is a lot of fun in learning at Swall and Studium, through the wide range of activities there that 'stimulate... thinking and a desire to speak and write' (Jone). However, further, according to one Studium informant there is also embodiment.

these activities give 'a feeling ... inside your whole body (that you don't get) just reading' (Joan). You feel 'respect and commitment from the teachers' (Beiha) and a sense of 'reward from the education as the activities help support a new understanding' (Mamud). A group of students who were talking to each-other about some word-card activities at Studium said the following:

> You help each-other ... (It) helps you focus ... You don't feel as tired ... '
> (Joan). 'You come at the problem from a different direction or through a
> different work ... It's hard to explain ... It's fantastic and you can put them
> in the right order and look at the word (and) create your own solutions ...
> I kept getting them right and afterwards I wrote them down and learned
> the words ... and could make new sentences with them ...'   (Mohani).

Teachers and students at the two sites thus emphasise (both verbally and in action) a position where communication and language learning 'are seen to increase with a transition from monological to dialogical activity' (Sue). As Annie, a Studium teacher put it, 'learners learn better when they start to actively exchange information with each-other and their teachers ... as they can then discuss interesting problems ... and the content they are working with in an active, dialogical communication process'.

These are statements that again express a social-cultural and constructivist commitment to creativity in the curriculum. They add a new communication theoretical dimension to the teachers' phenomenological theory. However, just as important to the teachers is the idea that the learning processes described 'don't (just) develop ... They have to be coaxed and scaffolded' (Sally). There is an active professional role for the teacher to play in other words, in relation to the development of the students and her learning skills and knowledge. But it is not of the formal kind:

> The teachers share a common idea expressed in a common narrative
> that 'every learner can learn creatively if favourable conditions ... can be
> formed' (Sue) (but they also believe) that these skills and abilities will
> not develop 'simply on their own' (Ingrid). As Sharon put it, 'variations in
> the environment, varied approaches to work and multi-sided involvement
> help ... But these activities ... have to be thought through, planned and
> evaluated ... They don't just happen ... Students are recognised as having

'a natural lust to learn (but as also) needing help in their learning in order
to learn well ...' (Sandra).   (Field-notes)

The ideas expressed here are in line with Vygotsky, Luria and Davydov,
according to sources like Säljö (2000) and Zaporozets (2005), but they also fit
well with Marx comments in the German ideology, concerning how the leading
role in mental development belongs to human interactions where the learner
actively assimilates the social experience and material and spiritual culture
accumulated by previous generations (Säljö, 2000; Zaporozets, 2005; Vygotsky,
1992). This differs strongly from other interpretations of the new curricula in
Sweden based on a concept of the spontaneous development of inborn capacities,
according to which the teacher need not teach, but needs only to arrange
conditions for a manifestation of personality, with this then forming grounds
for performances that are taken as natural expressions of an inner motivation
(Dovemark, 2004a). The teacher informants haven't just stepped aside to create
an imaginary room for learners to learn freely and individually in. They have
taken command over a new role where they help students to recognise, identify
and or produce spaces for learning creatively. And they then engage with them
in practices 'that are devised to help them ... use these spaces as productively as
possible' (Sally).

   Some specific techniques were important for creating conditions for these
kinds of creative learning according to the informants. They involved using
variations in the curriculum such as didactic games and different forms of
practical, social and artistic activities (visits to art galleries, drawing, photography
and theatre) 'to stimulate both ... active language use, cognitive activity and
intellectual development' (Sandra). But they also included things like active
story telling, extending the senses used in language teaching and making
spaces for professional contact and professional intimacy (see also Jeffrey and
Woods, 2003). However, the presence of a shared narrative, from the level of the
leadership function down to the 'shop-floor', was also an extremely important
item. This suggests something of a new leadership style—a kind of narrative
leadership—that may be positively associated with the development of shared
commitments, responsibility and involvement to support a more creative
teaching-learning venture (Beach, 2006b).

Story telling

As suggested in Beach (2006b), story telling was a very important tool of creativity and was used both in *passive forms*, where teachers use story telling to convey a message or illustrate an example of language use, and active forms. In the active forms students were encouraged to tell stories, 'sometimes fictional sometimes about their own lives' (Sharon) to other class members, either 'as an exercise in Swedish vocabulary (and) presentational skills' (Sally) or, and above all, 'as something that gives students ownership over what is taken up (and) a creative space (for) language use and experimentation' (Sally).

A good example of active story making came from Studium North where a site-newspaper was produced. This newspaper 'was a student product' (Laura, the teacher in charge of the newspaper project) that made use of computers and the facilities of the study resource centre, 'to give learners tools by which (to) develop and share experiences and information' (Rosie, teacher) when 'making a meaningful content for language (learning) in an engaging and fun way' (Laura). However, the newspaper isn't just produced by students it is also put to work. A class was observed working with the newspaper:

> Laura collected (new) words that students had found from ... 'The Vale' ... by asking them (to) write them on the whiteboard (and) she then talked about the words with them by asking if anyone could give an example of where they had seen the word ... other than in the newspaper and could compare this ... They discussed and gave uses of the word in sentence form, which were displayed also on the white-board, and the students were then asked to 'invent and try out new sentences on each-other' (Laura) and to come forward and write a sentence ... on the board ... When the board was full of sentences the students were asked 'to write them down in their exercise books' ... and Laura went round (to) correct sentences (and) locate and contrast understandings of different meanings ... These sentences formed the next part of the lesson ... in which students who had written them read them out and were asked about (them) by other students who were also asked if they could think of new examples ...

As described above, using the Studium newspaper involved all of the previously mentioned elements of interrogation, collaboration, negotiation and motivation to stimulate cooperation and creativity in order to first develop and then focus on something meaningful in the life of the school. However, it also involves trust in the learner. The students are trusted to work together and use their knowledge to further stimulate individual and group imagination. The intention is to encourage 'a dare to try approach to language (through) the development ... of knowledge (and) the fabrication of stories related to it' (Laura). It is about the valorisation of personal forms of knowledge in collective meaning making within a formal educational context.

Extending the senses used in learning

Extending the senses in learning was 'another common technique for promoting creativity in learning' (Sharon). It was particularly prolific at SWALL, where it was most clearly visible in field materials concerning the use of drama, art, sport, cookery, tactile work and rhythm, which were also the most common examples. In them learning 'is not just seen and treated as headwork (but as) an aesthetic ... physical and bodily experience ...' (Sharon). A field-note extract provides a description:

> There is (an) 'emphasis on embodiment as both an aspect of ... professional ideology and as an element of the most recent proposition in adult education ...' (Sally) ... A run-about game, stamping and clapping, a cookery group, football, small-drama, mime and didactic games are included. Music is played, touch is incorporated (and) we regularly do stretching and coordination activities ...' But there is also a social aspect (and) the ideas and practices (of) brain gymnastics' (Sharon) ... Emphasis is on the physical and emotional environment (and) the importance of enjoying learning ... The assumption of successful learning seems to be of a 'natural' process of meaning making in everyday life ... A starting point is that 'we cannot fail to be creative ... when making sense of our daily experiences and events around us' (Sally) ...

These things illustrate the willingness to experiment in the spaces available at SWALL as 'an outcome of specific practical-pedagogical theories developed from professional education and ... reflections over experienced student needs and responses' (Sandra). The following diary extract considers this further:

> The activities at SWALL are not ones that just anyone would be likely to think of or use. They reflect pedagogical convictions and beliefs formed

in praxis and require both materiality, familiarity, training and experience. They suggest that teachers have a very definite consciousness about what they are doing and that this awareness has been formed in the workplace but is 'aided by' formally acquired knowledge and activities that are also well documented and evaluated.

All the SFI teachers at SWALL have passed an initial teacher education programme and have further professional education experiences from universities in relevant subjects (languages, psychology, pedagogy, language pedagogy, linguistics, drama are common examples). Several of them are members of the Society for Effective Affective Learning (where they have obtained yet further formal and informal education and training). They also have metres of files about theorised forms of practice artistry to teach by, which also document the outcomes of their work in ways that can be (and are) shared and collectively evaluated in weekly staff conferences. Broadening the sensory base of teaching-learning activities enables students to ... laugh, talk, jump, sing, mime and learn in school. But this isn't just play. It is part of a thought through curriculum.

The SWALL and StudiumF teachers all express an awareness that 'the main education policy discourses in Sweden today talk about the importance of promoting flexibility, individual responsibility and the mobilisation of local and self- regulation in SFI, 'which is now to proceed from the motivation and interest of the students themselves' (Ingrid), 'through self-regulation, responsibility and an ability to find their own knowledge' (Sue). However, these teachers also point out that they were convinced of this already 'during their time at Komvux' (Sue) and also that 'without a guiding pedagogical theory (and) the experience and understanding of what different kinds of professional pedagogical engagement with different (types of) learning subjects involves' (Sam), the official discourse only points at a practical solution to practical problems rather than at deep changes to the foundations of a philosophy of practice. Since their time at Komvux the teachers thus have had 'a clear definition of learning opposing both behaviourist and laissez-faire interpretations of the new curriculum' (Sam).

Two teachers from SWALL used the example of the kinds of special knowledge required when working with 'new readers' to illustrate this point. As they put it, several issues are involved here, including 'developing phonemic hearing skills and analysing the phonetic composition of words' (Sandra). These are not the kinds of knowledge 'just anyone is likely to have' (Sally). 'They require education, practice and experience to be grasped and used well' (Sue).

> Teachers say they extend learning into broader sensory areas for three reasons. The first is that through their education and experience, they believe the quality of learning is simply improved by this ... The second concerns the humanist aim to develop a new classroom order with a view of the learner 'as a creative individual ... who can be supported in their learning ... to learn better' (Sally) ... The third is that students are 'resources ... not impediments to learning' (Sue). As Sally put it, extending the sensory base extends also 'the range of activities (students) learn through (and) can influence'. (Fieldwork Diary)

These kinds of ideas have been expressed regularly by the teachers in the present investigation (see also Beach, 2006b). For instance, as Sue and Sam put it (both from SWALL) 'each student has a talent that needs favourable conditions to develop and teachers have an important role in helping students to learn and in helping them make sense of their learning outcomes' (Sally).

Students as resources: from language workshop to study hall

One thing that should have become clear is that the teachers in the investigation have interpreted their work to involve finding ways to help students to become effective as an active resource in their own (and each-other's) learning without abandoning them 'simply to their own devices in their learning' (Sam). This is fully in line with the aims and intentions of the most recent adult education proposition (Government Proposition 200%1: 72) and 'new directives for SFI (from) the National Schools Agency' (Betty). However, what is also suggested is that this commitment was clear for the teachers before these new policies were published, even as far back as the early nineties according to several informants and sources, where promoting students as creative and self-supported and self-supporting learners 'was the basic form of education in SFI in what we called the study hall approach' (Betty). This approach was used in the groups visited at Studium and was characterised in field-notes as follows:

> The students (are) working ... I was waiting for them to start, expecting some kind of formal signal from teachers that the working day had begun ... but instead students just came in and started working ... Kath (the

teacher) was ... sat next to a Somali woman (who) seemed to be reading something ... Kath nodded and the lady wrote something on the stencil sheet (and then) looked up again ... Kath nodded, the lady's head went down (angled) toward the dictionary ... and she began to write again ... Only a few words and then a (smile) a question ... and then more writing ... A student (at the table nearest me) seemed to be looking into space and moving her lips ... Then she looked down at the sheet, moving her lips again and her finger across a line of text ... Then she looked up and moved her lips again ... 'She is reading to herself' Kath said. 'They are trying to learn a text so they can talk about it and present it ... Then they will fetch the file from the shelves over there and we will (record) that they have completed the work ... After that they go and get another stencil and do the work activities, either on their own or together ...

According to Annie, another StudiumF teacher, the advantages with the study hall approach are as follows: students 'have responsibility for the order and pace ... They can start to work as soon as they arrive (and) can concentrate on what they feel they need to work on'. However, as also noticed through several weeks of participant observation, there is even a system of management to guide them through the course on the basis of systematic work and a local curriculum that is aimed to help students develop key knowledge and skills. Students work independently, in self-sustained ways for quite long periods of time. But there is always teacher support available and students also help each-other a lot. A diary extract read:

> The study hall activities formed the kernel of work in SFI (which) was generally done with two or three teachers present as facilitators and evaluators of practice (and) with access to a wide range of materials ... There was regular collaboration between students (rather than what is common in 'usual' school contexts, which is competition) and reciprocity in interactions between students and between students and teachers characterised the lessons ... Teachers monitored, assessed and commented on student work, but they also took out smaller groups for direct teaching for an hour at a time two or three times a week.

Elementary/intermediate students more often than others engaged in the form of work described above according to field-notes, diary extracts and local policy documents. Betty said this was because they benefited from having some basic foundational knowledge. 'You could say they were introduced to the approach in the introductory groups and then learned to use it extensively in the elementary intermediate ...' she said.

The study hall system was researched mainly by watching student progress through the documentation available (Beach, 2006b). But a supply teacher and a 'new teacher' were also 'tracked' through a morning of work each, as a test of how the system gave 'natural support and a framework for action ... to the teachers as well ...', as Annie had put it. When doing this it was noted how the teachers were able to find their feet and quickly pick up the routine so that by the end of the first morning they could not be visually identified as out of place or lost in the activity compared to other teachers. It seems as if there is professional autonomy, self-control and reward in the routines used and that these are exercised in the interests of students by their educators. The following diary extract provides some further characteristics:

> The kind of commitment described above 'to involve (students) actively in their learning ... with constant support and encouragement is again typical of a socio-cultural approach to second language acquisition ... It sees the socio-cultural milieu (including individual differences, language acquisition contexts and actual learning outcomes, ongoing activities and 'learning products') as highly important for promoting successful learning and importance is attached to humanist aspects such as making things relevant and authentic. The approach stands clearly against both a behaviourist approach (based on linear stimulus-response-reinforcement models) and models of genetic language acquisition where learning is simply 'triggered' by the environment ...

As also stated in Beach (2006b), McGee (1999) refers to Krashen (1985) in support of a socio-cultural (constructivist) approach to second language learning. Krashen stated that people are able to creatively build and develop second languages when they obtain relevant input and stimulation from teachers and the environment, and when affective filters are lowered so as to help let this input in. Also noted is that this kind of intentional, theorised-practice-artistry takes preparation, education, time, effort, negotiation, reflection, knowledge and experience. This applies also according to Krashen (1984), McGee (1999), Berhanu (2001) and Carlson (2002).

Contradictions in practice

Four things may be noted from the discussions above concerning the structural orthography and the social order of creativity in classroom work. In line with also Jeffrey and Woods (2003) these concern the presence of and attention to issues of negotiation, interaction, thoughtfulness, reflection, authenticity and reciprocity. They have been expressed by informants in relation to interrogation (curiosity), collaboration, education, negotiation and motivation and are visible firstly in that a theoretically (educationally and experientially embodied and) informed form of negotiated relevance in the curriculum normally under girds classroom activities and that secondly, most of the time teachers 'allow (this) to grow forth (naturally) out of their everyday engagement in classrooms with students' (Sally), whose own first hand 'experiences, knowledge, values and practices are given sufficient space to influence and enter the formal curriculum' (Sue). However, at times teachers don't do this, but instead become coerced, for one reason or another, to commit to other things (Beach, 2006b). This occurs 'usually at times when performance requirements are (for some reason) high' (Annie), such as examination times and inspection periods. A diary text read:

> Examinations, inspections ... and submission of tender all create adverse conditions ... in that attention is directed not at authentic practices, (reciprocity and) negotiation but at external signals and performance factors ... Having to meet external demands (is an obvious pressure). However, skirting negotiation was (also) done in one of two other ways according to field-notes. These are (i) by teachers 'acting on direct orders from above' (Annie) and 'delivering a curriculum item or package' (Kath) or (ii) by them 'taking it upon (themselves) to ... select and lift in a specific content (and) *decide by themselves what is relevant* for (students) to learn' (Sharon, Kevin) ... In both (these) cases reciprocity and negotiation are suspended and the extent to which SFI students really are co-determiners and creative makers of knowledge in their education is questionable, as they are primarily knowledge recipients ... exposed to principles of meaning that they do not control ... In these ways the basic (classroom) values of the teachers are being contradicted in and by their own chosen practices ...

Krashen (1984) suggests that the absence of negotiation will always be problematic for learner creativity in second language learning as the possibilities to live out humanist and constructivist values in the curriculum are undermined through objectification and a loss of personal control and autonomy and a subsequent reduction of the presence of the self in the education context (McGee, 1999). This problem is one of alienation. It can become very severe.

According to the investigation alienation is pending in particular if and whenever there is a tendency to valorise western culture at the expense of what key social actors like media workers and teachers regard as the less sophisticated alternatives of the culture of the students (Carlson, 2002; Beach, 2006b). In these circumstances the content that is selected to help form a bridge between cultures in language and social learning actually becomes a barrier instead (Tesfahuney, 1998; Berhanu, 2001; Carlson, 2002). The following field-note extract picks up a little on this issue:

> Sandra (wanted) to open up horizons to issues of western humanism, equality and so forth ... She had the best of intentions (to) show the women in particular ... but also the men, the freedom and commitment to gender equity given by Swedish Law and social values and traditions ... But Beiha seemed almost to be in tears after the session (with the shawl) and Mamud was 'both angry (and also) very upset' about the way he felt that 'values ... that (he) didn't endorse (were) simply forced onto (him) as a member of particular race of people' at the same time as he had to admit that 'the values were ones (common) in his country' ... These are dominant values of dominant groups he added, but 'they are not every-one's values (and) we interpret them very differently ... just as Christians do regarding eating fish on Fridays' (Mamud) ... Being stigmatised is what Mamud said he felt and added 'it upsets you and puts you off ... You feel sad (insulted) and disrespected ... You don't feel like coming back just afterwards but usually it's not like this so you do ... It's only sometimes it is like this' ... Moreover, data would suggest that it is only when trying to solve a practical problem in the curriculum by for instance using media representations as 'a quick fix (of) *meaningful content* based on what the curriculum specifications determine we must take up' (Sharon), that these things ensue ... Normally they do not ... Negotiation is more common ...

Implied above is that the teachers at SWALL and Studium normally 'travel together' in the sense interpreted by Kvale (1995), across the educational terrain with their students, by negotiating value practices and constructing content with them, rather than simply telling them what's right and how they should be. This is about the authentic self seeking reciprocity and help in the potentially racist terrain of representations in the selection of content (and when checking if these selections are reciprocally valued). It is essential according to the investigation data and is best negotiated from within the 'flow' of the learning context.

Fitting the moment is a term used for this notion of reciprocally negotiated action (Jeffrey and Woods, 2003; Beach, 2006b). Fitting the moment requires the meeting of selves in line with Krashen (1984), Kvale (1995) and McGee (1999) earlier, but it is also a difficult and demanding skill, not just in a multi-/inter-cultural context, but perhaps particularly there (McGee, 1999; Berhanu, 2001; Carlson, 2002; von Brömsen, 2003; Eilard, 2004). It requires cultural competence and awareness from teachers and means that their professional knowledge base has to have a very broad foundation not only in subject, pedagogical, curriculum and organisational knowledge and skills, but also in personal political, ideological, class, gender and (inter-)cultural ones as well (von Brömsen, 2003; Dovemark, 2004a, Beach, 2006b; Lunneblad, 2006).

Such demands on teachers' knowledge and skills are somewhat reflected in the extended conceptions of teaching and learning discussed in recent curricula and government propositions in Sweden for both the school and for teacher education, which allude to how teaching requires subject knowledge, curriculum knowledge, political sensitivity and an ability to empathise and build human relationships (Dovemark, 2004a; Wass, 2004; Beach 2006b). But what is not discussed in these documents are the means by which these things are obstructed. Nor is it discussed what kind of education teachers need in order to be able to work well within culturally complex circumstances.

As also Lunneblad (2006), Carlson (2002) and Eilard (2004) have put it, complex learning contexts demand far more from teachers than them being just good people (also Beach and Carlson, 2005 and Beach, 2006b), as the value practices of 'just good people' are always likely to be put under threat in pressured circumstances. What is required is instead professional training, extensive knowledge and skills and appropriate material contexts to shore up specifically humanist values and traditions; all of which have been pointed out as essential qualities. Value practices are more stable and resilient when shored up by appropriate social relations and material arrangements that have been made resilient to depersonalisation (Mac An Ghail, 1988; Eilard, 2004; Carlson, 2002; Jeffrey, 2006; Beach, 2006b).

Jeffrey (2002) has made similar comments to these. Firstly when he noted how creative and experienced teachers in education contexts with committed students will always try to find ways to make even the most difficult circumstances into positive learning environments in relation to their most important personal and collective values and ideals; secondly when he pointed out that this 'effort' is often under threat and has to be fought for in conditions of economic steering and new management (Troman and Woods, 2001; Jeffrey, 2002; Jeffrey and Woods, 2003). When teachers are 'coerced into effectiveness' and are forced to include a specific content and ideas outside of negotiation, this seems to compromise the affective dimension and affect the attainment possibilities of humanist intentions and creativity aims in ways that have negative effects on humanism and creativity (Beach, 2006b).

Conclusions

The chapter illustrates several issues. Amongst these is willingness amongst the teachers in the investigation to experiment in the spaces available for educational interchanges with students. Also present is a suggestion that this is an outcome of specific practical-pedagogical theories that have been developed from professional education and reflections over experienced student needs. There is also an emphasis on embodded learning experiences as part of this theory and several innovations in the curriculum that reflect the theory, or are at least compatible with its main elelements, have been grafted into everyday work to facilitate the development of desired outcomes. Music is played, touch is incorporated but there is also a social aspect as well as an emphasis on not just the physical but also the emotional environment. The need of enjoying learning is stressed and the assumption of successful learning seems to be of a 'natural' process of meaning making in everyday life in which the students themselves are the main resources.

The successful activities at the sites, in the sense that the activities maintain an active contact with the aims of creativitiy and the foundation of humanism, are not ones that just anyone would be likely to think of or use we suggest. They reflect pedagogical convictions and beliefs formed in praxis and require familiarity, training and experience. They suggest that teachers have a very definite consciousness about what they are doing and that this awareness has been formed in the workplace but is 'aided by' formally acquired knowledge, documentation and evaluation. All the SFI teachers in the investigation have a formal teacher education and further professional education experiences from universities. They also have metres of files about forms of practice artistry to teach by, which also document the outcomes of their work in ways that can be studied and shared as part of a thought through curriculum.

Finally, the ideas expressed here refer to a specific context. However, they also concern the position of creative agency in education more generally and suggest that whilst teachers, as agents make their own local pedagogical identities and practices, what must also be remembered is that the contexts in which these identities, activities and practices are made are not always freely chosen. Agency is a situational, conditional, contingent and struggled for facet of life. It is not a universal, historically and materially independent fact that can be easily realised. The chapter suggests that teachers, as agents, need help through their professional education in recognising what spaces for positive action are available and how to use them in line with their shared values. Also suggested is that within commodity forms of education humanism and creativity will usually be opposed.

Chapter 8

Accommodations of creativity discourses

As presented already several times in this book, educational policy in Sweden is presently very clear about the importance of learner creativity and the development of individual responsibility for education. A particular discourse has developed around these issues (also Lindblad et al., 2005), which we have called the creativity discourse. The creativity discourse is a current mainstream educational discourse in Sweden (Lpo 94/98; Lindström, 2002; SOU 1999: 63; Gustafsson, 2003; Dovemark, 2004, a, b). However, this discourse exists within, around, combined with and alongside other discourses in a complex order of discourse and the practices of educators and learners who are contrite to try to put creativity to educational use (Jeffrey and Woods, 2003; Jeffrey, 2006). In this chapter we hope to provide contextual knowledge about creativity practices for education planners, practitioners and researchers based on long-term ethnographic research from an ongoing investigation financed by the Humanities and Social Sciences section of the Swedish Research Council. Marianne Dovemark, Elisabet Öhrn and Dennis Beach, all from Borås University College, and Jan Gustafsson, of Göteborg University, have been involved in the research. Dennis Beach and Marianne Dovemark are the joint authors of the chapter.

The policy discourses of creativity and performativity in education

When thinking about creativity we feel concepts like imagination, ingeniousness, innovation, inventiveness and originality are useful, as creativity in essence means having the skills and imagination enough to be *genuinely productive* (Beach, 2006a). Such words as inspired, talented, resourceful, fecund, fertile and fruitful also spring to mind, as opposed to their opposites, imitative, uninspired, infertile and unimaginative and the main education issue becomes one of the valorisation of authentic, personal forms of class-cultural capital and experience as educational knowledge (Jeffrey, 2006). Local interpretations of the new policy implications in the creativity discourse are in line with this. They have been expressed as follows (also Dovemark, 2004b):

We want to create ... a school (with) individual ... freedom of choice (and) responsibility for the curriculum where students determine where and when they learn ... Our aim is to help students to be motivated, alert, inquiring, self-governing and flexible users as opposed to just recipients of knowledge. It is in their best interests but demands their responsibility and flexibility as well. (Stina: Teacher)

Performativity is the second discourse and has been described by Jeffrey (2002) and Ball (2003) as both a culture and a technology of performance assessment that employs judgements, comparisons and displays of ability as a means of incentive, control and exchange based on material and symbolic rewards and sanctions that are often flagged for as elements of freedom of choice and as a means towards raising effectiveness. It is becoming the predominant and hegemonic discourse according to some sources, partly because of the traditional roles schools have played in the reproduction of a capitalist economy of signs, symbols and practices within the school infra-structure (Baudelot and Establet, 1974; Bourdieu and Passeron, 1977; Beach, 1999, 2003a, b; Dovemark, 2004, a, b) and partly as a response to tighten product control to compensate for looser (more flexible) procedural control through creativity (Seltzer and Bentley, 1999; Craft, 2002; Jeffrey and Craft, 2001; Paulsen, 1996; Lindström, 2002; Persson and Thavenius, 2003; Lindgren, 2001; Leach, 2001). Schools are 'traditionally' part of a superstructure of comparisons. Grading, differentiation and the ideological 'normalisation' of inequality are common. In them there is therefore always tension in practice in the crossfire of performativity and creativity that will go all the way throughout school history and all the way down to epistemology (Brosio, 1994; Beach, 2003c, 2006a; Korp, 2006; Båth, 2006). Our research aims to identify and empirically compare the tensions, constraints and compatibility between policies of creativity and performativity and their respective discourses in schools. One teacher informant expressed aspects of the tension to us as follows:

This job is about helping students recognise (and show) their abilities (by) making the best of what they have to get a good return ... from their education ... It's about giving them freedom to grow and guidance in helping them do well so they can show they are interested, motivated and able individuals ... I have to help students be inventive and produce new knowledge (and) they also have to show they can become ... effective learners ... They don't all have the ability or ... recognise the need to invest time and effort. But the ones who do have to be allowed to move on at a faster pace ... It's all about gearing the curriculum to their abilities to move and grow ... Their level is reflected in their performances and interests ...

(Sture)

As well as fairly clear articulations of a general conservative and traditionalist position in opposition to progessivism and creativity, there is at the same time here some evidence of weak classification and framing and in a sense therefore of hybridity (Barker and Galasinski, 2001). This is something that also previous research has identified (Beach, 2001; Gustafsson, 2003). Hybridity and hybrid texts and practices are important concepts to the research because of this, and can, by reference to Barker (2000) and Pieterse (1995), be described as social practices where text, talk and action evolve between alternative discourses in ways that help form and express new constellations of thought or new combinations of ideas (Jeffrey, 2003). In this chapter we aim to consider the principles of formation of hybridisations, in relation to the new school discourses of creativity and performativity with a focus on how teachers do and talk about their work.

Empirical focus

The broader framework of the project on which the present chapter is based empirically comprises four researched contexts. These are an adult education SFI class, one grade eight class in each of two comprehensive schools in a West Swedish town (pupils aged 13-14), and a pre-school-school integration classroom comprising pupils aged between 6 and 8 in another town in Western Sweden. From the project the two eighth grade classes are focussed on most. The classes are from schools that stand about a kilometre apart. Both have 1-9 intakes. They have been given the names Granskolan och Tallskolan. About 350 pupils attend each school.

Although they stand in fairly close proximity to eachother the catchments of the two schools differ in several ways. Granskolan's pupils come predominantly from a 'white', 'Nordic', middle-class area, composed predominantly of detached and semi-detached houses, whilst Tallskolan's pupils came from rented, high-rise accommodation in an area where the first language of many homes is not Swedish (50%). Moreover, Granskolan had twice as many pupils in year 8 as Tallskolan and income levels were higher in the vicinity of Granskolan. These are common patterns in the cultural geography of Sweden and other European countries at the present time that have been shown to, time and again, correlate with significant qualitative differences in the quality of the education available in the local school system (von Brömsen, 2003; Lynch, 2006; Lunneblad, 2006).

Main current outcomes of analysis

The stories developed from the data produced within 'ethnographically embedded participation' in the research sites we have visited have, after a provisional analysis, been grouped into three broad and overlapping constellations. One of these deals with the activities of schooling from a pupil perspective, one deals with things more from a teacher perspective and the third looks at relationships to the broader political economy of signs, symbols and economic exchange in Sweden as a restructuring welfare State society. All three constellations have been drawn on to inform the present chapter, which has however heavy emphasis on the second of them.

The chapter is organised conceptually around three main themes. These represent the present analytical outcomes of the investigation and refer firstly to issues of *reclaiming the teacher role* through practices and technologies of *re-traditionalisation*. This is linked to the second theme which is concerned with *the role of policy as text* in this practice. Here we consider how teachers make policy texts into resources for supporting, executing or providing motivations for; but rarely for critiquing, challenging and consciously changing; their practical ideas. In particular we consider how the new aims and grading criteria from the school curriculum are used as motivational devices for teachers towards students and in relation to their own work. Thirdly we consider *ambivalent social practices* in relation to the above two themes, where teachers have declared other points of departure, interests and professional values and commitments to the common ones. An emphasis on the secondary school level needs to be borne in mind. It is quite plausible, even according to the suggestions given in the chapter, that this sector of the school is more traditionalist and subject bound than the lower portions of the school system.

Reclaiming a teacher role

Dovemark (2004, a, b) and Österlind (1999) have both demonstrated how pupil activies in the formal school are often composed of what Carlgren (1997) terms 'individual work'. In this situation the pupils work alone and the teachers provide active support (Näslund, 2001) and take what they sometimes term as a supportive role (Beach, 2006a). However, in the present investigation many of the teachers have shown a different tendency in relation to their observed interaction with students and their descriptions of what they feel teaching should involve, and have expressed that they, in response to earlier developments, have 'begun to take back an initiative' (Signe) with respect to their work 'and have started to increasingly reclaim a more traditional teacher role' (Stina) with 'more subject knowledge emphasis' (Stina) and 'greater control and assessment of pupil learning' (Signe).

This idea can also be constructed through an analysis of field-notes and objective observations of classroom practices. Far greater numbers of lessons are predominantly teacher led today than was the case three to five years ago, not just according to teacher voices but also according to our collective observations over the past 8 years in school contexts. Teachers in the two schools control work 'far more now than they have done in the recent past' (Stina) and in Bernsteins (1990) terms there has definitely been a significant re-strengthening of standard classification and framing practices. One of the school management team expressed this when she said, 'we have got past the stage where there was a lot of individual work and a lot of free choice'. There has been a switch in emphasis 'from total freedom (to) performance control'. This is in accordance with an affirmation of the performativity culture as the new hegemonic culture of schooling. It matches Bernstein's notions of retraditionalisation (Bernstein; 2000; Beach, 2003c; Dovemark, 2004a; Beck and Young, 2005; Båth, 2006). Re-traditionalisation is in line with one of the current discourses (performativity) but not the other (creativity). Teachers have expressed things as follows:

> Stina has definitely taken charge during this lesson and has occupied the front spaces of the room where she has used the display facilities available to ... control and direct the pupils through whole class communication ... She has encouraged questioning about things and in this sense encourages active responsibility, but in the main we can talk in terms of formal direction giving and the provision of instructions as the dominant modality ... Stina has shown things to the class, she has talked to them and written on the board what they need to do and know ... This requires a lot of the students in terms of listening skills ... but very little inventiveness and creativity ...   (Fieldnotes 2005-10-10)

We don't have lengthy sessions ... We have shorter, more distinctly bounded lessons and more often provide common steering several times a lesson ... We rarely did this before, when we were taking the supportive, less leader-like role ... But when we had longer periods and a supportive role we found that we 'lost' many pupils ... We now feel that it is better to collect them together ... Some of them can only concentrate for short periods and they can get lost without help ...

We've gone back to how we used to work many years ago ... We have tightened up again ... We give a clear framework for the pupils. We use the formulation of clear aims as a way of doing this ...   (Svante)

There are however some significant differences between the ways in which teachers have reclaimed a traditional professional role.

Reclaiming professionalism in the assessment of pupil knowledge

Reclaiming something usually implies bringing it back from an undesirable state or restoring it to a previous more desirable condition. But it can also mean regaining possession of something or freeing it from some kind of danger through a particularly directed course of action. This is how we have interpreted talk about reclaiming the teacher role by many of our informants. That is, as implying a rescue or recovery of a former concept of the professional self, which aligns closely with a 'traditional' concept, from a condition of absence, ambiguity or threat (also Beach, 2003c). Several teachers talked about this when they emphasised the need to remain in focus and be clearer (than previously) about the formal demands that are placed on learners if they are to do well and 'to be on the mark subject wise' (Sture). The following comments by four teachers may help illustrate:

We have to set limits ... We can't only attend to the social side. The big problem is that we can trick both the parents and the pupils by lulling them into thinking mediocre performances will do and that it is simply a personal choice what you become in the future ...   (Sivert)

Being professional is about developing a focus and being selective ... You can't get involved in everything. I make it clear to the pupils ... And I don't try to take onboard issues that I know I can't resolve ... This wouldn't be right toward the pupils or myself ... I can tell pupils who they need to talk to about certain problems and I can help them book times with these people but I can't solve everything myself ... It isn't reasonable. We have to focus on the job of teaching and helping them learn and develop their knowledge ...   (Stina)

I don't want to know all there is to know about every pupil ... Sometimes I have to stop pupils telling me things if it can work against them ... I tell them, I have to grade you, are you sure you should really be telling me this. I try to keep their conflicts outside classrooms (and) concentrate on (developing and assessing) their knowledge ...   (Sture)

These pupils are sufficiently motivated for me to be able to help them ... Of course I try to ... show them all respect ... I do this better if I don't get involved in everything and try to deal with that others are there for ... It's about making our roles clear ... We should work mainly with the formal knowledge aims ...   (Sigrid)

The development and assessment of pupil knowledge is a central concept above. However, there is also an emphasis on the value and importance of the new grading criteria formulated in the most recent school curricula and making the demands these imply for pupils clear. Indeed just these items; i.e. clear demands and the conception of a more focussed teacher role dealing more with the development and assessment of pupil knowledge in relation to a new set of performance related aims; seem also to be mutually reinforcing.

This notion of resonance is something that has also been referred to in two recent theses by Helena Korp (Korp, 2006) and Jörgen Tholin (Tholin, 2006). As Korp and Tholin suggest, the formulation of education aims expressed in the new school curricula motivates and supports the grading and assessment of pupil knowledge as a key aspect of professional work. And as they point out, although this is clearly in a sense a reactionary backlash and a return to visible pedagogies of control based on individuated forms of organic solidarity, this aspect of a new performativity discourse also expresses core aspects of a new professional role for many teachers in a manner they conceive of as worthwhile (Beach, 2003c). This was also clear from field-notes:

The pupils are in the science lab and the teacher is at the front, by the board. She says ... 'We (the teachers) have a new task to develop you as young scientists' ... 'You are to learn to explain scientific phenomena in everyday language ... but to explain some things we have to go into a lot of detail ... right down to the level of particles. You have to explain the different particles in a natural way' ... Both of these points are concerned with the syllabus and the way it deals with knowledge about the atom. The teacher then goes through the syllabus with the pupils and is very careful to point out exactly what the pupils are expected to know for obtaining different marks ... Most of the pupils ... listen attentively and most of them make notes ...　　　　(Field-notes 05-10-04)

The teachers we have spoken with described activities like the ones they are involved in as intended 'to motivate the pupils to become engaged in the specific content areas included in the syllabus' (Stina). But in this sense, the activities are also a problem as they encourage closure, passification and the acceptance of the knowledge areas signified as important by the teacher, as essential and non-negotiable. So although they are expressed as motivational devices and technologies of communication 'that operate in the interests of all pupils' (Sivert), such activities are actually (also) technologies of power that enable teachers to act as a main intermediary in the control of what pupils are to do and learn in the formal school. Teachers have described why they do this. Mimetic isomorphism as opposed to creativity is clearly predominant:

These things are actually in the syllabus and the aims ... It is very important ... They should really work this way much earlier ... as well. But it's first when they start to be graded formally in grade 8 that we start to work through the syllabus in this way with them showing the demands as a form of motivation ...　　　　(Sigrid)

Sigrid went to great lengths to emphasise both to us as researchers and to the pupils that the presentation of the syllabus and its aims and contents was not simply a personal choice, but rather something that was part of the official framing of school work in new school policies. And as mentioned earlier, in this sense formal policy texts are being drawn into social and discursive practices as a means to help lend support to a chosen course of action that is felt by the agent in question to be in that agents (and her/his charges) best (professional) interests.

Written policy becomes in this way an artefact (and resource) in the enactment of power and control (Bernstein, 1990). It represents rules of practice.

Alternative positions and practices

Not all the teachers went to the same lengths of strengthened classification and framing in talk and action in the interests of heightened control over the student and the classroom, nor felt this was a good way of working. There were great differences in fact. These were expressed to a degree between younger and older teachers (Beach, 2003c), but more particularly between the teachers of younger and older children, the former of whom expressed opposition most clearly. They wanted 'more freedom of choice, more independent work for pupils ... and more creativity in the curriculum' (Rosaline), and they also expressed reluctance toward grading and assessment, which they said they did not feel should be the primary indicator of professionalism nor the main constituent of the activities of professional teachers. Their opposition showed itself in different ways. One way was in the choice of which school classes to teach. One teacher (Marie) said she had 'deliberately elected to work with younger classes' so she could 'avoid the control and emphasis on grading, instruction and assessment' (i.e. the imperatives of performativity culture). For her teacher professionalism 'should not be about the control of pupil knowledge (but about) supporting all round pupil development and each pupil's intellectual choices and preferences'. This suggests *flight* to the lower-elementary school as one way of coping with a strong imposition of performativity culture in the upper-school.[11]

The kind of 'attitude and reluctance to conform to performance assessment (shown) by teachers in early grades' (Sture) was seen as a problem by many of the teachers of the older children. Three spoke as follows:

> The problem is that the teachers of the younger kids ... don't see their task in the same way as we do ... There are criteria even for the younger classes but these teachers often just ignore them ... Grading and assessing pupils is something that all teachers should become engaged in as a professional

11 By this we mean fleeing employment in the upper-years of the secondary school for work in the middle school or even first school grades. This kind of flight compounds the problems of creativity in the upper-grades of the school rather than alleviating them, as it helps to 'drain' the upper reaches of the education system of qualified, motivated and committed progressive teachers in a manner that may bed for a reactionary traditionalist practice of as yet unforeseen proportions. This problem may become particularly acute in the future as the new government clearly articulates a very reactionary and retrograde education politics based on policy articulations that clearly expound the value of individuated organic solidarity and its control technologies.

duty ... regardless of which school class they work with' Not to realise, accept and respond to grading and assessment ... is to trick the pupils and do them a disfavour'.   (Sture)

This reluctance not to grade in the earlier classes is silly ... It is their job as well. I think that if we (teachers) are clearer in our messages earlier, right from the start ... there are a lot of parents who would want to help. The problem is we are not clear enough. Particularly with the younger ages ... Many skills are missing ... There are too many pupils as far up as eighth grade who have incomplete reading and writing skills, particularly writing ... Too much energy goes into just being able to get through the text ...   (Sigrid)

Several pupils on the recent Stenein test only got up to level 2. If these problems had been made clearer to the parents and pupils earlier ... they could perhaps have got some useful help ... Parents want to help ... but they can't unless they know that the child needs help (and) what kind of help they need and in relation to which skills and areas ...   (Stina)

There is an emphasis here on clarity of communication around performance issues. This was also visible in field-note extracts like the following:

To get the pupils to understand what the teachers place judgement on, Signe copied the grading criteria ... and gave them to the pupils for them to refer back to when they 'revise or assess their performances ... and grades'. But they are also used to assist teacher judgements regarding the work of the pupils 'who are also judged and marked in relation to them' (Stina). Signe, after having spoken for a while about the content of the thematic studies, pointed out for the pupils that 'this work goes on for several weeks ... so write things up in your work plans so you know what is expected ... You need to know what you want to aim at, G, VG, MVG ... and what is required of you at these levels' ... Signe described what had been on the 7th form syllabus. She emphasised the content in the 9th grade and the first year upper-secondary level. She pointed out particularly the common presentation of aims for the maths courses in year 9 and the year 1 upper secondary A course. She used these descriptions to motivate the content in year 8 and pointed out that the present course is often regarded as the

most difficult and that the level they are working at is above the work needed for a basic pass. As she put it, 'it's for those who try a little harder'.
(Field notes 05-10-12)

Although always present to some degree, the intense focus on communicating grading criteria and aims wasn't as apparent everywhere. At Granskolan for instance the pupils were split into two different groups according to judgements about the academic subject related and social skills of the pupils (Stina) and the group which the teachers had assessed as the weaker, did not obtain the same descriptions as did the other group, particularly with respect to the higher achievement levels of VG and MVG, nor were they presented with such descriptions as regularly. These types of differences in demands, presentations and expectations in communication have also been noticed elsewhere and written on previously as aspects of the links between school practices and both cultural and social reproduction (Dovemark, 2004a, b; Beach and Dovemark, 2005b). What is instigated is a form of pupil differentiation.

> The grouping is based on directly measured performances and on so called 'attitudes shown towards their work' (Stina) by the pupils ... Different aims were used ... The 'advanced group' worked with 'ambition aims' and from a more advanced book than the other group, who worked with 'attainment aims' (strävansmål resp. uppnåendemål) and a simpler text-book (Stina). The pupils in the advanced group were also constantly egged on and coaxed to intensify performances because of future educational requirements ...   (Field-notes 2005-10-20)

The observations in the lower group at Granskolan, about there being no references given to future studies and far less emphasis on grading requirements at the higher levels of distinction (VG) and above (MVG), also characterised conditions more generally at Tallskolan. At Tallskolan differences are also noted in terms of the concepts of difficulty and ability, where Tallskolan's pupils are often described by their teachers in relation to some kind of difficulty or other (language, concentration, both, other), as opposed to Granskolan's pupils, who are often described in relation to positive abilities (e.g. an ability to concentrate, focus, make the right choices and work hard), high levels of motivation and positive attitudes. Moreover, there was less obvious emphasis on performance criteria by the teachers generally at Tallskolan. This applies even amongst the pupils, who rarely referred to making the same rational choices of gearing effort to high level performances and a future career choice.

> *Jerker*: What do you have to do to pass maths?
> *Teacher*: 'Go to the notice board. I've posted everything there ... in the box'. (J goes and checks)
> *Jerker*: ' ... change units ... I can do that ... area and circumference ... I can do that ... (He continues through the list and says finally) 'That's alright. I can do this'. (Jerker leaves the room. The teacher comments after the lesson)
> *Teacher*: It's quite strange really ... Jerker could easily get VG or even MVG ... but he just isn't bothered'.   (Field notes 051108)

Differentiating practices in so-called mixed ability contexts have also been noticed previously. For instance Beach and Dovemark (2005b, c), Becker (1952), Keddie (1984), Sharpe and Green (1975), Tickle (1983), Korp (2006) and also Beach (1999a, b, 2001, 2003a, b), have found these treatment differences between groups that have been labelled by teachers as strong or weak respectively.

Performance criteria and a carrot and stick mentality

As stated above, particularly for the 'upper-group' at Granskolan, teachers emphasised the formal course aims from the school curriculum regularly, 'as a motivation device' (Sture), and continually stressed their relevance to and for pupils 'who wanted to get on and obtain good grades' (Stina). And this also seemed to work in the manner intended, particularly amongst the pupils labelled and treated as highly motivated. These pupils seemed able to internalise these values and re-express them in what were judged as 'appropriate ways'. For instance, they often stayed behind after school and lessons at break- and lunchtime, to take part in any extra curricula work presented as significant for higher level course content, even though much of the time many of them really 'didn't need to do this extra work in order to get the good marks they were looking for' (Stina). The following field-note extract (05-12-05) pertains to a full class presentation by a teacher during a lesson with the 'top maths group'.

> 'We have the green course for VG and MVG ... and this, multiplication with variables, which is really quite advanced, is part of it. You don't

actually need it for VG but I'll go through it ...' None of the pupils get up. The teacher starts by writing: $5(x+4)-2(7-2x)=3(2x+3)$. 'These kinds of questions are worth more points than the others on the test' (Sture). The pupils watch the teacher's demonstration intently, writing down what he writes down and listening to what he says. A pupil asks if the yellow course only gives a distinction (VG) ... The teacher answers, 'yes, if you want more then it's the green course you need.' Another asks if the green course will give MVG. The teacher answers, 'yes you can get MVG there (but not on the yellow). It's to do with your analytical capabilities'.

The performance aspects emphasised in Granskolan's 'upper-group' are actually very problematic as they can tend to encourage mimetic learning practices. This is contradictory towards creativity aims and practices according to our analysis, as by coupling content to the aims and grading criteria in this way the teachers not only make it difficult for the pupils who want to do well to question content selections (Beach and Dovemark, 2005b, c), they also significantly reduce spaces for creative agency and independence, both of which are key issues in the formulations of the creativity discourse in current policy texts (Craft, 2002; Jeffrey and Craft, 2001; Paulsen, 1996; Lindström, 2002; Persson and Thavenius, 2003; Lindgren, 2001; Leach, 2001; Beach, 2004a, 2006a, b; Jeffrey and Woods, 2003). Conformity and blind obedience becomes a requirement of formal success. Moreover, prior to major tests and examinations this mimetic tendency is intensified as 'entire lessons are commonly focussed on test content and questions, which are in their turn related, verbally by the teacher, to the course aims' (field-notes).

'This next test will be quite a big one' (Teacher). 'Remember the course aims ... We went through what was needed to get a distinction ... but I want to also go through what you need to do for MVG.' Stina goes through the requirements ... in order to 'serve the pupils ... with what they need to do well ...' (Stina). And most pupils note down what they are ... There are a few questions but none of them offer any significant challenge to the selection of content as such ... They are more to do with which content areas will be tested   (Field-notes 05-10-10)

The teacher gathers the pupils in front of the whiteboard. She draws two circles and writes the percentages for sea and land ... and for the Atlantic and Pacific oceans respectively. 'These are things that might come on the test'. The pupils seem very focussed. (Field-notes 05-11-29)

Several pupils have already asked about tomorrow's test. ... They seem a little uneasy and ask a lot of questions ... The teacher is a supply teacher and can't answer all of them and the pupils express frustration: 'Are we going to have the test tomorrow anyway?' one pupil asks. The supply teacher says: 'Yes, according to Stina you should already know what's going to be on the test'. There are loud protests: 'We haven't gone through all of it'. All the activities in the rest of the session and all of the talk is focussed on the test. Particularly in subjects like maths with the 'upper-group', but also quite often in mixed group (i.e. the normal class) contexts in other subject areas, most of the Granskolan teachers wrote regularly on the board what was likely to come up in future tests. They also emphasised to the pupils that 'if they wanted to do well' they should 'make sure (they) copied it down' (Siw). (Field-notes 05-10-11)

These are elements of a mimetic culture of performativity. This culture has been described by Jeffrey (2002) as originating in a principle of governance that enables strictly functional relationships to develop between the State and its outside environments over and against other control technologies (Ball, 2003). However, what we are suggesting mainly here is that performativity has begun to develop from a technology toward being a culture of regulation and incentive, as a means of control, as a means of attrition and as a means of change, based both on motivation, control and material and symbolic rewards and sanctions. In this culture of performativity a 'carrot and stick' mentality predominates in expressions about work and work relations and the performances of individual subjects or organisations serve as measures of productivity, as displays of 'quality' or as 'moments' of qualification, promotion or inspection that encapsulate the value of an individual or organisation within a particular field. We are also suggesting that a performativity culture seems to be an infertile place for anything but fetishised forms of creativity in learning and that it characterises work in school; particularly for successful students and very particularly for these groups close to larger tests and examinations.

Teacher ambivalence

The main dimension of ambivalence we noted in our investigation related to a conflict between creativity and freedom on the one hand and performance control and assessment on the other. This was expressed in fact by all teachers more or less, but particularly teachers of younger pupils and particularly regarding the descriptions of aims and grading criteria in the new curricula and how these were 'used ... to discipline and control (rather than support) learning practices' (Marie). However, even teachers of older pupils who otherwise re-traditionalised the teacher role occasionally spoke in this way. An experienced need to be fair as well as expressions about problems of contradictions in policy and the stress of personal relations and an affective dimension figured regularly here. A normative belief in real individual differences between pupils stabilised contradictory practices within the educational context:

> It's really odd. The general aims on creativity and responsibility are supposed to be superior to the specific course aims. But it doesn't work out right. The pupils know that grades are set on the basis of the specific course aims. We have tried to set grades based on group work. But like poor Ida ... She got in a group where she did all the work ... She did fantastically well. But the final result ... was very different than it would have been if she had chosen her partners herself.   (Stina)

> If you didn't have to all the time assess and grade their work maybe you could be more relaxed and sort of meet them more ... on a different plain ... There's a kind of conflict ... You want to be a pedagogue but you have to be a judge and jury ... You can disappoint a lot of the pupils (and) it can be difficult ... with pupils who you like and think a lot of ... You don't want to disappoint them ...   (Sigrid)

Some of the pupils are described by teachers as finding it easy to decode demands and to come with appropriate responses. These are often described as the 'strong (resursstarka) pupils' (Signe). However, several teachers also expressed pupil differences as on the one hand natural but at the same time as a problem. And they also expressed an experience of a kind of time pressure that was partially caused by these differences (Lindqvist, 2002; Nordanger, 2002;

Dovemark, 2004a). This time pressure 'stops everyone being as fully successful as they might otherwise have been' (Sture):

> Some find it easy to break the code and it doesn't really matter so much then, they'll do well anyway ... But for the others it's harder ... and can take a long time ... years even to grasp it all (and) that's where the problem lies ... Capturing (and helping) also this 50% who don't find things so easy is quite difficult ... (Sigrid)

> There is a bit of a dilemma for us teachers ... you want to achieve so much but there isn't time for all of them. There is a dilemma of trying to individualise all the time ... You have to make the demands clear. You mustn't trick them into thinking they are not there ... Some will naturally do better than others ... Grouping as we do allows everyone to work at their level and get further in less time ... (Signe)

The ambiguity toward the new aims formulations and the descriptions of grading criteria and the ways they are used never really seemed to deepen in any radical kind of sense, but usually seemed to just ebb out, given time. This point was also made by the teachers themselves in fact. However, by not engaging critically even the ambiguous teachers in the end contribute, materially and ideologically, to the formation of a new commodity culture of schooling in Sweden and its differentiation processes, even though they may do so more passively than their actively retraditionalising colleagues.

Discussion

We have taken the secondary school teachers' actions and comments in the present investigation to have generally tended to express desires toward reclaiming a more traditional teacher role, by which we mean to some degree rescuing of a former concept of a professional identity as a *subject teaching, learning and assessment expert*, from what was described as 'a quagmire of multiple ... overlapping (and) ambiguous practices (of) recent years ...' (Signe). This new traditionalism is talked of by them as specifically suitable for the present educational moment, particularly in respect of the new curriculum (see also Beach, 2003c and Båth, 2006). However, as well as having restorational qualities toward one set of previous aims the process almost totally ransacks the immediate past of teacher professionalism, by 'clarifying the disparate contents of the previous teacher role with its emphasis on social aspects as unnecessary and unsuitable' (Sture). The new struggle is 'to form a clearer focus on the role of the teacher in terms of the individual knowledge development and assessment of pupils' (Signe). The teacher as mediator and assessor of knowledge performances becomes central. Strong classification and framing supersedes weak as a current general tendency (Båth, 2006).

The descriptions of course aims and grading criteria became a key intellectual resource in relation to the *re-traditionalisation* practices noted (also Korp, 2006) according to our observations and interviews and their analyses. This also represents a swing back from the more recent personalised forms of organic solidarity in curriculum activities to individuated forms with characteristics of professional identity asserted not unlike those described for the teacher group known as the 'new-realists' in Mac An Ghails (1988) earlier ethnography, 'Young Gifted and Black'. However, in addition, older teachers also seemed to describe a new return to old-disciplinarian principles.

Old disciplinarian and new-realist perspectives share several points of resonance in relation to concrete activities and practices according to Mac An Ghail (op cit.). For example, in both situations there is an emphasis on the exchange rate value of education (product value) as opposed to educational processes (Beach, 2003c; Båth, 2006). Examination based performances and grading related attainments are primary (Beach and Dovemark, 2005b, c), particularly in schools where the dominant pedagogy is favourably rationalised and operationalised in concrete terms even by the pupils. This is the case at Granskolan amongst those individuals who have become part of the 'fast-stream' in the upper-group in subjects like maths.

A performativity culture is emphasised in the spaces of interaction in the curriculum in the circumstances of new realism and old-disciplinarianism. 'Measured Performances' are what count in everyone's minds eye, and these things are also what are made to count in the material practices of the school. Moreover, even the concept of creativity can become absorbed into the predominant culture of performativity in these conditions, as grade pressure and other performance demands begin to compromise the social identities, social relationships and learning practices of learners (also Vygotsky, 1926; Dovemark, 2004b; Beach and Dovemark, 2005b). There is an element of potlatch about this. The use value of education is expressed by students here almost exclusively in terms of an exchange value. The 'gift' of education is fetishised and the aim becomes to consume education simply in order to get good grades (Beach and Dovemark, 2005b, c).[12] School becomes a place that exists primarily for getting a qualification.

As we have also written in Beach and Dovemark (op cit), Vygotsky quoted William James' work in relation to such points as these and suggested that grading students is probably the most salient micro-contradiction of a free educational context and the valorisation of creativity. This is a point that has also been made by Pablo Freire (1971), when he suggested how grading significantly objectifies free performances in a way that combines all the negative aspects of praise and censure, until students begin to learn solely for the sake of either obtaining good grades or avoiding bad ones. This brings us to the condition of alienation and the question of why 'good' school students learn posed by Beach (2001, 2003a, b, 2006a) and Beach and Dovemark (2005b). Do they learn out of a love of learning, out of a natural impulse to learn something with a real use-value or because of an internalisation of externally motivated hegemonic values? That is, do they learn for external rewards under conditions where there is no real joy or value in learning for its own sake.

Conclusions

We want to make just a couple of brief observations at this point. The first is about the new ideas about creative learning in the Swedish school (Kommunförbundet, 1996; Skolverket, 1992:2; SOU 2000: 39; Lindensjö and Lundgren, 2000; SOU 1990:20; Dovemark, 2004, a, b; Beach and Dovemark, 2005c; Beach, 2006a). These aims are related to phenomena such as pupils taking responsibility for there own learning and making schools into places in which they can display new skills (Lundahl, 2001; Dovemark, 2004, a, b). However, we feel that the re-traditionalisation we have noted countermands these aims at the same time as a predominant performativity culture even transforms creativity and twists its skill development into particularly objectified connotations and forms. Creativity is transformed to fit the dominant hegemonic discourse of performativity, which has become once again (or has perhaps simply remained) the predominant cultural marker of the school reflected in the voices of its teachers (Dovemark, 2004a, b; Beach, 2003c, 2006a).

12 These are of course points that have been made before in education; not the least by Vygotsky (1926/1992) who recognised that questions of free (liberating and empowering) education will only be fully resolvable first after the problems of the social order have been resolved. In Vygotsky's words, until this point every attempt at constructing emancipatory ideals for education will be a utopian dream; a point commonly forgotten in the context of education today (also Brosio, 1994).

The second of our points, which was made in a similar fashion by Sharpe and Green in relation to progressive education as far back as 1975, concerns the 'new' ideas for creativity in learning that are reflected in National Curricula. These policy statements relate to such things as students developing capacities to take personal responsibility for learning, by taking part in education planning and assessment by choosing and evaluating courses, subjects, themes and activities for themselves to their own satisfaction. They describe schools as needing to create conditions for the development of new capacities amongst students (Lundahl, 2001; Dovemark, 2004, a, b). However, whilst this 'new school idealism' describes an increase in delegated responsibilities to the learner (and the local arena more generally), and symbolically ascribes value to self-determination, the bulk of the empirical evidence suggests to us that there is a tension between this *idealism* and a discourse and practice of performativity, which is historically deeply engrained in individuated forms of organic solidarity in the formal culture of the official school, toward which many teachers appear to be retraditionalising at the present time (Bernstein, 1990, 2000). The performativity discourse helps transform creativity at the level of social practice. Hybrid forms of discourse and hybrid practices develop between the discourses of the personalised forms of organic solidarity of creativity discourse(s) and the discourses of individuated forms of organic solidarity of the performativity discourse(s).

These conclusions make the creativity aims of education reform problematic concerning how to enable students to establish a positive social identity through being able to take charge of their own learning so they may valorise their own class-cultural capital and values as valuable education content (or educational capital). Rather than this, particularly the most successful students seem to be *encouraged* to some degree *to become* rote-learners, objects for instruction and targets of evaluations that grade and separate them for specialised treatment through performances related to the reproduction of (external) authority knowledge. Both they, and creativity policies, become in other words assimilated in a new performativity culture of schooling.

Finally, particularly at Tallskolan but also to a degree at Gran-, there were pupils who in a sense 'lived outside of' the predominant cultural understanding of school as a place that functioned primarily in terms of a fetishised exchange value system, as an element of a performativity culture. Jerker was one such pupil. All the teachers pointed out that he had great ability but little interest in applying this ability to his school work and above all his performances. He was satisfied with a pass, but by being so he also points out how it is not the intellectual abilities of agents that at first hand determine their performances, as in more liberalist understandings of school. There is more to performance based standards and selections than the establishment of a meritocratic hierarchy of ability.

Chapter 9

Teachers and new education aims

The school reforms and reform proposals of the recent period, such as Lpo 94/98; Lpf 94; Lpfö, 98; Government Proposition, 1990/91: 18, 1999/2000: 135, 200%1: 72, 2004/05: 162 and SOU 1999: 63, have implied significant changes to official teacher roles and responsibilities in school that have required modifications in respect of ideologies of practice and concepts of good learners and good learning (Beach, 2003c; Dovemark, 2004a). Although there is also a reactionary backlash, as described in the previous chapter, teaching and learning are now never the less officially discoursed very differently than they were fifteen or twenty years ago (Lindblad et al., 2005). Good learners are now described in formal policy, as creative, self-reliant and discerning consumers and producers of knowledge rather than pliant good listeners and avid reproducers of official curriculum content and teachers' ideas (see also Bernstein, 2000 in respect of generic skills in the curriculum; Båth, 2006), and good teachers are described as mentors, who facilitate students in their education in relation to the students' goals, values, interests and commitments (Skolverket, 1992, 1995, 2000; Lindqvist, 2002; Lundahl, 2001, 2002a, b; Lindensjö and Lundgren, 2000; Lindblad et al., 2002, 2005; Sundberg, 2003; Beach, 2001, 2003a, b). Learning has formally become a negotiated, constructive and interactive element of a new culture of schooling (Nordanger, 2002; Gustafsson, 2003; Dovemark, 2004a).

The present chapter uses interview and conversation materials produced during ethnographic engagements in three schools to provide a more bottom-up account of what the new ways of discoursing learning mean for teacher identities and teacher work. These extracts, supplemented by conversation materials and contextualising participant observations, have helped us identify a number of different ways in which teachers express their subjective understanding with regard to things like the role of the teacher and new teacher and student identities. A summary of a common kind of expression is provided by the following comment by a teacher informant:

Decentralisation and the new curriculum is supposed to mean more individual responsibility and freedom of choice (to) students and teachers ... But it also means more work and being constantly available ... The pupils are supposed to become more inquiring and self-governing ... However, putting aims into practice is complex ... Not all students are able to respond to the new situation and we also have other demands that require us to be more than just mentors to them. We still judge and grade them and this is more complex than before ... The different ideas don't gel easily in practice ... On the one hand we are facilitators supporting them in creating knowledge on the other mentors who lead projects and monitor development ...   (John)

This comment begins to introduce what, in our investigations, has become a central element of analytic interest, the relationship between two potentially competing policy discourses in which the new global creativity and flexibility discourse is being challenged and perhaps, as described in the previous chapter, practically compromised by a discourse of performativity and its related social practices. This kind of policy interference is not uncommon. As also Loxley and Thomas (2001) have suggested, layers of policy often conflict with one another in these kinds of ways. However, these authors also add that behind the seeming conflict of policies and ideas is a common new right interest in education and its relationship to the national economy. Education is becoming a global economic issue of outstanding proportions and, partly in order to fulfil a new discourse of stakeholder welfare in times of public service crisis and partly in order to fulfil an emphasis on individualism and the free market (Loxley and Thomas, 2001; Beach, 2005b), is being increasingly opened up by national and international policies and policy discourses to private interests and enterprises (Beach, 2004b). Life-long education consumption has become a significant source for the furtherance of economic accumulation for private organisations.[13]

The rise and rising tensions of neo-liberalism in education

Despite the side heading above, it is our conviction that although the currently bouyant education discourse places education as a 'fresh produce' and situates practices of choice, creativity, self-determination and individual responsibility in education at the centre of curriculum development as an effect related to the

---

13 This is not a new idea. As also Angus (2005) points out, sites like schools both reflect structural features of society and contribute to their formation (Beach, 2005b). Angus quotes Bowles (1991) in this respect with regard to how, in the insidiousness of the market context, people learn to function in particular (market oriented) ways (Beach, 2004b). We become what we might otherwise not have and build social arrangements which we might otherwise have opposed (Angus, 2005, p. 199).

economisation of society as a whole, the new policy context of education should not simply be seen as a smooth and easy transition to neo-liberalism. There is too much confusion for this to be the case and there are certainly too many centrally placed education bureaucrats, researchers, tacticians and politicians who are genuinely committed to further both the development, application and effects of direct democracy in education as well as through it (Brosio, 1994; Dovemark, 2004a). Furthermore, schools have previously been socially rationalised and even physically regioned as differentiating agencies within the fields of tension between different (most usually neo-conservative, but also sometimes even progressive) premises to those currently advanced.

The presence of competing discourses and contradictory policies, traditions and material structures and practices provide a somewhat uneasy structure for neo-liberal ideas and Sweden's comprehensive, upper-secondary and infant/ nursery school teachers also most often hold competing views of pedagogy (both with each-other and with respect to the new neo-liberal concept of public choice theory: also Beach, 2003c; Korp, 2006) that resonate as well, or even better, with other educational discourses and practices than those of neo-liberalism (Dahlberg and Lenz-Taguchi, 1994; Calander, 1999; Hansen, 1999; Davidsson, 2002; Dovemark, 2004b, Beach, 2000, 2003a, b; Gustafsson, 2003). The rise of neo-liberalism inside education is in this sense a sign of a struggle of the times whose discourses are political and ideological expressions of a dominant economic power's self-understanding of current needs and interests. But the rise of neo-liberalism is also only one sign. It is not the only possible sign or necessarily most desirable sign for all. And even if it is a very logically reasonable outcome of education in late capitalism it is not necessarily the most logically reasonable outcome and it can be opposed. Thus, although new school policies stress individual freedom of choice and responsibility (which can also be expressed as the non-liability of a third party; Beach and Dovemark, 2005b), private enterprise and other neo-liberalist ideas, there also seems to be tension, contradiction, ambivalence and hybridity as well (Gustafsson, 2003; Beach, 2003c; Beach and Dovemark, 2005b, c). This was also suggested in teachers' and head-teachers' voices in our research:

> Although I now feel heavily committed to the (new) package ... I remember that I also used to feel almost equally committed to the ... older upper-secondary school as well ... I used to ... teach in a ... traditional manner (and) responded very well to the students who buckled down to

... demands ... The new context doesn't suit everyone ... It's not working for everyone ... There are some problems ...   (Kim)

I have always approached the students' knowledge and performances from a position of authority ... There are ... limits that must be set on their freedom to choose ... There are fundamentals in subject areas that have to be covered and there is also the issue of individual differences that lead some to work hard and others to always choose an easy route ... It is important (they) develop positive relationships to learning, because learning is a life-long project nowadays. But I still think about teaching strategies and students acquiring the right skills ... These are though of a different kind and are developed from a different perspective and to different ends than before ...   (Carole)

What we think we can identify in statements like these is not pure reproductions of either a discourse of creativity or one of performativity, but rather more subtle hybrid comments and ideas. This occurrence is in line with Chouliarki and Fairclough (1999), who have suggested how text, talk and action are always articulated inside a mix of meaning constructions that reflect ambivalence or uncertainty regarding legitimate practices in a given practical arena (Bernstein, 1990, 2000; Gustafsson, 2003; Båth, 2006). In these conditions there is usually a great deal of uncertainty and contradiction and suggestions about freedoms to create new pedagogical practices that valorise self-reliance, personal values and creative education projects, will always coexist with discourses and practices that are imbued with very different values and ideologies (Jeffrey, 2003; Brosio, 1994; Beach, 2000, 2003a, b; Gustafsson, 2003; Beach and Dovemark, 2005b). Or as one teacher put it:

We are caught between things in the passage of time and are unsure ... It is difficult and complex ... On the one hand it's all about the learners and we are in the background ... The learners interests are in focus. On the other hand we have to assess their performances according to clearly defined knowledge criteria ... We have to assess and grade them and also account for the grades we set ... We can be challenged ... This is uncertainty not flexibility ...   (Ben)

The concept of over-determination derived by Althusser (1969) from the work of Freud comes to our minds when we consider the situation suggested here. Over-determination refers to a complex 'multiple causation of events' from different levels of practice, where every aspect or part contributes in its own right to determining the character of the whole (Beach, 2000). However, what over-determination in effect means is that the outcomes of social processes in culture cannot be predicted easily and fully known in advance. All available cultural positions and resources and the use of symbolic force are important (Bernstein, 1990, 2000; Bourdieu, 1996; Willis, 2000; Dovemark, 2004a, b; Gustafsson, 2003) and education agents are restrained not only by their assigned or experienced economic position and 'individual', intellectual possibilities and skills, but also by contingent forces (including discursive ones) and the material and political possibilities these support or oppose. Contradictions occur within contexts of over-determination, as well as between its different levels (Gustafsson, 2003). Issues of survival and economic production are primary, but the superstructure also exercises an important partially autonomic influence.

Reactions to neoliberalism on the ground

The teachers in our investigation have reacted differently to the challenge of the new school context and its requirements on them as professionals (also Nordanger, 2002; Linqvist, 2002). In Beck and Young's (2005, p. 189) terms, some of them have sensed *a loss of academic authority* as disciplines begin to be officially expressed as less important and increasingly fragmented, temporary and weakly insulated (also Beach, 2003c). Whilst others have celebrated the anticipated and experienced changes by openly declaring the obsolescence of accumulated knowledge. However, despite the obvious differences, there is a common logic to all of this. Although never fully stable, subject and academic departments never the less helped some relatively stable professional identities for teachers to develop as local subject experts and this encouraged a subject loyalty that the new discourses seriously destabilise by questioning the accepted value of subject/disciplinary knowledge (Bernstein, 2000, p. 59) in a way that leads not only (or perhaps even first and foremost) to an abandonment of these former identities and the values they stood for, but also, as suggested in the previous chapter as well, even to a possible reactionary backlash and re-traditionalisation of professional identity in line with subject teacher ideals.

The following table suggests something of how the hybrid conditions were represented by teachers in the present investigations in terms of their expressed ambivalence to, support of or criticism toward the new policy accounts of the importance of increased student responsibility and self-determination in the curriculum. Although some ambivalence is unavoidable, the table suggests two things in particular. Firstly that although teachers are not simple re-producers of pre-existing value discourses, they do express views formed at points between the two competing discourses of re-traditionalisation (including aspects of performativity) and neo-progressive renewal (Båth, 2006) or creativity. Secondly that although there are mainly differences between the sets of comments presented, there are also points of agreement.

Table 9.1: Retraditionalisation and renewal

Field	Re-traditionalisation	Renewal
Classification and Framing of Knowledge	(T)eaching involves helping them grasp what (we) already know ... Students need ... to listen to what is right from the field of knowledge and do the correct things in the right way to learn ... Subjects and disciplines are still what are most important to learn ...	We have to include students more actively and recognise (their) knowledge, skills and interests ... They need to be active producers and consumers of knowledge ... not empty recipients ... New content areas are more important than old subjects ...
Rules of procedure, institution, practices, governance and regulation	We have to base our work on the disciplines because (otherwise) other interests will become more ... compelling and this can be a problem ... I know from experience it happens ...	We need to identify and overcome obstacles (to) creativity and self-discipline and recognise ... that successful learning is accomplished actively, creatively ... and by exploration ...
Social relations of learning	Students get frustrated with-out ... firm guidance. (We) can empower (them) but this is a question of having discipline, knowledge and a realism of judgement ... We are experts ... They learn better from us than from each-other ...	We have to change our relationship to learning ... We must set them free (and) focus on ... engaging, coaching ... and counselling ... We must become ... facilitators (and) help them to choose what is right *for them* ...

One issue around which there is convergence between the two columns above is on the issue of individualisation in the curriculum. This issue is also mentioned as a normalising element in the previous chapter and in principle all teachers seem to support it as an ideal. We described this in field-notes as follows:

> Pitching things at student levels is present everywhere (and) is taken (by teachers) to imply independent work from the pupils and that they, with age, will learn how to take individual responsibility for an expanded freedom of choice. Themes like 'meeting students at their level' and creating conditions for individual choices and responsibility are things that have been emphasised ... for 'providing learners (with) the chance to work in line with ... self-understood, notions about their individual needs' (Annette) so that they 'can ... work with what they are best at and in ways they feel is best themselves ...' (Julie) ... These 'messages' are in line with concrete statements in policy texts ... But they are also often in distinctly individuated rather than personalised forms ... They are about individuation in the curriculum in the sense that students should be allowed to work 'at their own pace with things they think they can be successful with ...' (Agneta). They are also 'personalised' though, in the sense that there is an intention (and anticipation) that 'they will experience that they own their education' (Agneta) ... The 'personal' and the individualisation issues become aims and consequences (that) take (specific) forms when ... some children (in teachers' terms) learn well and ... quickly and others learn less well, less often and more slowly. Here it is expressed that 'some children are just stronger learners than others and some need more time than others' (Agneta) ... Culturally produced differences (in performance) in school are interpreted and inscribed in practice as natural differences between children ...   (Field-notes)

Two distinct moments of individualisation are included in comments from teachers according to the above. On the one hand is an element of individualisation in relation to student interests in the selection of content. On the other individual differences are allowed to determine the pace at which and the depth to which students work in both common and separate content areas (Beach, 1999a, b, 2001; Korp, 2006). And it is here the hybrid form becomes interesting. Because brought together, the two elements become a third, new, contingently operating educational force (Bernstein, 1996) in which individual skills and competences are understood to enable some selections for some students but not for others. In this sense individualisation becomes an aspect of differentiation, to paraphrase Lundahl (2001), which in its turn becomes accepted as an obvious and natural outcome of schooling. It is an aspect of a pedagogical arbitrary (Bourdieu and Passeron, 1977) around individuation and personalisation in the curriculum.[14]

New modalities of differentiation and social reproduction

Differentiation is suggested above as a logical outcome of education according to teacher expressions with an obvious material base in schools (Beach, 1999a, b, 2001, 2003a, b, c; dovemark, 2004a, b; Beach and Dovemark, 2005b, c). Moreover we are not the only researchers who assert this. Although we may put things slightly differently to others, differentiation in Sweden's schools has also been described in research by Lundahl (2001), Bliding (2004), Staberg and Assarsson (1997), Svensson (2001, 2006) Svensson and Reuterberg (1998), Tholin (2006) and Korp (2006), who all give examples of how teachers describe differences between students in terms of concepts of 'strong' and 'weak' student categories, which are thus basically both *emic* (belonging to a community's own expressive forms) and ubiquitous 'member categories' that denote key characteristics of a 'standardised relational pair' that provides insight into a grounded or *anchored relationship* and the type and the depth of particular qualities that are linguistically central to a social practice or field (Mäkitalo, 2002; Bliding, 2004). A fieldwork diary extract on this read:

> Performances are expressed as 'natural indications ... both of the abilities and of the motivation pupils have for their work' (Laurie). 'We grade (kids) on their work ... It's our job ... But it is also for their benefit as well, and for the good of (society) too ...' (Beth) ... So behind the social and symbolic (class) violence that is done to children in school, and despite teachers recognising that violence is being done ... lies a kind of self-

14 Because of this schools will still continue to grade and separate children within new creativity practices and differentiation is thus not a linear characteristic only of the re-traditionalisation and performativity discourses alone, but exists rather across and between both it and the creativity discourse. As one teacher put it in a staffroom conversation at Sci High, 'kids are different (and have) different abilities and interests.... It is perfectly natural that they perform differently in different subjects' (Liz, Sci High). A colleague added, 'they show their abilities in school performances and we help them identify their capabilities and channel their commitment to do well... Differences are natural and a sign of effort, ability (and) good teaching...' (Brian). Individualisation is 'about teaching to individual interests, skills and capabilities... so students can identify their potential to work and can work to fulfil their potential' (Liz).

expressed notion of an altruistic identity ... Teachers say they do the things they do ... for the good of the children and the benefit of society ...

We were surprised by the conviction teachers expressed with respect to the differentiation process as something that only had positive value so we asked some of the teachers about it. One teacher, Annika, gave a response that summarises the main points from all the teachers we spoke with:

> Strong pupils ... grasp how things work and how to do tasks ... They take responsibility and hand in work on time ... others take longer ... Because you have to give so much time to the weaker pupils (the good ones) get less attention ... I would like more time so we can work with the weaker pupils ... without the good ones having to suffer ... In that way (we) can do a good job (and) they (can) fulfil their potential ... Everyone benefits! The pupil, the school, society ... Standards will improve over time ...
> (Annika)

When comparing Annika's response with those from other teachers, there was no utterance by anyone that would question the basic commitments expressed of 'meeting pupils at their level (and) catering for their interests, desires and commitments' (Carl) to help them 'find a right level for their future ambitions and potential' (Betty) and the improvement of standards. However, whilst this kind of position can be seen to be in line with organising work 'to enable all pupils to be creative (and) have the best possible individual conditions for *their own* learning ... in their own way' (Jean) and can be interpreted as claiming individual differences as 'having naturally valid ... foundations' (Carl), it can also be seen in another way, *as perpetuating and reinforcing social selection* based on principles that, although they are cultural in origin, are also ideological, hegemonic and reified (i.e. given a natural, objective status).

What teachers actually describe when they talk about how they 'try to organise a milieu in which each student can find a space to study in a way that is compliant with their needs and interests' (Carole) so personal forms of class cultural capital can be positively valorised is related to two issues. Firstly that 'society needs the right person in the right positions and educations' (Brian) and secondly that 'it is only in this way that the students can be made familiar with what their real level is' (Brian). This is very important to teachers (Dovemark, 2004a). For they also express that it is only when the students 'know where their real level is ...

that they are able to accept a faster or slower pace (and) learn optimally' (Brian). In this way individuation as differentiation is a highly ideological, hegemonic and confused practice that appeals to dominant class interests. For instance in the following way:

> We help them find their right level and work with their interests ... Strong pupils ... take responsibility and produce (good) work ... others don't ... There'll always be weak and strong students (and) we have to help them find their right level and interests and fulfil their potential as far as is possible ...
> (Lena).

Given the social order of capitalist societies this can be understood as a very reactionary statement. But what is perhaps more important than making such a recognition, is to point out that pupil differentiation exists not just because our society demands it, supports it and defines it as inevitable (Poulantzas, 1974), but also primarily because teachers play an active and conscious role in it, which they can therefore also resist if they are given good reasons for doing so.

What we mean by the above statement is that the ethnography suggests that teachers are active agents in school based differentiation practices, but that they engage in these practices for the wrong *objective* reasons *as* living *subjects*, in that they engage in them because of an expressed need to feel they are doing what can be termed as 'altruistic work' in the interests of pupils 'by grading intelligent performances well ... and others less so' (Jean). In this sense, by feeling that they 'highlight (and) help pupils expand their natural abilities' (Carl) the teachers are able to believe that 'grading and differentiation ... is done for the good of the student and of society' (Brian), when of course *objectively* it is not. It is done in the ideological interests of the dominant class (and cultural) fractions. Some teachers seem to be able to recognise this whilst others don't.

> There is a value collision ... We say we are giving them space to do their own thing but we aren't ... We are still grading them through their abilities (and) performances ... This time though not just on the basis of them being able to answer our questions ... There is still this (but) there is also our judging their abilities to show us how they have become committed as self-learning individuals and can be graded as such ...   (Gunnar)

Work is always graded individually ... The students undertake individual learning projects and are then assessed on the basis of their performances. First (on) the degree to which they commit to ... school (i.e. attitudes) and secondly in terms of a formal product ... There are obvious contradictions between these practices ...   (Laura)

We have tried to give students responsibility ... They control very much the time (but) even to a degree content as well ... It is uncertain (though) and with some classes ... it doesn't work because (we) haven't trained them well enough ... There should be degrees of freedom that allow more work with one subject than another at times and they should be able to make these decisions themselves ... We should serve them with less ready mades ... But we have to teach them how to learn ... and how to choose (and) we also grade them on how and what they choose as part of this ...   (Harald)

Representations such as those provided above, as also suggested by Lindblad et al. (2005), need to always be understood according to a dual constructive axis. On the one hand is the narrative or discursive territory that gives addressed items their specific significances (also Willis, 2000). On the other hand is the 'medium' in which the specific accounts are 'realised' and 'come to life'. This means of course that the power of knowledge to shape, reshape, preserve and control 'what is there' and what might come into existence is heavily contingent (Baker and Gosinski, 2001) and changes in the knowledge base (in terms of competence, capacities and epistemological orientations) must always be viewed as a complex phenomenon, dynamically interrelated to structural as well as operational changes within the environment, as well as broader changes within the system of knowledge production itself (Gibbons et al., 1994; Nowotny et al., 2001; Lindblad et al., 2005). We have a responsibility to help change understandings of individu(alis)ation and the interests in which it operates under different contingent circumstances and conditions.

'Changing contexts' 'changing discourses' changing roles

One very significant change in the teacher role that has been consistently pointed to by the teachers in our investigations, is that 'teachers are now expected to be ... guides and mentors who help children choose what and how to learn in their education ...' (Marge). However, at the same time they also show how teachers, at least in their own view, 'must also teach pupils ... how to make right decisions ... so they can be assessed and graded on a fair basis' (Marge) and 'can develop a life-long lust for learning' (Agneta).

> We have responsibility that the pupils make progress and have the right attitude ... The work involves having discussions so they understand how to make the right choices, what these choices are and what the consequences are ... We need to say when their choices might not be suitable ... We are still involved ... We give feedback and signal ... what they need to do (and) how good they are ...   (Agneta)

> We provide access to frameworks of values and practices within which they make their choices ... We can be clear about where we want them to go and why this is important ... This is why we need clear guidelines ... Not to rob them of the right to take charge of their education but to help them to do this and to help us be fair to them when we assess what they have done, how they have gone about this and what they have arrived at ...   (Gunnar)

In some ways this all rings true with formal creativity policy as expressed in for instance Skolverket (1992, 1996, 2000). Both students and teachers have been delegated more responsibility for determining the content and form of an education than before, and there has been a shift in emphasis from the reproduction of specific skills and knowledge to the production of generic skills and competences. However, how much of this is 'genuine' ownership and control in a context of schooling in capitalist society is questionable. In this kind of context creativity aims, practices and outcomes can always become re-inscribed in ways that on the one hand help to (re)affirm a basic hierarchy of difference and on the other contribute to the further escalation of already existing and recognised differences in the body of the society as a whole. And in this scenario the middle and upper-middle classes may tend to always be discoursed as creative whilst the lower become discoursed as reproductive.

Thinking in the long-term (and) global context of the neo-liberal (economic) restructuring of education and the capitalisation of learning may make the consequences of this recognition clearer. In these circumstances, although taking charge of ones learning is formally expressed as a motor for learning and a motivational device, when we all become motivated and lustful consumers of education both the content and form of what is consumed as well as both attitudes to and pace of consumption become foundations for differentiation (Sharpe and Green, 1975; Lundahl, 2001; Dovemark, 2004a, b).

Several contradictions in expressions of lived learning found in the data support our suggestions regarding the above point. Examples include the fact that the labels of self-determination and self-realisation are rhetorically used at the same time as the learning situation is *materially* alienated (Beach, 1999a, 2003a) and that students are described as taking charge of their learning, but often do so mainly for the sake of obtaining good grades or avoiding bad ones (Beach and Dovemark, 2004a, b, 2005b). That is, they do not learn for the joy of learning for learning's sake or for valorising a personal class-cultural identity. Education takes on an economic (market) form (if only symbolically at times) in relation to actual school practices (Beach, 2003a).

One teacher (Brian) and one student (Klara) gave similar expressions in separate interviews along these lines (see also ch 4). Klara described how 'freedom in learning presents a great opportunity to show what you can do ... and if you don't take this chance it is either because you can't ... or aren't interested in doing well'. She added that if you don't make the most of your opportunities ... you only have yourself to blame'. Brian's comments fit well with this. As he put it, 'schooling and society are complex and competitive (and) it is ... in everyone's interests to compete (and) do as well as they can ... based on (their) best interests, abilities and motivation' (Brian). He added that 'taking an active responsibility is a new feature of performance ... and a factor in student differentiation'.

Deviant cases

Voices like Brian's (above) are not the only voices present. As in the previous chapter there are others that account for things in other ways. For instance, as one teacher said; 'setting standards is unavoidable in performance cultures such as the ones that have developed in education recently ... not just here but also across Europe' (Patrick); and his words shadow comments by several researchers recently. There seems in education to currently be a technology, a culture and mode of regulation that is pervasive across nations and that reaches into the hearts, minds and planning of working professionals, parents and students (Gordon et al., 2003; Jeffrey, 2002, 2003) based on new principles of governance for the ordering of (school) knowledge, practices and also pupils in school (Lundahl, 2001). To use Patrick's words:

We have to set standards ... because our bosses (and parents) have standards that they apply and that we are judged by and although we have our own professional values and beliefs ... we don't always have the strength of conviction or the consistent practices and support to back these up ... Although I don't see any problems in letting the children talk about pop-music ... while others might be studying the structure of middle-age settlements, and having them then share the ideas they have developed with each other, the rhetoric is one thing and the support systems ... are separate issues ...   (Patrick)

Patrick says something important we feel about the problem of policy *formation* at what is sometimes termed the *phenomenological* level, where intentions to change education are influenced through the co-presence of competing ideas and practices as aspects of a repertoire of actual and virtual possibilities that are recognised and culturally supported at a given moment. As he points out, prevailing conditions, traditions and beliefs help to normalise some kinds of thinking and some forms of behaviour and weaken others (Beach, 1995). And he suggests that teachers are not not in full control of the situation they are acting in and are often restricted through a legacy of their own concepts, beliefs and traditions (myths, ritual and witchcraft; i.e. hegemony) as well as those of others.[15] Teachers are thus not bound to merely respond to policy prescriptions. They could also resist them.

Woods and Jeffrey (2002) make statements with bearing on the above when they describe how teachers have had to reconstruct their identities in response to the reconstruction of an education system where holism, humanism and vocationalism have been challenged by a new social identity. They add that in trying to resolve the dilemmas this brings about, teachers have engaged in identity work characterised mainly by partitioning off self-identity with a risk of an inauthentic subject position to follow. The 'real self' is, as they put it, withheld and set to one side (Beach, 2003c). Practices become both impersonal and inauthentic in these circumstances.

15 Our research suggests that through restructuring the value practices and beliefs of organisations begin to change in ways that are congruent with the requirements of corporate law (conversion, accumulation, limited responsibility) and market conventions (Skolverket, 1992, 1996; also Bernstein, 2000; Beck & Young, 2005). But our research also says that such things can be resisted once they are recognised for what they really are, actually imply and genuinely represent.

Discussion

The image generated within new school policies (e.g. Skolverket, 1992, 1995, 2000; SOU 1997: 21; Prop. 1997/98: 6; SOU 1997:21; Lindblad et al., 2002) is one where control over the curriculum is said to have moved from the State to individuals in situations where students are to look for their own knowledge and develop a lust for learning in ways that shift 'the root-metaphor of learning' from transmission to creativity and construction. There is a heavy emphasis on communication, interaction, culture, identity and context, and traditional ways of teaching and learning in schools have been challenged and widened at the level of formal discourse (Gustafsson, 2003). However, whilst there is a rhetoric about the value (and future need) of active and creative learners (and of extended conceptions of teaching and learning that 'match up to these ideals'), this is a rhetoric of ideas not a description of material conditions nor of their contradictions in practice. Beyond the ideas are the current social and material relations of education.

Just about all the chapter data can be interpreted to support the above suggestion, in that the teachers have in their own speech acts at some point and to some degree always without fail spoken about three cornerstone values for conceptions of professionalism and professional work when describing what they feel are the key elements of the new school policy vision. This applies equally well to teachers who have been supportive of the new aims as it does those who are negative or ambivalent. These cornerstone values are firstly, the need to become co-creative and interactive knowledge workers in school with colleagues and students who are 'instrumental' in the production of the conditions of production for new kinds of learner subjectivity, new learner identities and new professional identities. These new identities have then been couched in a second element of discourse about the learners' inner power to learn and 'lust for learning'. In this element of discourse students are to learn how to become responsible consumers of education who can identify needs and can make 'the right choices' in their education. This element is tied to a third element of discourse about individualisation and the 'right for every student to choose' to perform in the new education economy in line with their best interests, as 'strong/good' and 'slow/weak' learners who show their 'abilities to ... come up with the goods' (Brian) within the 'grading culture' of schooling generally. These 'structuring (and suturing) discourses' operate within and not just despite progressive discourses of practice from infant to comprehensive and upper-secondary levels, supported by 'functional' concepts and technologies of distinction and difference such as performance, ability and motivation.

Role conflict and identity confusion, but also a 'hidden' or perhaps 'misrecognised' power to resist, is thus what we feel is described by teachers in our investigation. Furthermore, this confusion and contradiction, as well as the possibility for resistance, also basically complies with what has been reported by other researchers (e.g. Lindqvist, 2002; Nordanger, 2002) and research from other countries, such as from primary and middle schools in Europe (Beach, 2005a) and the UK (Hargreaves, 1986; Jeffrey and Woods, 1998; Troman, 1997 and Woods and Jeffrey, 2002). All this research describes the teacher's subject position as in the grip of modes of information that pull in different directions (also Woods and Jeffrey, 1998 and Woods et al., 1997), that mask resistant agency possibilities and that help different practices to result in consistencies and various forms of structural isomorphism.

Althusser's concept of *interpellation* (a speculative function of ideology) may help us to understand more about these processes. Interpellation refers to the mechanisms behind structures of representation in both discursive and ideological terms, and brings both the material and symbolic functions of ideology together within the same framework, in the creation of a subjectivity that is accomplished by ideologies hailing us through our senses at the same time as we are also forced to engage in meaning making processes from within the specific social and cultural practices we participate in. This is what pressured professionals like teachers do everyday, day in, day out (Jeffrey and Woods, 1998; Troman, 1997; Woods and Jeffrey, 2002; Lindqvist, 2002; Nordanger, 2002; Beach, 2003c). And in these circumstances each individual subject is always at one and the same time 'exposed' to numerous ideologies (and discourses) that are at odds with each other in terms of the ways in which they are resonant or not with what is recognised as right (Barker and Galasinski, 2001), by corresponding with cultural narratives (moral codes, professional ethics or even plain common sense). Interpellation is always part of a struggle between competing 'regimes' of truth in this respect (Bernstein, 2000).

This is also at least partially in line with Fairclough (1993, 1995), who situates the concepts of discourse and ideology as inter-changeable in terms of the ways they function in the articulation of meaning (Wass, 2004; Båth, 2006). Discourse comprises parole, the surface form of text, and langue, a deep structure or contextual system of representation that has developed socially in order to communicate meaningfully about specific topics. It is not just a text, but rather a communicative structure of practice by means of which social relations are established and maintained in ways that 'permit' some forms for the ordering of knowledge and some forms of pedagogical communication but not others (Bernstein, 2000, p. 86) and, therefore and there after, also some kinds of professional identity and identity change but not others (Beck and Young, 2005; Båth, 2006). And this is also what the present chapter has been about. The way discourses and ideologies can work at both the rudimentary level of psychic identity and drives, the level of discursive formation and the level of the formation of practices that ultimately help to constitute a social field (Bourdieu, 1996, pp. 201-203).

However, our point here is that social relations, such as those of education production, are not only made transparent through the use of discourse, there is also a duality of discourse and representation, as discourses (as ideological, social and textual practices) link language with the social realm and foreground the nature of understanding, to paraphrase Helmstad (1999), as a system of meaning making constituted by signifying and ideologically mediating practices and structures that constitute the beliefs that people both communicate outwardly and use in order to understand themselves inside a cultural (language) system (Bernstein, 1990, 2000). In this interplay both the production and interpretation of meaning are constrained by being socially constructed from within the signifying practices by which individuals form the objects of which they speak as they speak and act, in relation to historically specific sets of truth claims and finite bodies of rules in organisations that authorise some specific performances and articulations but not others.

What we could equally well be describing here is the issue of hegemony. Hegemony is a concept developed in a close relationship to Marxism to describe the ways in which the ruling classes maintain their rule by ideological means rather than through the use of overt physical (e.g. military) force, with the help of other classes whose own actual material interests are different, but who never the less become convinced to act in ways that are not genuinely beneficial to them. Hegemony is in this sense a form of alliance by means of which a particular class assumes a position of leadership over other classes by guaranteeing them certain (falsely represented) benefits, so as to be able to secure public political power. It is not so much a question of false consiousness as it is of (deliberate) ideological manuipulation and abuse. Hegemony works exactly by being ambiguous and distorting!

In the presently researched contexts our analyses suggest that teacher voices about the new school vision are hegemonically constituted primarily between two competing regimes of ideas within a specific ideological context (the neo-liberal restructuring of capitalist schooling) as part of a continual struggle over what counts as valid teacher work and correct ways of approaching the curriculum issue, that in the end actually come to mean (support and lead to) more or less the same thing; school based social and cultural reproduction based on amended forms of individuation and differentiation. These discourses are (mainly) those of old-conservative and new-liberal pedagogy respectively (with an odd sprinkling of constructivism and progressivism, Gustafsson, 2003) like those previously maintained by competing factions of the middle classes described by Bernstein (1990), who also suggested that neither of the discourses would favour a radical 'under-class pedagogy' under present historical conditions.

This idea about the domination of education by 'interests' emanating from the upper-classes mediated by the middle-, so that education 'works' in dominant class interests and against the interests of subordinate groups, is also 'backed up' in terms of class related patterns of education qualification produced in the schools we have done our research in. This has also been shown in other chapters and in other research in Sweden by for instance Dovemark (2004a, b), Staberg and Assarsson (1997), Svensson (2002, 2006), Svensson and Reuterberg (1998), Båth (2006), Korp (2006) and Beach (2001, 2003b), who have all shown that there is a vast contradiction between an educational rhetoric that stresses self-determination, individual creativity, personal responsibility and equal opportunities for all, and actual education conditions and possibilities within the Swedish capitalist social-democratic State that, for structural and cultural reasons, always finally denies such possibilities at the very same time as this denial is also itself disguised (Poulantzas, 1974; Willis, 2000; Brosio, 1994; Beach, 2001, 2003b). They suggest that although the experiences of young people (and their teachers) in school may have changed quite radically over the last two decades, through processes of social reproduction life chances have remained highly structured along class, racial and gender lines in school.

And here we have the ultimate contradiction in relation to teachers' voices in the present investigation. As we have seen things intimated in the voices of teachers in this chapter, they still seem to express it as possible for individual students to obtain a positive subject identity in school on the basis of a valorisation of their own personal class-cultural labour power and values. But as we see things mediated in actual practices, this positive valorisation is always negated (as an empirical fact) whenever (and if ever) the personal values and commitments of students (and/or also teachers for that matter) 'contradict' the values, interests, official knowledge and knowledge practices (and above all interests) of the dominant (now corporate) classes in our (now global) society. This is an issue not only of hegemony but also ideological domination. It is also very obvious in relation to education development globally and locally today.

Conclusions

The curriculum ideas reflected in the new policies for Sweden's schools, teachers and students are all elements expressed formally in the various National Curricula since 1990 (see also Skolverket, 1992, 1996, 2000) in statements relating to such things as students developing capacities to take personal responsibility for learning, by taking part in planning and evaluation and by choosing their own courses, subjects, themes and activities. And they also reflect policy writing at the political level of the education system internationally, as exemplified in writing such as OECD (1992) and (1995), which states that individual schools should create their own profiles and help individual pupils to influence the content of their studies' (OECD 1995, s. 137). These documents continually exhort the 'willingness and ability of individual citizens and families to take responsibility for choices and priorities of their own' (OECD 1995, s. 86) and their ideas have filtered through things like official national propositions (SOU 1992: 94; DsU, 1987: 1, 1995: 5, 2001: 19) and reports (e.g. Skolverket 1992, 1995, 2000) to the curricula and arenas of action comprised by schools and colleges, where they are developed into new working activities for a modern education.

The present chapter concerns the workings of ideology and discourse in the circumstances of (competitive) education (in a late-capitalist context) in relation to the above policy expressions and is about the conditions of development for the new forms of practice artistry called for by policy, as well as new forms of professional identity that can be linked to such policies. It identifies issues of repression and reproduction in these respects as well as active penetrations of the contradictions embedded in education messages in present circumstances, and thereafter also suggests some possibility for creative agency and active resistance, even if (and as) these possibilities are seriously compromised by the workings of hegemony (Sarup, 1978). In this sense the chapter also suggests something of how agentic possibilities become missed or (alternatively) misrecognised.

There is thus at least one important point in the chapter. This point is double edged. It is that although cultural agents (in this case teachers) are active in the making of their own (local) cultural identities and practices, they are also restrained in their actions, because they are positioned in and inherit rather than create the traditions and categories that are immediate in any given social-cultural context and this is important regarding the subject positions and practices that become apparent to and taken up by them.

These ideas support something expressed first by Marx over 100 years ago (in the Brumaire) about how, although individuals may be the makers of their own history, they do not make this history just as they please or under circumstances chosen freely, but under conditions and circumstances given and transmitted from the past that can at times weigh like a nightmare on efforts to make history move in desired directions. This doesn't paint an easy picture with regard to the realisation possibilities of pastel coloured versions for a new school vision, but it might suggest something of the struggle needed to rename and overcome the problems of such aims for teachers.

As Troman (2005) suggests, teachers face threats to their identity through the ways in which abstract(ing) systems operate (also Beck and Young, 2005), but these threats and disruptions also throw up new challenges that also lay open some new possibilities. A clear identity (such as a clearly defined teacher role) is no longer given by the direct rules and regulations of traditional institutions and cultures. There are different options but choices are complex and what the right choices are might not be so obvious at first glance. Active agency is still a possibility within neo-liberal education restructuring but it needs to be recognised and struggled for. Through such things as hegemony, as an issue of power, agency is constantly struggled for. It is never freely given and is continually shadowed by its opposite.

Moreover, within agency there always lies the possibility of the formation of a reactionary force, and indeed just this kind of reactionary agency is predominant in school practices according to teachers' descriptions of the aims and outcomes of their situated struggles over practice in the present chapter. This reactionary agency is particularly expressed in respect of the decriptions of a retraditionalising tendency at the level of professional drives and identitiy commitments and is also suggested in the previous chapter. Retradtionalisation seems to be (theoretically and practically) highly resonant with the commitments, technology and culture of performativity and antagonistic towards creativity discourses, cultures and practices.

Chapter 10

New schools and new pedagogy?

The research we have presented has focussed on a series of related ethnographic investigations of how several educational institutions have dealt with knowledge production, processing, acquisition, critique, and dissemination at times of social, economic and political change with regard to the steering principles of education and the discoursing of education policy. It has been about how education districts, regions, schools, school classes and study groups import, construct and evaluate knowledge, talk about education elements and form the spaces in which the values, discourses and practices of education production form links to cultural and social reproduction, as well as how these links are experienced, challenged, resisted, reviewed and renewed by teachers and students in their daily work and understanding (Beach et al., 2004; Troman et al., 2006). The analysis has suggested that educational institutions as well as education discourses and practices are places where knowledge and learning appear in both 'use-value' and commoditised forms, as genuinely useful skills, competencies and understanding on the one hand, and as a means to acquire, develop, hone and improve status and employment possibilities through the accumulation of educational capital on the other.[16] This is perhaps the first message of the present book. It concerns the flows and transformations of educational ideas and forms of capital in education practices.

The second message concerns the root-metaphor of schooling in Sweden, which is often described in school reforms, reform proposals and commentaries as having been shifted from a transmission metaphor to a metaphor of construction (see also Säljö, 1992, 2000; Gustafsson, 2003). As both formal policy and school leaders and teachers have expressed it (Beach, 2003c; Dovemark, 2004a), cognitive perspectives on knowledge, learning and development that emphasised personal skills and internal traits dominated previously, but now a heavy emphasis is also placed on discursive and socio-

---

16 Instrumentalism is in tension here with the creative fabrication of new knowledge of different forms with other potentials for valorisation than simple exchange value, which implies that although new school policies suggest that control over the curriculum has changed from the State to the individual in a situation where students are to, with help and guidance from teachers, look for their own knowledge and develop, *a lust for learning* (Dovemark, 2004a,b), these aims are not straightforwardly lived out.

cultural perspectives and the importance of communication, interaction, creativity, culture, identity and context (Gustafsson, 2003). The present chapter makes further considerations as to why such policies are articulated and heard just now, in just the ways they are, and in whose interests they seem to operate. However, it also sets the new formal discourse into its political economic and cultural and symbolic moment. This moment is one of tension and inter-textuality with other current discourses. Particularly the discourse of performativity has been considered in the research presented here.

The new school discourses of performativity and creativity in education in our analysis of them seem to borrow from previous discourses of individuated and personalised forms of organic solidarity in education as expressed by Bernstein (1990) and visible and invisible modes of control. These discourses sometimes go under the terms of traditional and progressive education or power centred and person centered education, after Carl Rogers (1969; Beach, 1995). The concept of retraditionalisation from Båth (2006) using Bernstein (2000), as well as Beck and Young (2005), has been important in the analyses in respect of the relationship between traditionalism and the performativity discourse in the schools we have done research in.

The invisible pedagogic codes of the progressivist discourses of the past were, in Beach (1995, 1997 and 2000) described as the opposite of the dominant university instructional code and its *visible pedagogies*, which were also described in relation to a number of clear parameters. These included a *context of reproduction*, which was said to comprise strongly physically and socially regioned spaces from which clear ideas about what counted as valid knowledge and knowledge practices were projected over students in strongly classified and framed instruction. They included also representations of knowledge as *facts* that are simply to be taken over by those exposed to them, whose abilities to meticulously reproduce these facts are then also directly tested in grading and assessment exercises. They included specific forms of *communication* between transmitters and receivers of knowledge and a two step delegation of authority. Tutors spoke, students listened and reproduced tutor mediated knowledge when so requested. There were also said to be clearly demarcated *boundaries* between different contents. These boundaries were monitored and maintained by tutors through rules that regulated the legitimacy of both written and spoken texts; what was able to become valid discourse. The mimetic characteristics of the *learning* taking place were also described. Finally, there was also a distinctive *expression of value* amongst successful students. Content value was described in exchange value terms and as high.[17]

The new school discourses of performativity (visible pedagogic code) and creativity (self-regulation, invisible self-governance, personal choice in the curriculum, constructivist fabrication of knowledge etc.) are suggested throughout the empirical chapters of the book to be extended in their relationships to traditionalism and progressivism, and like these two older discourses, they are also said to be in some ways in tension with each-other, with little evidence of a positive relationship between them that might favour creative forms of agency and authenticity. These elements of the creativity discourse become instead accommodated to the requirements of commodity culture. This is the third message emanating from our serial ethnography,[18] which thus describes how new curriculum ideas have developed on the ground in the changing relationship between the State, professional agencies, market interests and individuals. These descriptions help constitute a fourth message of the book. This message suggests, as particularly in the first four chapters, how previous discourses of traditional schooling have been replaced by outwardly self-monitored activities and discourses of self-determined learning in what seem to be more progressive contexts, but in fact are not necessarily so, as the education researched has been continually caught between the discourses and hybrid practices and ideologies have developed.

This suggestion in some senses seems to support notions of educational change and curriculum development proposed by critical cultural relativisits like Michael Apple. According to Apple, instead of schools reproducing an exact reflection of norms of behaviour, attitude, and ideological dispositions, individuals within schools possess sufficient agency and consciousness to undermine the direct reproduction of dominant economic relationships through institutions (Apple, 1995, 1982). However, our research is not totally in line with the cultural relativist position, as our research shows quite clearly that local discourses and practices are very often highly socially reproductive and seriously challenge the modern concept of an equal, fair and inclusive education for all. In this sense the research suggests that schools in Sweden are still active agencies of social reproduction (Beach, 2005b), where it is still easier for middle class

---

17 It is in these senses that we feel we can talk about re-traditionalisation in the present research, in that what has been noted is in many ways a return to the appropriation of the above forms of pedagogical communication and control. Re-traditionalisation has been discussed in relation to student learning, student self-identity, student evaluation, teachers' professional concepts and concrete classroom practices.

students with high levels of social and cultural capital 'at home' to be successful in school (also Staberg and Assarsson, 1999; Svensson, 2002, 2006; Svensson and Reuterberg, 1998; Dovemark, 2004b; Dovemark and Beach, 2004; Beach, 2001). In the era of restructuring, in other words, inequalities are maintained and not challenged by teachers and students in school and as we imply, differences in education inclusion and attainment seem still to be clearly related to social backgrounds.

As suggested earlier, ours is primarily a Marxian analysis in the senses outlined by Engels (1969) in a letter to Borgius, where he addressed the role of the economic base in relation to the political superstructure. Engels suggested how political, juridicial, philosophical, religious, literary, artistic, etc., development is not based directly on economic development, as the economic situation is not *the cause of super-structural developments*! It is only active in them. Engels wrote, it 'is not that the economic situation is *cause* while everything else is only passive effect. There is, rather, interaction on the basis of economic necessity, which *ultimately* always asserts itself. So it is not that the economic situation produces an automatic effect. People make their history themselves, in a given environment, and on the basis of already existing actual relations, among which the economic relations are the most decisive ones.

The reproductive character of schooling is in our view related to its task as the provider of a differentiated corpus of labour to fuel and manage the fires of living labour power and production. This task remains 'intact' even at the present time, even if there has been some modification to some of its fundamental classifications as education has begun to take on new economic meanings as a cultural commodity with both symbolic and economic exchange values. It has become a commodity with direct links to economic production in ways hither-to-for unseen in Swedish education politics. Moreover, differentiation is tied to the new consumerist role of education subjects (learners) in the new educational economies of signs and symbols (Båth, 2006). It selects out who is suitable for what kind of education for what type of future in the new knowledge society on the basis of attitudinal attributions based on observed and recorded consumerist behaviour (i.e. choices). These things are touched on in several empirical chapters. They take us to the next message of the book, which concerns agency (for both teachers and learners) and the line between active agency and passive compliance.

As is also made explicit in the final three empirical chapters, as well as in Dovemark's recent thesis (Dovemark, 2004a), the dividing line between active agency and passive compliance is neither sharp nor distinct. For as these works suggest, whilst the capacity to act as self-regulated learners in school is apparent in school practices, it has also, *at the same time*, become a new instrument of differentiation (also Lundahl, 2001). Moreover the reverse also applies. Creativity is becoming an educational commodity with an exploitable symbolic exchange value that far outstrips its other forms of value. Educational creativity is becoming heavily involved in socially reproductive practices (also Willis, 1977, 2000) as part and parcel of the contradictory position of democratic schooling under capitalism. As Apple (1995, p. 53) puts it, on the one hand the school must assist accumulation by producing agents for a hierarchical labour market and cultural capital for technical/administrative knowledge but at the same time, our educational institutions must also legitimate ideologies of equality and class mobility, and make themselves seem as positive as possible to as many classes and class segments as possible (also Brosio, 1994). The need for *economic* and ideological efficiency and stable production tends to be in conflict with other *political* needs. What we see is the school attempting to resolve what may be the inherently contradictory roles it must play (Apple, op cit).

The complications of restructuring

This side-heading brings us to the next message of the book. Restructuring in education in Sweden is a *complicated issue*. And it is not just about State childhood and youth schools. It is also about independent childhood and youth schools and both public and independent schools for adults. Some of the chapters have focussed on the latter in particular. They have described how restructuring in adult education has been locally motivated by a rhetoric concerning a form of 'new capitalism' that tries to profit from claims about there being an increased demand for more highly educated and motivated employees, who are able to use more autonomy in applying working life skills in combination with flexible technology, and how, in order to thrive in our 'new' global economy—defined by the innovative application of knowledge—future citizens must be able to do more than simply absorb and feedback information (Seltzer and Bentley, 1999). This is about how discourses are created and manipulated to play on human emotions and create or support specific influences and ideologies.

However, in addition to the discursive dimension there is also a material one. Nowadays there is a course that can be bought for just about everything and everyone as part of a new consumerist approach in education. But not everyone gets to eat from the high table and some people profit more than others; some directly, some indirectly; from the new forms of education governance and practices. This is the next message! Education has become a cultural commodity that can be recognised as connected to new forms of production of labour power and economy (i.e. productive labour) in new labour processes in Sweden, which are also becoming more abstract, cognitive and immaterial as automation and computerisation invade production industry at home at the same time as many manual jobs are moved to cheep labour markets. As part of a new global, capitalist economy of goods, signs, symbols, artefacts and practices economic production has increasingly swarmed out of factories and economic accumulation in Sweden now develops more from within the interstices of civil society than ever before (Beach, 2004b, 2005b).

The changing conditions of production have (had) consequences for how we might understand the new unifying concepts of education change in Sweden and should, according to our research and this book, be taken as *local and national responses* to supranational conditions (Dovemark, 2004a). For instance, both national policy texts (like the various school curricula) and supra-national ones (like e.g. OECD 1996, 2000a, b) have emphasised the need for a reduction in central and rules regulation and an increase in delegated responsibilities, goal-rationality, self-determination and freedom of choice in education. And a new politically expressed interest has become extensively voiced for *what learners should become* (i.e. creative, self-reliant and *discerning consumers and producers* of knowledge) rather than what they should know for a lifetime of productive work. What they should become is new education consumers eating selectively from mixtures of starters, main courses and desserts that are sufficiently varied as to be massively abundant and totally available at almost all times on the bourgeoning education markets.

Education is ever increasingly becoming business—worldwide, nationally and regionally (Hill, 2006). Discourses filter down through global cultures and into the local arenas, where they are re-spoken (Dovemark, 2004a) and come to fuel the changes described as necessary and desirable by the powerful groups. This is in essence how hegemony tends to work according to for instance Fairclough (1989), where it is less a form of ideological domination (as in more orthodox Marxist perspectives) than a form of leadership that operates through the full spectrum of *the economic, political, cultural and ideological domains of society*, including education. As Allman (1999, p. 105) expressed it, the term describes moral and ethical leadership as a means by which consent is organised.

Hegemony is a form of leadership. It can work by either domination or direction, through an imposition of ideological systems of belief and the absorption of potentially radical elements of thought into an existing framework. It is a form of *power over society as a whole* that is exercised by and in the interests of one of the fundamental economically-defined classes in society in alliance with other social forces. As we have suggested—both implicitly and explicitly—throughout the pages of this book the struggle over the definition of education is a key aspect of the struggle for hegemony in advanced societies. The book has been about these struggles and their resolutions at individual and group levels perhaps more than anything else.

However, hegemony is never fully sutured. It is part of a constant struggle for power and control and is only ever partially and temporarily achieved, through struggles over definitions and the content and meaning of ideas, in a form of *unstable equilibrium*. It is a form of leadership that operates by the consent of classes and blocs, who construct, sustain or fracture alliances that can then take on economic, political and ideological forms. It includes all the institutions of civil society and evidences some unevenness between different levels and domains.

Education, hegemony and neo-liberalism

Education in Sweden is suggested in the present book to be a clear part of a new global hegemony of economic neo-liberalism in the educational field where the 'images' of new education and new professionalism co-exist with other 'ways of talking' and acting (Beach, 2003a, b; Dovemark and Beach, 2004; Lundahl, 2001; Zackari, 2001; Dovemark, 2004a, b; Gustafsson, 2003). More materially rooted these provide contra-distinctive pictures *of life and learning* and corrections for over-idealised notions of school change. Education in these street level (emic) terms does not have 'value in itself', but is of 'instrumental value' only. This is the commodity value education has always had within capitalism according to Beach (2003a) that restructuring is changing only by tightening market relations and emphasising output control at the expense of process control. By describing some of these things ethnographically the present book suggests to some degree how the new global hegemony can be identified, deconstructed and challenged in local practices.

Of course we can still ask what is wrong with extending the application of market logic inside schools. The answer to this according to the present chapters is primarily two sided. It is that through the couple between the home/family and education via the circuits of accumulation in education, there is a tendency for the children of the better-educated families to constantly and consistently accrue better education qualifications and ultimately get better jobs, almost solely on the basis of their cultural and social capital and their respective rates of exchange within the new-school-curriculum context, thus perpetuating a cycle of social reproduction that overrides equity and equality (Bourdieu, 1984; Dovemark, 2004a, b). The introduction of the market function as choice of schools and not just choices in them extends this reproductive capability into the spheres of economic capital (Broady and Börjesson, 2005), not despite voucher systems and emotional capital but because of them (Ball, 2003; Beach, 2005b).

All the present research in Sweden related to education attainment in education markets suggests that the children of educationally and economically rich parents with high levels of social and cultural capital still tend to get educations that give better qualifications and future prospects than do the children of the educationally and economically poor parents. This runs in the face of expressed education policy from the mid forties onwards and the democratic principles of education in Sweden presented already in the introduction. It is a further characteristic of the contradictions of an education system that claims to serve all factions of society equally regardless of social inheritance but does not. This contradiction is the main consistent outcome and message of the book. An associated characteristic is also that these contradictions are usually denied by most of the teachers who monitor and facilitate them. Hegemony works in this sense as a silent vehicle, not just deliberately and directly through agents, but also in a sense through their un-reflected actions as well. Neither the creativity nor the performativity discourses (nor hybrids between them) appear to have much influence on this.

Concluding remarks

Current education reform in Sweden is formally characterised in terms of decentralisation, deregulation and the creation of quasi-markets to stimulate creativity, individual responsibility and efficiency (Lundahl, 2002a, b). However, as also Lundahl has expressed it, the creation of market solutions in public services is ironic according to the present book and the statement above, as it plays on and extends the differences and ineffectiveness it was meant to challenge, with this pedagogy again also then favouring dominant groups. Increasing numbers of people in school, adult and higher education now attend modular programmes and short courses—often termed flex-courses—that, although they are focused increasingly narrowly on the short-term needs of trade and industry rarely seem able to lead to stable jobs. These courses tend to age quickly and are increasingly being provided by independent, private and quasi-private organisations yet paid for publicly. They are also given *at the expense of* comprehensive humanist educations and a political education for social transformation (Allman, 1999).

Thorpe and Brady's (2003) view of the dominance of finance capital within cultural (including educational) politics today may explain some of the contradictions we have identified and described. Finance capital requires a flexible workforce not an educated workforce and would be unlikely to want to pay for a general, worthwhile education for the majority of individuals. This seems to be happening. Moreover, the interest of capital in education doesn't stop here. It is also ideological according to our analysis, i.e. concerned with the habituation of market thinking through language use, and material, concerned with the objectification of education and education practices and goods as commodities. This, together with the material objectification of educational practices (teaching, learning and administration), corresponds with the commodity problem of education that the present book attempts to describe.

The degree of contradiction in education in Sweden since restructuring is in the above senses expansive. Four principle areas demonstrate this. Firstly discourses of restructuring have been used to motivate a particular (neo-liberal) kind of education and have constantly advanced the capacities of individuals as agents who can (and should) choose for themselves and take responsibility for their own affairs. But as the chapters of this book suggest, the material reorganisation of education actually either denies people these very possibilities or steers choices in ideologically conditioned ways. Free and informed choices are not made! They are not even possible in many cases, as there are insufficient freely available functional informational modalities accessible to 'education consumers' to facilitate them. Furthermore, what choices are available are guided by common sense interpretations of dominant discourses and common sense is manipulated and ideologically normative in most cases (Beach, 2004b). Thirdly there is talk of increased senses of belonging and material inclusion in education. But this is simply not the case. The education system continues to differentiate and exclude, albeit to some degree on different grounds than before. Finally there is an increasing direct economic interest in education from organised capital. This interest is often seen as a sign of the superiority of capitalism above other forms of control but can be seen as evidence of its current crisis (Thorpe and Brady, 2003).

The suggestions of the book thus fit quite well with Marcuse's (1964) notion of cultural change and its relationship with social life more broadly, where culture is described as a historically distinguishable unity with two dimensions (Beach, 2004a). These are the common sense constructs and cultural categories that articulate experiences within complicated social processes on the one hand and the existing modes of economic and cultural production on the other (also Willis, 1999). Marcuse used the term *affirmative culture* with respect to this duality. Within it education restructuring would not be expected to primarily consist of a transformation of education services through direct takeover by corporate enterprise, as in common 'linear' understandings of this phenomenon, as the control implied is already prevalent (Brosio, 1994; McMurtry, 1998; Hill, 2001). But it would instead be an element of neo-liberalism that as Hursh and Camille write, would emphasise and mobilise resources for the further increase of individualistic private accumulation of education goods from public provision.

This is one side of education as a commodity problem. It is the side corresponding to education as accumulation as expressed through Freire's concept of banking forms of education (Allman, 1999). But there is also a second side. As suggested for instance in Beach (2005a) there is a long-term indication across Europe from the new political right to move service supply from the public sector to the private, by deregulating how private producers behave and by putting into question all collective structures capable of obstructing the logic of the market in educational contexts (Beach, 2004b).

This is also what is suggested to have occurred in vernacular forms in several chapters of the book. It suggests to us that educational re-culturing is a better descriptor of current developments than is education restructuring, as what the neo-liberal reconstitution of education consists of is an updating of key aspects of moral determination in line with the prevailing economic and ideological standards of global, neo-liberal, market capitalism. It suggests also that the creativity and performativity discourses are part of (rather than opposed to) these articulations.

Gramsci's and Friere's ideas about the power of ideology are relevant to this discussion according to Beach (2004a). This notion is embedded in a Marxian conception of ideology in which ruling ideas are nothing more than the ideal expressions of dominant social and material relationships that make the ideas of one (dominant) class the ruling ones in a scenario where subordinate classes are dominated because they are always immersed in production relations that lend them to reproduce ideas that support the dominant material relationships.

They suffer a contradictory consciousness. This consciousness can be challenged and changed. Both these points have been empirically and ethnographically described discussed in the present book.

Chapter 11

A short chapter on methods

There are several common definitions of ethnography, not one (Beach, 1997). Ethnography is not a uniform paradigm and the definitions 'target' and center upon different aspects of the ethnographic venture. One common 'target' concerns what ethnographers produce. A common definition here claims that ethnographers produce written accounts of cultures or cultural processes from records which have been made of events witnessed at first hand through participating in the daily round of life in cultural settings or that have been related by (other) first hand observers (cf. Sanjek, 1990). Another is as is expressed in Atkinson's (1990) terms, that ethnography is the textual reconstruction of reality. This fits in with the version presented by Hammersley and Atkinson, whose claim was that ethnography is just:

> (O)ne social research method, albeit a somewhat unusual one ... The ethnographer participates, overtly or covertly, in people's daily lives for an extended period of time, watching what happens, listening to what is said, asking questions; in fact collecting whatever data are available to throw light on the issues with which he or she is concerned.
> (Hammersley and Atkinson, 1983: 2)

That is, put simply, ethnographers gather and develop information about life-settings, the people in them, their expressions and activities, the artefacts they develop and employ and the ways in which they do these things, their rituals and their traditions (Geetz, 1973; Beach et al., 2004; Beach, 2005c). They then analyse, classify and communicate these materials as data (usually in written form—although video and film documentary are also used) to others (Beach, 1997; Dovemark, 2004a). Kuper (1989) put things as follows:

> Ethnographers ... deploy various techniques of observation, and return home with several packages of data. Each package, as a consequence of the observational technique from which it derives, has its own characteristics, and is in the first instance best summarised, or organised, in a specific ...

form ... (say) a set of jural rules, a series of case studies, statistical tables, genealogies, myths, etc ... .The next step focuses the data. This may be done in various ways, none of which is a priori most obvious or useful. One may focus the data around a cultural notion ... , or an extraneous problem ... , or a kind of activity ... , or a set of such activities defined by a common input or output (e.g. an economic system), or upon the constraints on the individual in pursuing particular goals. This list ... not exhaustive ... is usually chosen or justified on 'theoretical grounds' ... but the reason for the choice may be that this is what my professor is interested in, or this will shake the grant from the tree, or show people why they must revolt, etc. However, even if we accept the ... position that the choice of focus is ultimately moral and thus scientifically arbitrary, the fact remains that, once the focus has been selected, it imposes its own analytic imperatives. What the investigator does with it is largely determined by the content and nature of the data ... and the model-building techniques he (or she) has available for data of this kind.

(Kuper, 1989; 202)

As well as there being different foci and knowledge interests in ethnography as suggested by Kuper (above), ethnography is also conducted from different philosophical positions, such as postmodernism, symbolic interactionism, structuralism, neo-Marxism and so on. In education research, probably thanks to the Chicago school influences, symbolic interactionism is very common. This approach is exemplified in the Manchester school tradition including initially the research by Colin Lacey, Audrey Lambart and David Hargreaves and later, under the guidance of Lacey but now at Sussex University, Stephan Ball as well as by exponents at the Open University in Milton Keynes, such as Peter Woods, Martin Hammersly, Geoff Troman and Bob Jeffrey.

In symbolic interactionist investigations the central concern in ethnography is to display acts and show their meaning from the perspective of those who carry them out (cf. Blumer, 1969; Mead, 1934; Beach, 1997, 2003d, 2005c). This moves us beyond 'blackbox' positivist and behaviourist theory, and reasserts a legitimate interest in research for the role of agents in structuring processes and exercising power and domination, and helps locate the injunctions of power within social positions and between persons (Hammersley and Atkinson, 1983). Moreover, it does not view people as simple autonoms propelled blindly and can help us see resistance as a human possibility. However, there are some possible problems with this as these interests in agency may occur at the cost of an interest in structure and the agent, agents and agency may become the only thing of interest in the work (Beach, 2005c). Put very simply, if one believes there is more to life than agent and agency then symbolic interactionist forms of ethnography may be considered problematic.

The restrictions of interactionism have been pointed out particularly by critical ethnographers and anthropologists (e.g. Willis, 1977; Corrigan, 1979; Marcus and Fischer, 1986; Angus, 1986; Sharpe, 1993; Sharpe and Green, 1975; Lave, 1988; Beach, 1997, 2003d), holistic ethnographers (e.g. Lutz, 1993), as well as researchers associated with or following the Frankfurt School of critical theory (e.g. Young, 1989; Carr, 1995), who all criticise symbolic interactionism as inadequate for the development of social theory as it lacks a reflected notion of social-cultural totality or 'situation' which goes beyond the mind or consciousness of the acting subject (i.e. the situation as the actor understands it or phenomenological context in which he or she acts: cf. Young, 1989; Angus, 2005). This means there is no clearly articulated politically informed notion of structural formation, power or a macro-theory of society or culture to tie the research to and that the research therefore cannot legitimately pose the question why it is that certain stable institutionalised meanings emerge from practice rather than others, unless this is within the consciousness of agents themselves. As Angus (1986: 62) has expressed it, because action and meaning are explained in terms of their immediate context, both the prior knowledge of actors, and any link with a conception of a wider, external social reality, are denied preventing any understanding of the dialectic between continuity and change, and between human agency and social structure.

Focussing only on actor perspectives and meanings would be OK of course, if what was existentially important in the life-times of the living subjects and lives that we do research on was only that which exists in the mind of the acting subjects themselves. But of course existence transcends any naïve phenomenology of this kind and most rational scientists agree on this. What they don't always see is that un-reflected subjectivist ontology obliterates this and that in this process what disappears is also the simple empirical fact that, as well as acting on the basis of assumed mutuality and shared meaning and assumptions, humans can also act on the basis of the opposite condition: individual and shared cultural misunderstanding (Beach, 2005c). This is not to say that subjectivism has no place in ethnography, but rather that the aim of ethnography as a social science should not only be to show acts as understood, interpreted and articulated from the actor perspective, but also to suggest something of how these acts, although they are culturally produced, are produced under specific conditions that can incorporate elements beyond the actors present control and influence. This has also been indicated by Habermas's treatise on human knowledge interests (Habermas, 1972). Both subject (agent) and (agency) structure are important objects of knowledge in social science.

Critical ethnography

Critical ethnography is the research method we have employed in our research. This form of ethnography is both similar and different to the more common interactionist approaches. It has an aim to portray culture and culturally productive and reproductive processes and to produce speculative theories about logically possible forms of complex causality so they may be interpreted, deconstructed and changed. An important idea here is to help people to be able to see things in new ways and to become able to act on the basis of this knowledge, by using it as a means for framing future professional questions and future life projects. This involves uncovering the ideologies at play in the researched contexts.

Ideology, as Kincheloe and McLaren (1994, p. 141) suggest, 'are not simply deceptive and imaginary mental relations that individuals and groups live out relative to their material conditions of existence', but are actually inscribed in the materiality of social and institutional practices. The intention is to produce research which will illuminate the ways in which the ideologically formed understandings that are more commonly termed as knowledge can be seen as both a product and a part of the exercise of power. This power-knowledge contributes to the ways in which differently positioned groups become tied to local structuration processes and the issue is to begin to question a naturalised acceptance of these founding ideas and to show the effects of ideology formation on 'common' sense. Things can different from how they seem once alternative ideas are attached to the particularity of everyday experience (Åsberg, 1973). This is about showing the effects of perspective and position dominance to people and helping generate new outlooks.

Our commitment here has been influenced by Fay's (1977) examination of the social and structural conditions which both give rise to and 'normalise' the rules, actions and beliefs in a social order that dominant groups engender and benefit from (Beach, 1997, 2003d, 2005c; Dovemark, 2004a). But it is not just ideology criticism, as the aim is not just to show what the dialectics of human agency are that confound progressive attempts to reform a social order, but also to show something of the detailed technologies of how they work in specific local communities so they may be more clearly identified, challenged, opposed and changed in the development of a more practical critical subjectivity (Heron and Reason, 1997, Beach, 2003d; 2005c). The intention is to show the basis on which liberating decisions can be taken on the basis of local, complex and often ironic, collective and cultural forms of knowledge that are not reducible to the dominant forms. This knowledge is an essential tool for progressive and transformational political change.

There is a parallel here between Fay's analysis and Freud's psycho-analysis, which in Habermasian terms works in two directions. Firstly, by taking a point of departure in the neurotic behaviour of patients the analysis shows regularities between symptoms and extra-psychic circumstances. Second, by establishing dialogue with the patient the analyst attempts to penetrate behind the surface connections to grasp and reveal hidden motives and causes to help the patient change from a neurotic, blind commitment to a more rational choice (Beach, 1997, 2003d; Carr, 1995).

These ideas also liken Frieres (1970) notion of conscientisation, for, at the heart of Friere's critique of traditional science is the way in which its processes and products act to separate out from rational inquiry the inclusion of the subjects of the same, except in an objectified form. What is opposed here is clear in formulations of science such as science and value, observer and observed, knowledge and belief, researcher and researched (Beach, 1997, 2003d, 2005c; Carr, 1995). While an empiricist educational science seeks to replace the practical common sense knowledge of 'practitioners' with an 'objective' knowledge of science, critical ethnography seeks to encourage practitioners to treat their practical common sense knowledge as a subject of critical reappraisal. Critical ethnography opens an analysis towards the processes through which actors carve out and stabilise spheres of rationality and the processes through which such rationalised spheres can be recognised and challenged in terms of their value injunctions and implications (Carr, 1995; Beach, 1997, 2003d).

Summary

A form of theoretically informed critical ethnography of education with a basic foundation in modern neo-Marxist theory is the kind of ethnography that characterises the research behind the present book. It can be characterised by a number of points. One of these is an opposition to the idea of communities of elite groups conducting science on others. Instead of this, as a critical educational science, our research seeks to influence and/or establish critical communities of workers and professionals (e.g. students/pupils, teachers and educational administrators and politicians) to engage in processes of discussion, argument and critique toward the rational development of their values and practices so they may contribute to social change or transformation.

There are distinct validity forms for this kind of research (Beach, 2003d). These are located in forms of pragmatic (Kvale, 1995) and catalytic (Lather, 1986) validity, where knowledge is valid if it is integrated with and or instigates change that is sustainable and beneficial to economically disadvantaged and materially and ideologically exploited groups. The main intention is to undermine the limitations and restrictions of ideology and to deconstruct the expressed and understood limits of education renewal by exposing the contradictions located in time and space that either allow for or oppose the possibility for organisational and ultimately social transformation.

Our approach to critical ethnography is thus neither an advocacy of 'auto-ethnography' nor an open invitation to others to step into the vacuum created by removing the researcher from the ethnography scene (Beach, 1997). What is on offer is critical co-authoring and analysis of 'eventful' texts for the specific purpose of raising a critical (transformative) action potential. This is not an 'ethno-ethnographic' package awaiting deconstruction and subsequent repackaging. It is ethnography which thanks to joint effort on the part of critical co-workers, fulfils both 'scholarly' and 'local' prerogatives, by allowing each subject to speak in a way readers can hear, and by hearing can come to see several sets of conditions, lives and relations and their antecedents differently (Marcus and Fischer, 1986). It is primarily intended to form a basis for social action. As critical ethnographers we believe in the 'sanctity' of the dialectic relationship between individual agency, consciousness formation and the structural formations of the political economy. This is a belief formed around empirical and material knowledge, not just 'idealism' or ideology. It is based on evidence about the way agents make decisions that contribute to the reproduction of the social relations of capitalism in education interchanges.

References

Allman, P. (1999) *Revolutionary Social Transformation: Democratic Hopes, Political Possibilities and Critical Education*. Westport, Connecticut: Bergin and Garvey.

Althusser, L. (1969) *For Marx*. Harmondsworth: Penguine.

Althusser, L. (1971) Ideology and Ideological State Apparatuses, in Althusser, L., *Lenin and Philosophy and Other Essays*. London: New Left Books.

Althusser, L. (1976) *Filosofi från proletär klasståndpunkt*, Urval och redigering av G. Therborn. Bo Cavefors Bokförlag.

Angus, L. B. (1986) Developments in ethnographic research in education: From interpretative to critical ethnography, *Journal of Research and Development in Education*, 20(1): 34-47.

Angus, L. (2005) New methodologies, cultural analysis and the politics of research: Revisiting the lessons of critical ethnography, in Troman, G., Jeffrey, B. and Walford, G. (Eds) *Methodological Issues and Practices in Ethnography. (Studies in Education Ethnography Volume 11)*. Amsterdam, London and New York. Elsevier.

Apple, M. W. (1982) *Cultural and Economic Reproduction in Education: Essays on Class, Ideology and the State*. New York and London: Routledge and Kegan Paul.

Apple, M. W. (1995) *Education and power* (2nd ed.). New York: Routledge.

Atkinson, P. (1990) *The Ethnographic Imagination: Textual Construcions of Reality*. London: Routledge.

Ball, S. J. (1990) *Politics and Policy Making in Education*. London: Routledge.

Ball, S. J. (1994) *Education Reform: A Critical and Post-structural Approach*. Milton Keynes: Open University Press.

Ball, S.J. (1998) Educational studies, policy entrepreneurship and social theory. I R. Slee, G. Weiner and S. Tomlinson, *School Effectiveness for Whom? Callings to the School Effectiveness and School Improvement Movements*. London: Falmer Press.

Ball, S.J. (2003) The teachers' soul and the terrors of performativity. *Journal of Education Policy*, 18(2), 215-228.

Ball, S. J. and Larsson, S. (1989: Eds.). *The Struggle for Democratic Education: Equality and Participation in Sweden*. London: Falmer Press.

Barker, C. (2000) *Cultural Studies. Theory and practice*. London: Sage.

Barker, C., and Galasinski, D. (2001) *Cultural Studies and Discourse Analysis: A Dialogue on Language and Identity*. London: Sage.

Barrows, H. (1980) *How to Design a Problem Based Curriculum for the Pre-Clinic Years*. New York: Springer P. C.

Barrows, H. and Tamblyn, R. (1980). *Problem Based Learning: An Approach to Medical Education*. New York: Springer.

Baudelot, C. and Establet, R. (1971) Grundskolans funktion i det kapitalistiska skolsystemet. I Berner, B. Callewaert, S. and Silberbrandt, H. (1977) *Skola, ideologi och samhälle*. Stockholm: Wahlström and Widstrand.

Beach, D. (1995) *Making Sense of the Problem of Change: An Ethnographic Study of a Teacher Education Reform*. (Göteborg Studies in Educational Sciences 100). Göteborg: Acta Universitatis Gothoburgensis.

Beach, D, (1996) Socio-material structuration and education change. *Nordisk Pedagogik*, Vol. 16(4) pp. 203-213.

Beach, D. (1997) *Symbolic Control and Power Relay: Learning in Higher Professional Education.* (Göteborg Studies in Educational Sciences 119), Göteborg: Acta Universitatis Gothoburgensis.

Beach, D. (1999a) Om demokrati, reproduktion och förnyelse i dagens gymnasieskola, *Pedagogisk forskning i Sverige,* 4(4): 349 365.

Beach, D. (1999b) Matematikutbildningens politik och ideologi, *Nämnaren,* 26: 56-60.

Beach, D. (1999c) Alienation and Fetish in Science Education, *Scandinavian Journal of Education Research,* 43(2), pp157-172.

Beach, D. (2000) Continuing problems of teacher education reform, *Scandinavian Journal of Education Research,* 44: 275-291.

Beach, D. (2001) Alienation, Reproduction and Fetish in Swedish Education, in Walford, G. (Ed) *Ethnography and Education Policy. (Studies in Education Ethnography Volume 4).* Amsterdam, London and New York. Elsevier.

Beach, D. (2003a) Mathematics goes to market, in Beach, D., Gordon. T., and Lahelma. E. (Eds) *Democratic Education: Ethnographic Challenges,* London: Tufnell Press.

Beach, D. (2003b). The politics, policy and ideology of school mathematics, in Walford, G. (Ed) *Investigating Educational Policy through Ethnography. Studies in Education Ethnography Volume 8,* Amsterdam, London and New York. Elsevier.

Beach, D. (2003c) From teachers for change, *European Educational Research Journal,* 2(2): 203-227.

Beach, D. (2003d) A problem of validity in educational research, *Qualitative Inquiry,* 9(6): 859-874.

Beach, D. (2004a) The Public Costs of the Re-structuring of Adult Education: A Case in Point from Sweden. *Journal for Critical Education Policy Studies,* 2(1), www.jceps.com.

Beach, D. (2004b) Labs and the quality of learning in school science: Schools, Labs and creativity, in Troman, G., Jeffrey, B., and Walford, G. (Eds) *Identity, Agency and Social Institutions. Studies in Educational Ethnography* Vol. 10, Oxford: JAI Press.

Beach, D. (2005a: Ed) Work-package 2: Welfare State Restructuring in Education and Health Care: Implications for the Teaching and Nursing Professions and their Professional Knowledge, second deliverable in the EU sixth framework project Professional Knowledge at *Education and Health: Restructuring work and life between the State and the citizens in Europe* http://www.profknow.net/fs-results.html.

Beach, D. (2005b) Summarizing General Developments in Teaching and Nursing and Teacher and Nurse Education, in Beach, D. (Ed) *Welfare State Restructuring in Education and Health Care: Implications for the Teaching and Nursing Professions and their Professional Knowledge.* Second deliverable in the EU sixth framework project *Professional Knowledge in Education and Health: Restructuring work and life between the State and the citizens in Europe* http://www.profknow.net/fs-results.html.

Beach, D. (2005c) From fieldwork to theory and representation in ethnography, in Troman, G., Jeffrey, B., Walford, G., (Eds) *Methodological issues and Practices in Ethnography. Studies in Educational Ethnography* vol. 11, Oxford: JAI Press.

Beach, D. (2005d) The problem of how learning should be socially organised, *Reflective Practice,* 6(4): 473-489.

Beach, D. (2006a) Policies of Creativity and Practices of Opposition: The construction of student preferences for creativity in different forms of school-work within school classrooms, in Jeffrey, B. (Ed). *Creative Learning Practices: European Experiences.* London: Tufnell.

Beach, D. (2006b) Humanism and Creativity in Restructured Adult Education in Sweden, *Ethnography and Education*, 1(2): 143-54.

Beach, D. and Carlsson, M. (2004) Adult education by tender: A case study of effects of restructuring on education identities. *European Educational Researcher Journal*, 3(3): 674-690.

Beach, D and Carlson, M. (2005) Den samlade förnyelsen av sfi. *Utbildningsvetenskap 2005—Resultat dialog*, Stockholm: Vetenskapsrådets rapportserie 13: 2005.

Beach, D. and Dovemark, M. (2005a) L'educazione svedese verso un cambiamento? La riforma della scuola e della pedagogia, o nuovi modi per la riproduzione sociale (Swedish schooling in transition? New Schools and new pedagogy or new ways of continuing social reproduction) in Francesca Gobbo (a cura di) *Le scuole degli altri. Le riforme scolastiche nell'Europa che cambia*. Torino: SEI.

Beach, D. and Dovemark, M. (2005b) Kreativitet som kulturell handelsvara: en etnografisk studie om kampen om kreativitet, *Didaktisk Tidskrift*, 15(1-2): 5-17.

Beach, D. and Dovemark, M. (2005c) Creativity as a Cultural Commodity: An Ethnographic Investigation of Struggles over Creativity in Three Swedish Schools, *Journal for Critical Education Policy Studies*, 4(2), www.jceps.com

Beach, D., Gobbo, F., Jeffrey, B., Smyth, G., and Troman, G. (2004) Guest Editor's introduction, *European Educational Researcher Journal*, 3(3): 534-538.

Beck, J. and Young, M. F. D. (2005) The assault on the professions and the restructuring of academic and professional identities: a Bersteinian analysis, *British Journal of the Sociology of Education*, 26(2): 183-197.

Becker, H. S. (1952) Social Class Variations in the Teacher-Pupil Relationship, *Journal of Educational Sociology*, 25(4): 451-465.

Bentley, T. and Seltzer, K. (1999) *The Creative Age*, London: Demos.

Berhanu, G. (2001) *Learning-In-Context: An Ethnographic Investigation of Mediated Learning Experiences among Ethiopian Jews in Israel*, (Göteborg Studies in Educational Sciences 166), Göteborg: Acta Universitatis Gothoburgensis.

Bernstein, B. (1975) *Class, Codes and Control: Towards a Theory of Education Transmissions, Volume 3*, London: An Open University Press.

Bernstein, B. (1990) *Class, Codes and Control, Vol. 4: The Structuring of Pedagogic Discourse*, London: Routledge.

Bernstein, B. (1996) *Pedagogy, Symbolic Control and Identity: Theory, Research and Critique*, London: Taylor and Francis.

Bernstein, B. (2000) *Pedagogy, Symbolic Control and Identity: Theory, Research and Critique* (revised edition), Lanham: Rowman and Littlefield.

Bliding, M. (2004) *Inneslutandets och uteslutandets praktik*. (Gothenburg Studies in Educational Science 214), Göteborg: Acta Universitatis Gothoburgensis.

Bourdieu, P. (1996) *The Rules of Art: Genesis and Structure of the Literary Field*, Cambridge: Polity Press.

Bourdieu, P. (1997) The forms of capital, in Halsey, A. H., Lauder, H., Brown, P., and Stuart Wells, A. (Eds) Education, Culture, Economy, Society, Oxford: Oxford University Press.

Bourdieu, P. and Passeron, J. C. (1977) *Reproduction in Education, Society and Culture*, London: Sage.

Bowles, S. and Gintis, P. (1976) *Schooling in Capitalist America: Educational Reform and the Contradiction of Economic Life*, New York: Basic books.

Bowles, S. and Gintis, H. (1988) I Cole, M. (ed.), *Bowles and Gintis Revisited: Correspondence and Contradiction in Educational Theory,* London: Farmer Press.
Broady, D. and Börjesson, M. (2005) Gymnasiaskolans sociala karta (the social map of upper-secondary schools), *Utbildningsvetenskap 2005—Resultat dialog.* Stockholm: Vetenskapsrådets rapportserie 13: 2005.
Brosio, R. (1994) *A Radical Democratic Critique of Capitalist Education,* New York: Lang.
Brown, P., Halsey, A.H., Lauder, H. and Stuart wells, A. (1997) The Transformation of Education and Society. An Introduction, in A.H. Halsey, H. Lauder, P. Brown and A. Stuart Wells (eds.) *Education-Culture, Economy, Society,* Oxford: University Press.
Båth, S. (2006) *Kvalifikation och medborgarfostran. En analys av reformtexter avseende gymnasieskolans samhällsuppdrag,* (Gothenburg Studies in Educational Sciences 240), Göteborg: Acta Universitatis Gothenburgensis.
Carlén, M. (1999) *Kunskapslyft eller avbytarbänk? Möten med industriarbetare om utbildning för arbetet,* (Göteborg Studies in Educational Sciences 140). Göteborg: Acta Universitatis Gothoburgensis.
Carlgren, I. (1997) Klassrummet som social praktik och meningskonstituerande kultur, *Nordisk Pedagogik,* 17(1): 9-27.
Carlgren, I. (2000) The Implicit Teacher, in Klette, K. and Carlgren, I. (Eds) *Restructuring Nordic Teachers: An Analysis of Policy Texts from Finland, Denmark, Sweden and Norway,* (Report No. 10, 2000) University of Oslo: Institute for Educational Research.
Carlson (2002) *Svenska för invandrare—brygga eller gräns? Syn på kunskap och lärande inom sfi-undervisningen,* Göteborg: Department of Sociology, Göteborg University.
Carlson, M. (2004) Restructuring of Swedish Adult Education: the involvement of economists and politicians in education policy, in Troman, G., Jeffrey, B. and Walford, G. (Eds) *Identity, Agency and Social Institutions,* Studies in Educational Ethnography, vol. 7, Oxford JAI Press.
Carlson, M. (2005) Vuxenutbildningen går till marknaden—Omstrukturering och om-kulturalisering av utbildning. I R. Foss Fridlizius (red) *Vuxenutbildning i omvandling.* Rapport 2005: 3, Göteborgs Universitet. Institutionen för pedagogik och didaktik.
Carr, W. (1995) *For Education: Towards Critical Educational Inquiry,* Buckingham: Open University Press.
Chouliarki, L., and Fairclough, N. (1999) *Discourse in the late modernity: Rethinking critical discourse analysis,* Edinburgh: University Press.
Cole, M. (2003) Might It Be in the Practice that It Fails to Succeed? A Marxist Critique of Claims for Postmodernism and Poststructuralism as Forces for Social Change and Social Justice, *British Journal of Sociology of Education,* 24(4): 487-500.
Corrigan, P. (1979) *Schooling and the Smash Street Kids,* London: MacMillan.
Craft, A. (2002) *Creativity and Early Years Education,* London: Continuum.
Czarniawska-Joerges, B. (1988) *Att handla med ord.* Stockholm: Carlssons.
Dahland, G. (1998) *Matematikundervisning i 1990-talets gymnasieskola,* Göteborg, Inst. för pedagogik: Rapport 1998: 05.
Dale, R. (1997) *The State and the Governance of Education: An Analysis of the Restructuring of the State-Education Relationship,* in Brown, P. and Halsey, A.H. *Education-Culture, Economy, Society* Oxford: University Press.
DsU (1987: 1) *Ansvarsfördelning och styrning på skolområdet,* Stockholm: Utbildnings departmentet.

DsU (1995: 5) *Där man inte har något inflytande finns inte något ansvar-En översyn av elev−och föräldrainflytande i skolan,* Stockholm: Utbildnings departmentet.

DsU (2001: 19) *Elevens framgång−skolans ansvar,* Stockholm: Utbildnings departmentet.

Dovemark, M. (2004a) Pupil Responsibility in the Context of School Changes in Sweden: market constraints on state policies for a creative education. *European Educational Researcher Journal,* 3(3): 658-673.

Dovemark, M. (2004b) *Ansvar-flexibilitet-valfrihet. En etnografisk studie om en skola i förändring* (Gothenburg Studies in Educational Sciences 223). Göteborg: Acta Universitatis Gothenburgensis.

Dovemark M and Beach, D (2004) New aims and old problems in Swedish schools: Flexibility, freedom of choice and self-reliance in learning as part of social reproduction, in Troman, G., Jeffrey, B., and Walford, G. (Eds) *Identity, Agency and Social Institutions. Studies in Educational Ethnography vol. 7,* Oxford: Jai Press.

Eilard, A. (2004) Genus och etnicitet i en läsebok i den svenska mångetniska skolan. *Pedagogisk Forskning i Sverige,* 9(4): 241-263.

Engels, F. (1969) *The Condition of the Working Class in England.* London: Panther.

Eriksson, R. and Jonsson, J.O. (2003) Varför består den sociala snedrekryteringen? *Pedagogisk forskning i Sverige,* 7(3): 210-217.

Fairclough, N. (1989) *Language and Power,* London: Longman.

Fairclough, N. (1993) Critical discourse analysis and the marketisation of public discourse, *Discourse and Society,* 4(2): 133-168.

Fairclough, N. (1995) *Critical Discourse Analysis,* London: Longman.

Fay, B. (1977) *Social Theory and Political Practice,* London: Allen and Unwin.

Frejes, A. (2006) *Constructing the Adult Learner: A Governmentality Analysis.* (Linköping Studies in Education and Psychology 106), Linköping, Sweden: Linköping University, Department of Behavioural Sciences.

Freire, P. (1970) *Pedagogia do Oprimido.* (Sw. trans. 1972) Pedagogik för de förtrykta. Stockholm: Gummessons. English translation (1994), Pedagogy of Hope, New York: Continuum

Freire, P. (1975) *Utbildning för befrielse,* Stockholm: Gummessons Förlag.

Fullan, M. and Hargreaves, A. (1992) *Teacher Development and Educational Change.* London: Falmer Press.

Furlong, A. and Cartnel, F. (1999) *Young People and Social Change: Individualisation and risk in late modernity,* Buckingham: Open University Press.

Geertz, C. (1973) *The Interpretations of Cultures,* New York: Basic Books.

Gibbons, M., Limoges, C., Nowothny, H., Schwartzman, S., Scott, P., and Trow, M. (1994) *The new production of knowledge,* London: Sage.

Giota, J. (2001) *Adolescents 'Perceptions of School and Reasons for Learning.* (Göteborg Studies in Educational Sciences 147). Göteborg: Acta Universitatis Gothoburgensis.

Goodson, I. F. and Norrie, C. (2005) Case Report on Restructuring work life and Professions in Teaching and Nursing in England, in Beach, D., (Ed) *Welfare State Restructuring in Education and Health Care: Implications for the Teaching and Nursing Professions and their Professional Knowledge,* http://www.profknow.net/fs-results.html

Gordon , T., Holland, J. and Lahelma, E. (2000) *Making Spaces: Citizenship and Difference in Schools,* London and New York: St. Martin´s Press.

Gordon, T., Lahelma, E. and Beach, D. (2003) Marketisation of democratic education: Etnographic insights, in: Beach, D., T. Gordon and Lahelma. E.(eds.) *Democratic Education: Etnographic Challenges:* 1-12. London: Tufnell Press.

Government Proposition (1990/91:18) *Skolans ansvar och styrning*, Stockholm: Regeringskansliet.

Government Proposition (1995/96: 222) Sysselsättningspropositionerna, Stockholm: Finansdepartementet.

Government Proposition (1997/98: 6) Regeringens proposition om att införa förskoleklassen i det obligatoriska skolväsendet, Stockholm: Utbildnings-och kulturdepartementet.

Government Proposition (2000/01:72) *Vuxnas lärande och utveckling av vuxenutbildning.* Stockholm: Utbildnings-och kulturdepartementet.

Government Proposition (1999/2000:135) *En förnyad lärarutbildning*, Stockholm: Utbildnings-och kulturdepartementet

Government Proposition (2000/01: 72) *Vuxnas lärande och utvecklingen av vuxenutbildningen*, Stockholm: Utbildnings-och kulturdepartementet.

Government Proposition (2004/05:162) *Ny värld—ny hög*skola, Stockholm: Utbildnings-och kulturdepartementet.

Gramsci, A. (1967) *En kollektiv intellektuell.* Uddevalla: Bo Cavefors.

Gramsci, A. (1988) *Prison Letters*, London and Chicago: Pluto Press.

Green, A. (1999) Education and globalization: convergent and divergent trends, *Journal of Education Policy,* 14(1): 55-71.

Grundén, I. (2005) *Att återerövra kroppen: en studie av livet efter en ryggmärgsskada.* (Göteborg Studies in Educational Sciences 226), Göteborg: Acta Universitatis Gothoburgensis.

Gustafsson, J. (2003) *Integration som text, diskursiv och social praktik: En policyetnografisk fallstudie av mötet mellan skolan och förskoleklassen*, (Göteborg Studies in Educational Sciences, 190), Göteborg: Acta Universitatis Gothenburgensis.

Habermas, J. (1972) *Knowledge and Human Interests.* London: Heineman.

Hall, S. (1996) *Representation: Cultural Representations and Signifying Practices*, London: Sage.

Hammersley, M. and Atkinson, P. (1995) *Ethnography. Principles in Practice*, London and New York: Routledge.

Hargreaves, A. (1986) *Two Cultures of Schooling.* London: Falmer Press.

Hazel, E. (1990: Ed.) *The Student Laboratory and the Science Curriculum*, London: Routledge.

Helmstad, G. (1999) *Understandings of Understanding*, (Göteborg Studies in Educational Sciences 134), Göteborg: Acta Universitatis Gothoburgensis.

Henning-Loeb, I. (2006) *Utveckling och förändring i kommunal vuxen-utbildning —en yrkeslivshistorisk ingång med berättelserom lärarbanor.* (Göteborg Studies in Educational Sciences 237), Göteborg: Acta Universitatis Gothoburgensis.

Hill, D. (2001) State theory and the neoliberal reconstruction of schooling and teacher education: A structuralist neo-Marxist critique of postmodernist, quasi-postmodernist, and culturalist neo-Marxist theory, *British Journal of Sociology of Education*, 22(1): 135-155.

Hill, D. (2006) Education services liberalization, in Rosskam, E. (Ed.) *Winners or Losers? Liberalizing Public Services*, Geneva: ILO.

Hursh, D. and Camille, A. M. (2003) Neoliberalism and schooling in the US: How State and federal government policies perpetuate inequality, *Journal for Critical Education Policy Studies*, 1(2). http://www.ieps.org.uk

Jeffrey, B. (2002) Performativity and primary teacher relations, *Journal of Education Policy* 17 (5): 531-546.

Jeffrey, B. (2003) 'Countering student instrumentalism: A creative response', *British Journal of Educational Research*, 29(4): 489-504.

Jeffrey, B. and Woods, P. (1998) *Testing Teachers: The Effect of School Inspections on Primary Teachers*, London: Falmer Press.

Jeffrey, B. and Woods, P. (2003) *The Creative School. A Framework for Success, Quality and Effectiveness.* London and New York: Routledge Falmer.

Jonsson. M. (2004) *Kontrasternas rum—ett relationostiskt perspektiv på valfrihet, segregation och indoktrinerande verkan i Sveriges grundskola,* Akademisk avhandling. Umeå Universitet.

Keddie, N. (1984) Classroom Knowledge, in Hargreaves, A. and Woods, P. (ed.) *Classrooms and Staffrooms—the Sociology of Teachers and Teaching.* Open University Press.

Kincheloe, J. L. and McLaren, P. L. (1994) Rethinking critical theory and qualitative research, in Denzin, N. K. and Lincoln, Y. S. (1994: Eds.) *Handbook of Qualitative Research.* London and New York: Sage.

Kommunförbundet (1996) *En satsning till två tusen,* Stockholm: Svenska Kommun förbundet.

Korp, H. (2006) *Lika chanser i gymnasiet-En studie om betyg, nationella prov och social reproduktion,* Malmö studies in educational sciences. Lärarutbildningen. Malmö Högskola.

Krashen, S. (1984) *Writing: Research, Theory, and Applications.* Oxford: Pergamon Institute of English.

Kuper, A. (1987) *Anthropologists and Anthropology: The British School 1922-1972,* London: Routledge.

Kvale, S. (1995) *InterViews,* London: Sage.

Larsson, S. (1993) Initial encounters in formal adult education, *International Journal of Qualitative Studies in Education,* 6(1): 49-65.

Lather, P. (1986). Research as praxis, *Harvard Educational Review,* 56(3): 257-77.

Lave, J. (1988) *Cognition in Practice: Mind, Mathematics and Culture in Everyday Life,* Cambridge: CUP.

Lazzeretti, L. and Tavoletti, E. (2006) Governance shifts in higher education: a cross-national comparison, *European Educational Researcher Journal,* 5(1): 18-37.

Lindblad, S. (1994) *Lärarna, samhället och skolans utveckling,* Stockholm: HLS Förlag.

Lindblad, S, Foss, R. and Wärvik, G-B. (2005) Discoursing working life and professional expertise in Education and Health Care in Sweden in Beach, D. (Ed) *Welfare State Restructuring in Education and Health Care: Implications for the Teaching and Nursing Professions and their Professional Knowledge,* http://www.profknow.net/fs-results.html

Lindblad, S., Lundahl, L. and Zackari, G. (2001) Sweden: Increased inequalities—increased stress on individual agency, in Lindblad, S. and Popkewitz, T. (red.) *Education governance and social integration and exclusion: Studies in the powers of reason and the reasons of power,* Uppsala Reports on Education nr. 39. Uppsala Universitet.

Lindblad, S., Lundahl, L., Lindgren, J., and Zackari, G. (2002) Educating for the New Sweden? *Scandinavian Journal of Educational Research,* 46(3): 283-303.

Lindblad, S. and Popkewitz, T. (2003) Comparative etnography: Fabricating the new millennium and its exclusion, in Beach, D., Gordon, T. and Lahelma, E. (Eds) *Democratic Education: Ethnographic Challenges.* London: the Tufnell Press.

Lindensjö, B. and Lundgren, U. P. (2000) *Utbildningsreformer och politisk styrning.* Stockholm: HLS Förlag.

Lindqvist, P. (2002) Lärares förtroendearbetstid (Malmö Studies in Educational Research 165), Malmö: LHS Malmö.

Loxley, A. and Thomas, G. (2001) Neo-conservatives, neo-liberals, the new left and inclusion: stirring the pot, *Cambridge Journal of Education*, 31(3): 291-301.

Lundahl, L. (2001) Governance of Education and its Social Consequences: Interviews with Swedish Politicians and Administrators, in Lindblad, S. and Popkewitz, T. (eds.) *Listening to education actors on governance and social integration and exclusion.* Uppsala Reports on Education nr. 37, Uppsala Universitet.

Lundahl, L. (2002a) Sweden: decentralization, deregulation, quasi-markets—and then what? *Journal of Education Policy*, 17(6): 687-697.

Lundahl, L. (2002b) From Centralisation to Decentralisation: Governance of Education in Sweden, *European Educational Research Journal*, 1(4). 625-636.

Lunneblad, J. (2006) *Förskolan och mångfalden: en etnografisk studie på en förskola i et multietniskt område.* (Göteborg Studies in Educational Sciences 252), Göteborg: Acta Universitatis Gothoburgensis.

Lutz, F. (1993) Holistic Ethnography, in Hammersley, M. (Ed.: 2nd. edition) *Controversies in Classroom Research: A Reader.* Milton Keynes: OUP.

Mac an Ghaill, M. (1988) *Young, Gifted and Black: Student—Teacher Relations in the Schooling of Black Youth,* Milton Keynes, OUP.

Macdonald, B. J. (2003) Thinking through Marx: An introduction to the political theory of Antonio Negri, *Strategies*, 16(2):86-95.

Maki, R.H. (1998) Test predictions over text material, in Hacker, D. J., Dunlosky, J. and Graesser, A. C. (Eds), *Metacognition in educational theory and practice*, Mahwah, NJ: Erlbaum.

Marcus, G. and Fischer, M. J. (1986) *Anthropology as Cultural Critique,* Chicago: Unversity of Chicago Press.

Marcuse, H. (1964) *One-Dimensional Man,* Boston: Beacon Press.

Marton, F., Hounsell, D. and Entwistle, N (Eds) (1986) *Hur vi lär,* Stockholm: Rabén and Sjögren.

Mead, G.H. (1934/62) *Mind, Self and Society from the Standpoint of a Social Behaviorist,* Chicago: University of Chicago Press.

McGee, A. (1999) *Investigating Language Anxiety through Action Inquiry,* (Göteborg Studies in Educational Sciences 136), Göteborg: Acta Universitatis Gothoburgensis.

McMurty, J. (1998) *Unequel Freedoms: The Global Market as an Ethical System,* Toronto: Kumarian Press.

Millar, R. (1989) Bending the evidence: The relationship between theory and experiment, in Millar, R. (ed). *Doing Science: Images of Science in Science Education.* London: Falmer Press.

Mäkitalo, Å. (2002) *Categorizing Work: Knowing, Arguing, and Social Dilemmas in Vocational Guidance,* (Göteborg Studies in Educational Sciences 177), Göteborg: Acta Universitatis Gothoburgensis.

Nordänger, U-K. (2002) *Lärares raster. Innehåll i mellanrum.* Malmö studies in educational sciences, Lärarutbildningen. Malmö: Malmö Högskola.

Nowotny, H., Scott, P., and Gibbons, M. (2001) *Re-Thinking Science. Knowledge and the Public in an Age of Uncertainty,* Cambridge: Polity Press.

Näslund, L. (2001) *Att organisera pedagogisk frihet. Fallstudie av självständigt arbete med datoprstöd vid en grundskola.* Institutionen för beteendevetenskap, EMIR, rapport nr. 5, Linköpings Universitet.

OECD (1992) *The Swedish Way Towards a Learning Society.* Paris: OECD.

OECD (1995) *Reviews of National Policies: Sweden.* Paris: OECD.

OECD (1996) *Lifelong Learning for All—Meeting of the Education Committee at Ministerial Level, 16-17 January 1996.* Paris: OECD.

OECD (2000a) *From Initial Education to Working Life—making Transitions Work. The Final Report of the Thematic Review.* May 2000. Paris: OECD.

OECD (2000b) *Where are the Resources for Lifelong Learning.* Paris: OECD.

OECD (2002) Education at a Glance. OECD Indicators 2002. Paris: OECD

Peters et al. (2000) The Third World debt crisis : why a radical approach is essential, in *Round table : a quarterly review of British Commonwealth.* London : Oxford University Press

Pieterse, J. D. (1995) Globalization as Hybridization. I M. Featherstone, S. Lash and Robertson, R. (Eds), *Global Modernities.* London: Sage .

Popkewitz, T. (2000) *Educational Knowledge—Changing Relationships between the State, Civil Society, and the Educational Community.* Albany: State Univ. of New York Press.

Poulantzas, N. (1974) *Classes in Contemporary Capitalism.* London: New Left.

Rikowski, G. (2003) That other great class of commodities: Labour power as a sparke for igniting Marxist educational theory. Paper presented at the Marxism and Education, Revisiting Dialogues Conference, London Institute of Education, May 1st, 2003.

Rose, N. (1995) Politisk styrning, auktoritet och expertis i den avancerade liberalismen, in Hultqvist, K. and Petersson, K. (Eds). *Foucault—namnet på en modern vetenskaplig och filosofisk problematic.* Stockholm: HLS.

Rosskam, E. (2006: Ed.) *Winners or Losers? Liberalizing Public Services.* Geneva: ILO.

Sanjek, R. (1990) A Vocabulary for Fieldnotes, in R. Sanjek (Ed.). *Fieldnotes. The Making of Anthropology.* Ithaca och London: Cornell University Press.

Sarup, M. (1984) *Marxism, Structuralism and Education.* London: Falmer.

Sharpe, R. (2003) The Left in the Academy: demotivated withdrawal, passive complicity or soldiering on? Observations of an early retiree. Paper presented at the Marxism and Education, Revisiting Dialogues Conference, London Institute of Education, May 1st, 2003.

Sharpe, R. and Green, A. (1975) *Education and Social Control: A Study in Progressive Primary Education.* London: RKP..

Sohlman, Å. (1996) *Framtidens utbildning. Sverige i internationell konkurrens.* Stockholm: SNS Förlag.

SOU (1988: 20) *En förändrad ansvarsfördelning och styrning på skolområdet.* Stockholm: Utbildningsdepartementet.

SOU (1990: 20) *Utbildning för 2000-talet.* Stockholm: Utbildningsdepartementet.

SOU (1992: 94) *Skola för bildning.* Stockholm: Utbildningsdepartementet.

SOU (1996: 1) *Den nya gymnasieskolan—hur går det?* Stockholm: Utbildningsdepartementet.

SOU (1996: 22) *Om elevers rätt till inflytande, delaktighet och ansvar. Delbetäckande av skolkommitén.* Stockholm: Utbildningsdepartementet.

SOU (1997: 1) *Den nya gymnasieskolan—steg för steg.* Statens Offentliga Utredningar.

SOU (1997: 21) *Växa i lärande. Förslag till läroplan för barn och unga 6-16 år.* Stockholm: Utbildningsdepartementet.

SOU (1999: 63) *Att leda och lära—En lärarutbildning för samverkan och utveckling,* Statens offentliga utredningar (SOU) maj 1999 Utbildnings-och kulturdepartementet.

SOU (2000: 7) *The Long-Term Survey*. Stockholm: Finansdepartemenetet.
SOU (2000: 39) *Välfärd och skola*. Stockholm: Utbildningsdepartementet.
Skolverket (1992) *Towards Free Choice and a Market Oriented School*. Stockholm: Skolverket.
Skolverket (1996) *Skola för framtiden—tankar om gymnasiereformen*. Stockholm: Skolverket.
Skolverket (2000) *Life-long and Life-wide Learning*. Stockholm: Liber.
Staberg, E-M. and Assarssson, M. (1997) *Den breda vägen—flickor och pojkar om gymnasieskolans naturvetenskapsprogram*—The Broad Pathway: Girls and Boys on the Natural Sciences program in the Gymnasium—. Umeå: Pedagogiska Institutionen, Rapport Nr 118.
Stronach, I. (1993) Education, vocationalism and economic recovery: the case against witchcraft. *British Journal of Education and Work*, 3(1), 5-31.
Sundberg, D. (2003) The politics of time in educational restructuring, in Beach, D., Gordon. T., and Lahelma. E. (Eds) *Democratic Education: Ethnographic Challenges*. London: Tufnell Press.
Svensson, A. (2001) Består den sociala snedrekrytering? Elevens val av gymnasieprogram hösten 1998, *Pedagogisk Forskning i Sverige*, 6(2): 161-182.
Svensson, A. (2002) *Den sociala snedrekryteringen till högskolan—när och hur uppstår den?*. Rapport från Institutionen för pedagogik och didaktik, 2002:10. Göteborg: Göteborgs universitet.
Svensson, A. (2006) Hur skall rekryteringen till högskolans mest eftersökta utbildningar breddas? *Pedagogisk Forskning i Sverige*, 11(2): 116-133.
Svensson, A. and Reuterberg, S-E. (1998) How to get more students to science and technical programmes in higher education? Paper presented at the International Conference on Science, Technology and Society, March 16-22, Tokyo, Hiroshima and Kyoto, Japan.
Säljö, R. (1982) *Learning and Understanding: A Study of Differnces in Constructing Meaning from Text*. (Göteborg Studies in Educational Sciences 41), Göteborg: Acta Universitatis Gothoburgensis.
Säljö, R. (2000) *Lärande i praktiken: ett sociokulturellt perspektiv* (Learning in Practice: A Socio-Cultural Perspective). Stockholm: Prisma.
Tesfahuney, M. (1998) *Imag(in)ing the Other(s): Migration, Racism, and theDiscursive Construction of Migrants*. Diss. Uppsala University.
Tholin, J. (2003) *En roliger dans*. Borås: Institutionen för pedagogik, Högskolan i Borås.
Tholin, J. (2006) *Att kunna klara sig i ökänd natur: en studie om betyg och betygskriterier—historiska betingelser och implementering av ett nytt system*. Diss. Göteborgs universitet 2006. Borås: Högskolan.
Tickle, L. (1984) One Spell of ten Minutes or Five Spells of two...? Teacher-Pupil Encounters in Art and Design Education, in A. Hargreaves and P. Woods (ed.) *Classrooms and Staffrooms: the Sociology of Teachers and Teaching*. Milton Keynes: Open University Press.
Troman, G. (1997) Self-management and School Inspection: Complementary Forms of Surveillance and Control in the Primary School, *Oxford Review of Education*, 23(3): 345-364.
Troman, G. (2005) Primary Teacher Identity, Commitment and Career in Performative Cultures. Paper presented at the European Conference on Educational Research, 7-11 September 2005, Dublin, Ireland.

Troman, G., Jeffrey, B. and Beach, D. (2006) *Researching Education Policy: Ethnographic Experiences*. London: Tufnell Press.

Troman, G., and Woods, P. (2001) *Primary Teacher Stress*. London: Falmer.

von Brömsen, K. (2003) *Tolkningar, förhandlingar och tystnader. Elevers tal om religion i det mångkulturella och postkoloniala rummet.* (Göteborg Studies in Educational Sciences 201). Göteborg: Acta Universitatis Gothoburgensis.

Vygotsky, L. (1926) *Educational Psychology.* Translated by Robert Silverman (1992), Florida: St Lucia Press.

Wahlström, N. (2002) *Om det förändrade ansvaret för skolan. Vägen till mål och resultatstyrning och några av dess konsekvenser.* Örebro Studies of Education 3. Örebro University.

Wass L, K. (2004) *Vuxenutbildning i omvandling: Kunskapslyftet som ett sätt att organisera förnyelse.* (Göteborg Studies in Educational Sciences 219). Göteborg: Acta Universitatis Gothoburgensis.

Whitty, G., Power, S. and Halpin, D. (1998) *Devolution and Choice in Education: The School, the State and the Market,* Buckingham: Open University Press.

Whitty, G. and Power, S. (2003) Making sense of education reform: Global and national influences, in C. A. Torres and A. Antikainen (Eds) *The International Handbook on the Sociology of Education.* New York: Rowman and Littlefield.

Willis, P. (1977) *Learning to Labour: How Working Class Kids Get Working Class Jobs.* Farnborough: Saxon House.

Willis, P. (1999) Labor Power, Culture, and the Cultural Commodity, in: M. Castells, R. Flecha, P. Freire, H. Giroux, D. Macedo and P. Willis (Eds) *Critical Education in the New Information Age.* Lanhan and Oxford: Rowman and Littlefield.

Willis, P. (2000) *The Ethnographic Imagination.* Cambridge: Polity Press.

Woods, P., Jeffrey, B., Troman, G. and Boyle, M. (1997) *Restructuring Schools, Reconstructing Teachers: Responding to Change in the Primary School.* Buckingham: Open University Press.

Woods, P. and Jeffrey, B. (2002) The reconstruction of primary teachers identities. *British Journal of Sociology of Education,* 23(1): 89-106.

Yates, J.F., Lee, J.W., and Shinotsuka, H. (1996) Beliefs about overconfidece, including its cross-national variation. *Organizational Behavior and Human Decision Processes,* 65, 138-147.

Young, R. (1989) *A Critical Theory of Education: Habermas and our Children's Future.* New York: Harvester.

Zackari, G. (2001) Swedish school actors about education governance changes and social consequences, in Lindblad, S. and Popkewitz, T. (red.) *Listening to Education Actors on Governance and Social Integration and Exclusion.* Uppsala Reports on Education nr. 37. Uppsala Universitet.

Zambeta, E. (2004) Greek Education 1980-2001: From the demand for democratisation to the promotion of entrepreneurship, in Sakis-Karagiorgas-Foundation (ed) *Social Change in Contemporary Greece (1980-2001).* Athens: Sakis Karagiorgas Foundation.

Zaporozets, A. V. (2005) The pedagogical and psychoanalytical problems of child preparedness for school, *Nordisk Pedagogik,* 25(1): 36-43.

Åsberg, R. (1973) *Primary education and national development.* Göteborg: ACTA Universitatis Gothoburgensi nr.10.

Österlind, E. (1998) *Disciplinering via frihet—Elevers planering av eget arbete.* Uppsala: Acta Universitatis Upsaliensis. Uppsala Studies in Education 75.

www.ingramcontent.com/pod-product-compliance
Lightning Source LLC
Chambersburg PA
CBHW070916270326
41927CB00011B/2589

9 781872 767727